15,000 Spanish Verbs

fully conjugated in all the tenses using pattern verbs

SECOND EDITION

by Stephen Thompson, Ph.D.

Center for Innovative Language Learning
Washington, DC

Address all inquiries to:
Center for Innovative Language Learning
320 Independence Avenue, Southeast
Washington, DC 20003 USA

Library of Congress Catalog Card Number (LCCN): 99-90213

International Standard Book Number (ISBN): 0965141829

Publisher's Cataloging-in-Publication Data

Thompson, Stephen J.
15,000 Spanish verbs fully conjugated in all the tenses using pattern verbs/ by Stephen J. Thompson. - 2nd ed.
p. cm.
ISBN: 0965141829
1. Spanish language-Verb-Tables. I. Title.
PC4271.T47 1999
468.2'421

Printed in Canada

I hope this book makes your study and use of Spanish easier and more enjoyable.

To my parents, family, and friends, with love and gratitude.

For helpful suggestions, I wish to thank Mark Churchwell, Gilbert Galván, William Hermann, William Jennings, Lee-Alison Sibley, and Anton Trinidad.

My thanks to David Rabasca, without whose encouragement this book would not have come to fruition, and to Mark Churchwell for proofreading the final manuscript.

I wish to gratefully acknowledge Lee-Alison Sibley and her 150 7th and 8th grade students of Spanish in public school in Fairfax County, Virginia. For an entire school year, they used and successfully classroom-tested an earlier version of this book.

Your questions, comments and suggestions are welcome. Send them to the author at the address on the copyright page, or by e-mail to CenterLang@aol.com

Introduction

This book is easy to use. Just follow the three steps on the back cover.

Irregular letters in pattern verb conjugations are printed in red. Omitted letters are indicated by showing the next letter in red. This helps you find and learn irregular conjugations. No other book does this.

Spanish is a verb-rich language because descriptive, precise verbs are used more commonly than in English. This book makes learning Spanish more fun and relevant to your own life by helping you use verbs related to your own academic studies, hobbies, friendships, personal interests, job, and leisure activities. It does this by not restricting you to a particular, smaller set of verbs that may have been selected for inclusion in other conjugation books because they were more general and non-specific.

This book will take you further than other books because it:

- has more verb patterns;
- has more verbs keyed to those verb patterns;
- prints irregular letters in red;
- shows how to translate each conjugation;
- shows how to pronounce Spanish words; and
- describes in words what each pattern verb illustrates.

This book helps you learn and use the subjunctive mood by placing the subjunctive next to its counterpart indicative mood. If you are not ready to learn and use the subjunctive, just bypass the subjunctive conjugations. Placing the indicative and subjunctive side-by-side is important because in Spanish the subjunctive is used much more frequently than in English. It is used to express emotions, to indicate uncertainty (such as a future event), to signal doubt, and to make requests. So, when you want to speak and write more authentic Spanish, and when you want to more fully understand Spanish speakers and writers, this book can help you more than other Spanish verb conjugation books.

You can take this slim book anywhere for ready reference. It fits in a pocket, purse, briefcase, or backpack. The book fits nicely on a desktop and could find a spot next to the dictionary on a bookshelf.

This book makes a great gift to pre-teens and up, to beginning students of Spanish and fluent users of the language, including teachers, translators, travelers and those who use Spanish at home, work or with friends.

The subject and reflexive pronouns are on the page facing pattern 1 for easy reference. The subject pronouns are omitted from the non-reflexive conjugations in order to emphasize the verb forms.

On April 27, 1994, the Spanish language academies eliminated ch and ll as separate letters of the Spanish alphabet. Now ch and ll, at any place in a word, are alphabetized the same as in English.

15,000 Spanish Verbs
in alphabetical order

a

ababill-arse 80
abacor-ar 1
abadan-ar 1
abadern-ar 1
abagr-arse 80
abaj-ar 1
abaj-arse 80
abalag-ar 1
abalall-ar 1
abalandr-ar 1
abalanz-ar 21
abalanz-arse... 21
abal-ar 1
abalaustr-ar 1
abaldes-ar 1
abaldon-ar 1
abaldon-arse ... 80
abale-ar 1
abali-ar 9
abalien-ar 1
abaliz-ar 21
abaliz-arse 21
aball-ar 1
aballest-ar 1
abalsam-ar 1
abalser-ar 1
abaluart-ar 1
aban-ar 1
abancal-ar 1
abancuch-ar 1
abandaliz-ar 21
abander-ar 1
abanderiz-ar 21
abanderiz-arse 21
abandole-ar 1
abandon-ar 1
abandon-arse 80
abane-ar 1
abang-ar 51
abanic-ar 67
abanic-arse 67
abanique-ar 1
abant-ar 1
abañ-ar 1
abaraj-ar 1
abarand-ar 1
abarañ-ar 1
abarat-ar 1
abarat-arse 80
abarb-ar 1
abarbech-ar 1
abarbet-ar 1
abarc-ar 67
abarcuz-ar 21
abarlo-ar 1
abarlo-arse 80
abarquill-ar 1
abarquill-arse 80
abarrac-ar 67
abarrac-arse 67
abarragan-ar 1
abarragan-arse 80
abarraj-ar 1
abarranc-ar 67
abarranc-arse 67
abarr-ar 1
abarren-ar 1
abarr-er 2
abarril-ar 1
abarr-ir 3
abarrot-ar 1
ab-arse 80, and used in the positions in 14
abas-ar 1
abasoir-ar 1
abass-ar 1
abast-ar 1
abastard-ar 1
abastec-er 48
abastec-erse ... 48
abastill-ar 1
abastion-ar 1
abatan-ar 1
abat-ar 1
abatat-ar 1
abatat-arse 80
abate-ar 1
abat-ir 3
abatoj-ar 1
abatoll-ar 1
abayunc-ar 67
abdic-ar 67
abduc-ir 28
abebr-ar 1
abeit-ar 1
abeiz-ar 1
abejone-ar 1
abejorre-ar 1
abejuc-ar 67
abel-ar 1
abeld-ar 53
abellac-ar 67
abellot-ar 1
abemol-ar 1
aberenjen-ar 1
aberr-ar 37
aberre-ar 1
abes-ar 1
abesti-arse 80
abestion-ar 1
abetun-ar 1
abevigu-ar 1
abeyt-ar 1
abez-ar 1
abich-arse 80
abield-ar 1
abigarr-ar 1
abij-ar 1
abill-ar 1
abillit-ar 1
abin-ar 1
abisagr-ar 1
abisel-ar 1
abism-ar 1
abistern-ar 1
abistu-ar 1
abit-ar 1
abiyel-ar 1
abizcoch-ar 1
abjur-ar 1
ablact-ar 1
abland-ar 1
ablandec-er 48
abland-ir 3
ablaque-ar 1
ableg-ar 1
ablend-ar 1
ablent-ar 1
ablevi-ar 1
abluc-ar 1
ablu-ir 42
abneg-ar 62
abob-ar 1
abocad-ar 1
abocade-ar 1
abocan-ar 1
aboc-ar 67
abocard-ar 1
abocel-ar 1
abocet-ar 1
aboch-ar 1
abochorn-ar 1
abocin-ar 1
abodoc-ar 67
abodoc-arse 67
abof-ar 67
abof-arse 67
abofell-ar 1
abofete-ar 1
abogade-ar 1
abog-ar 51
abol-ir 4
aboll-ar 1
abollon-ar 1
abols-ar 1
abomb-ar 1
abomin-ar 1
abonanz-ar 21, and for its use regarding weather, see 45
abon-ar 1
abon-arse 80
abond-ar 1
aboquill-ar 1
abord-ar 1
abordon-ar 1
aborraj-ar 1
aborraj-arse 80
aborrasc-ar 67
aborrasc-arse 67, and for its use regarding weather, see 45
aborrec-er 48
aborreg-ar 51
aborreg-arse 51
aborric-arse 67
aborr-ir 3
aborron-ar 1
aborrug-ar 51
aborrug-arse 51
abort-ar 1
aboruj-ar 1

abos-ar 1
abostez-ar 21
abotag-ar 51
abotag-arse 51
abotarg-ar 51
abotij-arse 80
aboton-ar 1
aboton-arse 80
aboved-ar 1
aboy-ar 1
abozal-ar 1
aboz-ar 1
abrac-ar 67
abracij-arse 80
abrahon-ar 1
abras-ar 1
abravec-er 48
abraz-ar 21
abrech-ar 1
abrenunci-ar 1
abreton-ar 1
abrev-ar 1
abrevi-ar 1
abrez-ar 21
abribon-arse 80
abrig-ar 51
abrig-arse 80
abrillant-ar 1
abriol-ar 1
abrir 3, except the past participle is abierto
abro-ar 1
abro-arse 80
abrocal-ar 1
abroc-ar 1
abroch-ar 1
abrog-ar 51
abrog-arse 80
abrom-ar 1
abrom-arse 80
abronc-ar 67
abroquel-ar 1
abrotoñ-ar 1
abrull-ar 1
abrum-arse 80, and for its use regarding weather, see 45
abrut-ar 1
abruz-arse 21
absced-arse 80
abscond-er 2
absent-arse 80
absolutiz-ar 21
absolv-er 47, except the past participle is absuelto
abson-ar 25
absorb-er 2, plus the past participle absorto
absort-ar 1
absten-er 74
absten-erse 74
absterg-er 23
abstra-er 75, plus the past participle abstracto
abub-arse 80
abuch-ar 1
abuche-ar 1
abuen-ar 1
abuey-ar 1
abullon-ar 1
abult-ar 1
abund-ar 1
abuñol-ar 25
abuñuel-ar 1
abur-ar 1
aburel-ar 1
aburgues-arse 80
aburil-ar 1
aburr-ar 1
aburr-arse 80
aburr-ir 3
aburr-irse 82
aburuj-ar 1
aburujun-ar 1
abus-ar 1
abuz-arse 21
acabal-ar 1
acaball-ar 1
acaballer-ar 1
acaballon-ar 1
acabañ-ar 1
acab-ar 1
acabd-ar 1
acabdell-ar 1
acabdill-ar 1
acabel-ar 1
acabestr-ar 1
acabestrill-ar 1
acabild-ar 1
acabt-ar 1
acach-arse 80
acachet-ar 1
acachete-ar 1
acachorr-ar 1
academiz-ar 21
acadenill-ar 1
acaec-er 48, and for its use regarding weather, see 45
aca-er 20
acafel-ar 1
acaguas-arse 80
acairel-ar 9
acalabaz-arse 80
acalabrot-ar 1
acalambr-arse 80
acaland-ar 1
acald-ar 1
acalentur-ar 1
acalentur-arse 80
acallant-ar 1
acall-ar 1
acalor-ar 1
acalore-arse 80
acalug-ar 51
acamaleon-arse 80
acam-ar 1
acamastron-arse 80
acamellon-ar 1
acampan-ar 1
acamp-ar 1
acanal-ar 1
acanall-ar 1
acanastill-ar 1
acancer-ar 1
acancer-arse ... 80
acanch-ar 1
acandil-ar 1
acanelon-ar 1
acangren-arse 80
acanog-ar 51
acansin-arse 80
acansir-arse 80
acantale-ar 1, and for its use regarding weather, see 45
acantar-ar 1
acante-ar 1
acantil-ar 1
acanton-ar 1
acañavere-ar 1
acañone-ar 1
acapar-ar 1
acaparr-ar 1
acaparr-arse 80
acapill-ar 1
acapiz-arse 21
acapuch-ar 1
acapull-arse 80
acarabe-ar 1
acaramel-ar 1
acar-ar 1
acardenal-ar 1
acare-ar 1
acarici-ar 1
acariñ-ar 1
acarnaz-arse ... 80
acaron-ar 1
acarral-ar 1
acarr-arse 80
acarraz-ar 21
acarraz-arse 21
acarre-ar 1
acarret-ar 1
acarrete-ar 1
acarroñ-ar 1
acarton-ar 1
acaser-arse 80
acastill-ar 1
acat-ar 1
acatarr-ar 1
acatarr-arse 80

acontent-ar 1
acop-ar 1
acopet-ar 1
acopi-ar 1
acopl-ar 1
acoquin-ar 1
acor-ar 1
acoraz-ar 21
acorazon-ar 1
acorch-ar 1
acord-ar 25
acordel-ar 1
acordon-ar 1
acorn-ar 25
acorne-ar 1
acorral-ar 1
acorr-er 2
acorruc-arse 67
acort-ar 1
acortej-arse 80
acorull-ar 1
acorv-ar 1
acorz-ar 21
acos-ar 1
acosij-ar 1
acost-ar 25
acostill-arse 80
acostumbr-ar 1
acot-ar 1
acotej-ar 1
acotol-ar 1
acoyund-ar 1
acoyunt-ar 1
acrecent-ar 53
acrec-er 48
acredit-ar 1
acrianz-ar 21
acrib-ar 1
acribill-ar 1
acrimin-ar 1
acrioll-arse 80
acrisol-ar 1
acristal-ar 1
acristian-ar 1
acromatiz-ar 21
acruñ-ar 1
actit-ar 1
activ-ar 1
actualiz-ar 21
actu-ar 9
acuadrell-ar 1
acuadrill-ar 1
acuajaron-ar 1
acuanti-ar 1
acuart-ar 1
acuartel-ar 1
acuarteron-ar 1
acuartill-ar 1
acuatiz-ar 21
acub-ar 1
acubil-ar 1
acucham-arse 80
acuch-ar 1
acuchar-ar 1
acuchill-ar 1
acuchille-ar 1
acuchuc-ar 1
acuchuch-ar 1
acuci-ar 1
acuclill-arse 80
acud-ir 3
acuerd-ar 1
acuern-ar 1
acuerp-ar 1
acugul-ar 1
acuidad-arse 80
acuilm-arse 80
acuit-ar 1
acul-ar 1
aculebr-ar 1
aculebre-arse 80
aculebrin-ar 1
aculill-ar 1
acullic-ar 1
acull-ir 3
acultur-arse 80
acumb-arse 80
acumbr-ar 1
acumuch-ar 1
acumul-ar 1
acun-ar 1
acuñ-ar 1
acur-ar 1
acurcuch-arse 80
acurcull-arse 80
acurd-arse 80
acurr-arse 80
acurruc-arse 67
acurruj-arse 80
acurrull-ar 1
acuruj-arse 80
acus-ar 1
adagu-ar 7
adam-ar 1
adam-arse 80
adamasc-ar 67
adapon-er 57
adapt-ar 1
adarde-ar 1
adarg-ar 51
adarv-ar 1
adat-ar 1
adecen-ar 1
adecent-ar 1
adecu-ar 9
adehes-ar 1
adelant-ar 1
adelgaz-ar 21
adem-ar 1
adement-ar 1
adempribi-ar 1
adens-ar 1
adentell-ar 1
adentr-ar 1
aderez-ar 21
adestr-ar 53
adeud-ar 1
adherec-er 2
adher-ir 71
adhib-ir 3
adhort-ar 1
adiamant-ar 1
adi-ar 9
adicion-ar 1
adiestr-ar 1
adiet-ar 1
adiner-ar 1
adintel-ar 1
ad-ir 3, and used in the positions in 11
adivin-ar 1
adjetiv-ar 1
adjudic-ar 67
adjunt-ar 1
adjur-ar 1
adminicul-ar 1
administr-ar 1
admir-ar 1
admit-ir 3
adob-ar 1
adocen-ar 1
adoctrin-ar 1
adoj-ar 1
adolec-er 48
adolor-ar 1
adomicili-ar 1
adon-arse 80
adonec-er 48
adoniz-arse 21
adopt-ar 1
adoquin-ar 1
ador-ar 1
adormec-er 48
adorment-ar 1
adormil-ar 1
adormil-arse 80
adorm-ir 31
adormit-ar 1
adormit-arse 80
adorn-ar 1
ados-ar 1
adquir-ir 5
adr-ar 1
adriz-ar 21
adrog-ar 51
adscrib-ir 3, except the past participle is adscrito
adsorb-er 2
adstring-ir 3, plus the changes in red in 23
aduan-ar 1
aduc-ir 59, plus the past participle aducho
adueñ-ar 1
adueñ-arse 80
aduj-ar 1
adul-ar 1
adulc-ir 3, plus the changes in red in 46
adule-ar 1
adulter-ar 1
adulz-ar 21

aguald-ar ... 1
aguam-arse ... 80
aguamel-ar ... 1
aguand-ar ... 1
aguant-ar ... 1
agu-ar ... 7
aguard-ar ... 1
aguasali-ar ... 1
aguas-arse ... 80
aguat-arse ... 80
aguaz-ar ... 21
agudiz-ar ... 21
agüeit-ar ... 1
aguerr-ir ... 4
aguij-ar ... 1
aguijone-ar ... 1
aguil-arse ... 80
aguisc-ar ... 67
aguizg-ar ... 51
agujer-ar ... 1
agujere-ar ... 1
agujete-ar ... 1
agusan-ar ... 1
aguz-ar ... 21
ahaj-ar ... 1
ahax-ar ... 1
ahech-ar ... 1
ahele-ar ... 1
aherroj-ar ... 1
aherrumbr-ar ... 1
ahervor-arse ... 80
ahidalg-ar ... 51
ahij-ar ... 9
ahijone-ar ... 1
ahil-ar ... 9
ahiler-ar ... 9
ahinc-ar ... 8
ahit-ar 9, plus the past participle ahíto
ahobachon-arse ... 80
ahoc-arse ... 67
ahocic-ar ... 67
ahocin-arse ... 80
ahog-ar ... 51
ahoj-ar ... 1
ahombr-arse ... 80
ahond-ar ... 1
ahorcaj-arse ... 80
ahorc-ar ... 67
ahorm-ar ... 1
ahornag-arse ... 51
ahorn-ar ... 1
ahorquet-arse ... 80
ahorquill-ar ... 1
ahorr-ar ... 1
ahot-ar ... 1
ahoy-ar ... 1
ahuch-ar ... 9
ahuche-ar ... 9
ahuec-ar ... 67
ahuer-ar ... 1
ahues-arse ... 80
ahuev-ar ... 1
ahum-ar ... 1
ahume-ar ... 1
ahup-ar ... 1
ahus-ar ... 1
ahus-arse ... 80
ahuyent-ar ... 1
air-ar ... 9
aire-ar ... 1
aisl-ar ... 9
ajabard-ar ... 1
ajamon-arse ... 80
ajaquec-arse ... 67
aj-ar ... 1
ajardin-ar ... 1
aje-ar ... 1
ajedrez-ar ... 21
ajel-ar ... 1
ajeni-ar ... 1
ajerg-ar ... 1
ajeri-ar ... 1
ajeriz-ar ... 1
ajesuit-ar ... 1
ajetre-ar ... 1
ajicar-ar ... 1
ajigot-ar ... 1
ajil-ar ... 1
ajilguer-arse ... 80
ajin-ar ... 1
ajiron-ar ... 1
ajob-ar ... 1
ajonje-ar ... 1
ajor-ar ... 25
ajord-ar ... 1
ajornal-ar ... 1
ajot-ar ... 1
ajuanet-ar ... 1
ajuar-ar ... 1
ajubon-ar ... 1
ajudi-arse ... 80
ajuglar-ar ... 1
ajuici-ar ... 1
ajum-ar ... 1
ajum-arse ... 80
ajumpi-arse ... 80
ajunc-ar ... 1
ajunquill-ar ... 1
ajust-ar ... 1
ajustici-ar ... 1
alab-ar ... 1
alabastr-ar ... 1
alabe-ar ... 1
alacen-ar ... 1
alaching-ar ... 1
alachingu-ar ... 1
alaci-ar ... 1
alaci-arse ... 80
alacrane-ar ... 1
aladr-ar ... 1
alag-ar ... 51
alagart-ar ... 1
alagart-arse ... 80
alagun-ar ... 1
alambic-ar ... 67
alambr-ar ... 1
alambre-ar ... 1
alamp-ar ... 1
alance-ar ... 1
alandre-arse ... 80
alanz-ar ... 21
alaqui-ar ... 1
alaqu-ir ... 3
alarde-ar ... 1
alarg-ar ... 51
alarid-ar ... 1
alarm-ar ... 1
al-arse ... 80
alastr-ar ... 1
albain-ar ... 1
albañal-ar ... 1
albañe-ar ... 1
albañile-ar ... 1
alb-ar ... 1
albardane-ar ... 1
albard-ar ... 1
albarde-ar ... 1
albardill-ar ... 1
albarraz-ar ... 21
albayald-ar ... 1
albe-ar ... 1
albeld-ar ... 53
alberg-ar ... 51
albitr-ar ... 1
albogue-ar ... 1
albore-ar 1, and for its use regarding weather, see ... 45
alborot-ar ... 1
alboroz-ar ... 21
albrici-ar ... 1
albumin-ar ... 1
alcachof-ar ... 1
alcahaz-ar ... 21
alcahuet-ar ... 1
alcahuete-ar ... 1
alcaide-ar ... 1
alcalesc-er ... 2
alcalific-ar ... 1
alcaliz-ar ... 21
alcane-ar ... 1
alcanfor-ar ... 1
alcantarill-ar ... 1
alcanz-ar ... 21
alcatif-ar ... 1
alcayat-ar ... 1
alcohol-ar ... 1
alcoholiz-ar ... 21
alcontriz-ar ... 21
alcoravis-ar ... 1
alcorz-ar ... 21
aldabe-ar ... 1
ale-ar ... 1
alebr-arse ... 53
alebrast-ar ... 1
alebrast-arse ... 80
alebrest-ar ... 1
alebrest-arse ... 80
alebron-ar ... 1
alebron-arse ... 80
aleccion-ar ... 1
alech-ar ... 1
alechig-ar ... 1
alechug-ar ... 51
alechuguin-arse ... 80
alechuz-arse ... 21
alegaj-ar ... 1

alegam-ar 1
alegan-arse 80
aleg-ar 51
alegoriz-ar 21
alegr-ar 1
alejandr-ar 1
alej-ar 1
alel-ar 1
alend-ar 1
alendel-ar 1
alengu-ar 7
alent-ar 53
aleon-ar 1
alert-ar 1
alesn-ar 1
aletarg-ar 51
alete-ar 1
aleud-ar 1
alevin-ar 1
alfabetiz-ar 21
alfalf-ar 1
alf-ar 1
alfard-ar 1
alfarraz-ar 21
alfeiz-ar 21
alfeñic-arse 67
alfiler-ar 1
alfoli-ar 1
alfombr-ar 1
alfonse-arse 80
alforj-ar 1
alforroch-ar 1
alforz-ar 21
algali-ar 1
algalib-ar 1
algarab-ar 1
algarace-ar 1,
and for its use
regarding
weather,
see 45
algare-ar 1
algarrob-ar 1
algebriz-ar 21
algodon-ar 1
alhaj-ar 1
ahele-ar 1
alheñ-ar 1
alhere-ar 1
ali-ar 9
alicat-ar 1
alicore-ar 1
alicort-ar 1
aliebr-arse 80
alien-ar 1
alif-ar 1
alig-ar 51
aliger-ar 1
alij-ar 1
alijar-ar 1
aliment-ar 1
alimon-arse 80
alind-ar 1
alinder-ar 1
alindong-
arse 51
aline-ar 1
aliñ-ar 1
alion-ar 1
aliquebr-ar 53
alis-ar 1
alist-ar 1
alivian-ar 1
alivi-ar 1
aljafif-ar 1
aljami-ar 1
aljofar-ar 1
aljofif-ar 1
aljoroz-ar 21
allamar-arse 80
allan-ar 1
alleg-ar 51
alloc-arse 67
allug-ar 1
almacen-ar 1
almacig-ar 51
almade-arse 80
almadi-ar 1
almagr-ar 1
almarbat-ar 1
almen-ar 1
almendr-ar 1
almiar-ar 1
almibar-ar 1
almidon-ar 1
almirante-ar 1
almizcl-ar 1
almogavare-ar ... 1
almohace-ar 1
almohadill-ar 1
almohaz-ar 21
almoned-ar 1
almonede-ar 1
almorz-ar 39
almosn-ar 1
almuerc-ar 67
alobad-arse 80
aloball-ar 1
alob-ar 1
alobreguec-
er 48
aloc-ar 67
aloj-ar 1
aloj-arse 80
aloll-ar 1
alom-ar 1
alomb-ar 1
alon-ar 1
along-ar 24
aloquec-erse ... 48
alor-arse 80
alot-ar 1
aloy-ar 1
alparce-ar 1
alpargat-ar 1
alpistel-arse 80
alquil-ar 1
alquitar-ar 1
alquitran-ar 1
altan-ar 1
alt-ar 1
alte-ar 1
alter-ar 1
alterc-ar 67
altern-ar 1
altibaj-ar 1
altiv-ar 1
altivec-er 48
aluci-ar 1
alucin-ar 1
alud-ir 3
alueng-ar 1
alufr-ar 1
aluj-ar 1
alumbr-ar 1
alumin-ar 1
alun-ar 1
alun-arse 80
aluniz-ar 21
alustr-ar 1
aluz-ar 21
alzaprim-ar 1
alz-ar 21
amachambr-ar ... 1
amachambr-
arse 80
amachet-ar 1
amachete-ar 1
amachimbr-
arse 80
amachin-
arse 80
amachorr-
arse 80
amaciz-ar 21
amacoll-ar 1
amadaj-ar 1
amadall-ar 1
amadam-
arse 80
amadiz-ar 21
amadrig-ar 51
amadrin-ar 1
amaestr-ar 1
amafi-arse 80
amagall-arse ... 80
amag-ar 51
amagost-ar 1
amain-ar 9
amaitin-ar 9
amaiz-ar 35
amajad-ar 1
amajan-ar 1
amalay-ar 1
amaldit-arse 80
amalgam-ar 1
amalhay-ar 1
amalign-arse ... 80
amallad-ar 1
amall-arse 80
amalvez-arse ... 21
amamant-ar 1
amanceb-ar 1
amanceb-
arse 80
amancill-ar 1
amane-ar 1
amanec-er 48,
and for its use
regarding
weather,
see 45
amaner-ar 1
amangual-

arse 80
amaniat-ar 1
amanill-ar 1
amanoj-ar 1
amans-ar 1
amant-ar 1
amantill-ar 1
amanzan-ar 1
amañ-ar 1
amapol-arse 80
am-ar 1
amar-ar 1
amarchant-
arse 80
amarec-er 48
amarg-ar 51
amargue-ar 1
amarguje-ar 1
amarill-ar 1
amarille-ar 1
amarillec-er 48
amarin-ar 1
amariz-ar 21
amarom-ar 1
amarr-ar 1
amarreque-ar 1
amartel-ar 1
amartigu-ar 7
amartill-ar 1
amas-ar 1
amat-ar 1
amayorazg-
ar 51
amazacot-ar 1
ambici-ar 1
ambicion-ar 1
ambicione-ar 1
ambient-ar 1
ambl-ar 1
ambul-ar 1
ambut-ar 1
amech-ar 1
amedrant-ar 1
amedrent-ar 1
amel-ar 53
amelcoch-ar 1
amelg-ar 51
amell-ar 1
amenaz-ar 21
amengu-ar 7
ameniz-ar 21
amenor-ar 1
amenorg-ar 51
ament-ar 53
amer-ar 1
americaniz-
ar 21
amerit-ar 1
ametal-ar 1
ametrall-ar 1
amezquin-
arse 80
amezquind-
arse 80
amig-ar 51
amilan-ar 1
amillar-ar 1
amillon-ar 1
aministr-ar 1
aminor-ar 1
amist-ar 1
amitig-ar 51
amnisti-ar 9
amobl-ar 25
amoch-ar 1
amodorr-ar 1
amodorrec-
er 48
amohec-er 48
amohin-ar 9
amohos-ar 1
amohos-arse ... 80
amojam-ar 1
amojel-ar 1
amojon-ar 1
amol-ar 25
amold-ar 1
amolel-ar 1
amoll-ar 1
amollec-er 48
amollent-ar 1
amollin-ar 1,
and used in
the positions
in 45
amon-arse 80
amoned-ar 1
amonest-ar 1
amont-ar 1
amontazg-ar 51
amonton-ar 1
amoñ-ar 1
amorag-ar 51
amorat-ar 1
amorc-ar 67
amordaz-ar 21
amorec-er 48
amorg-ar 51
amorgon-ar 1
amorill-ar 1
amorr-ar 1
amorrin-ar 1
amorriñ-arse ... 80
amorron-ar 1
amorrong-
arse 51
amortaj-ar 1
amortec-er 48
amortigu-ar 7
amortiz-ar 21
amorug-arse 51
amosc-ar 67
amostaz-ar 21
amotin-ar 1
amov-er 47
amoz-arse 21
ampar-ar 1
ampi-ar 1
ampiel-ar 1
ampli-ar 9
amplific-ar 67
ampoll-ar 1
ampr-ar 1
ampuch-ar 1
amput-ar 1
amuch-ar 1
amuebl-ar 1
amuel-ar 1
amuf-ar 1
amugron-ar 1
amuj-ar 1
amul-ar 1
amullic-ar 67
amunicion-ar 1
amunuc-arse ... 80
amuñij-ar 1
amurall-ar 1
amur-ar 1
amurc-ar 67
amurill-ar 1
amurr-arse 80
amurri-arse 80
amurriñ-arse ... 80
amusg-ar 51
amusti-ar 1
anac-er 48
anade-ar 1
anadi-ar 1
anagramatiz-
ar 21
analiz-ar 21
anaranje-ar 1
anarquiz-ar 21
anascot-ar 1
anastomiz-
arse 21
anastomos-
arse 80
anatematiz-
ar 21
anatomiz-ar 21
anc-arse 67
anch-ar 1
ancho-ar 1
ancl-ar 1
ancle-ar 1
ancor-ar 1
andaluz-arse 21
andami-ar 1
and-ar 10
andarague-ar 1
andaregue-ar 1
andarieg-ar 1
andig-ar 1
andivel-ar 1
andone-ar 1
andorre-ar 1
ane-ar 1
anebl-ar 53
anecdotiz-ar 21
aneci-arse 80
aned-ir 3
aneg-ar 51
anej-ar 1
anestesi-ar 1
anex-ar 1
anexion-ar 1
angarill-ar 1
angarille-ar 1
angel-ar 1
angeliz-ar 21
angeliz-arse 21
angost-ar 1
angusti-ar 1

ar 1
apesar-ar 1
apescoll-ar 25
apesg-ar 51
apestañ-ar 1
apest-ar 1
apestill-ar 1
apetec-er 48
apezon-ar 1
apezuñ-ar 1
apiad-ar 1
apian-ar 1
apicar-arse 80
apicon-ar 1
apil-ar 1
apilg-arse 51
apilgu-arse 80
apilon-ar 1
apilong-arse 51
apimpl-arse 80
apimpoll-ar 1
apimpoll-
arse 80
apiñ-ar 1
apiñusc-ar 67
apioj-arse 80
apiol-ar 1
apip-arse 80
apiporr-arse 80
apirab-ar 1
apiramid-ar 1
apire-ar 1
apirgüin-arse ... 80
apison-ar 1
apit-ar 1
apitigu-arse 7
apiton-ar 1
aplac-ar 67
aplac-er 11
aplan-ar 1
aplanch-ar 1
aplant-ar 1
aplantill-ar 1
aplasm-ar 1
aplast-ar 1
aplatan-ar 1
aplaud-ir 3
aplay-ar 1
aplaz-ar 21
aplebey-ar 1
aplic-ar 67
aplom-ar 1
apoc-ar 67
apoc-arse 67
apoch-arse 80
apochong-
arse 51
apocilg-arse 80
apocop-ar 1
apod-ar 1
apoder-ar 1
apoge-ar 1
apolill-ar 1
apolism-ar 1
apologetiz-ar ... 21
apologiz-ar 21
apoltron-ar 1
apoltron-arse ... 80
apolvill-arse 80
apomaz-ar 21
apomp-ar 1
aponch-ar 1
apontoc-ar 67
aponz-ar 21
apop-ar 1
apopoch-
arse 80
apoquec-er 48
apoquin-ar 1
aporc-ar 67
aporism-arse ... 80
aporrace-ar 1
aporr-ar 1
aporr-arse 80
aporrat-ar 1
aporre-ar 1
aporrill-arse 80
aport-ar 1
aportill-ar 1
aporuñ-ar 1
apos-ar 1
aposent-ar 1
aposesion-ar 1
apost-ar 25
apostat-ar 1
apostem-ar 1
apostill-ar 1
apostill-arse 80
apostoliz-ar 21
apostrof-ar 1
apotenci-ar 1
apotinc-ar 1
apotinc-arse 67
apotr-arse 80
apotrer-ar 1
apoy-ar 1
apoz-arse 21
apreci-ar 1
aprehend-er 2
apremi-ar 1
aprend-er 2
aprens-ar 1
aprension-
arse 80
apres-ar 1
aprest-ar 1
aprestigi-ar 1
apresur-ar 1
apret-ar 53
apretin-ar 1
apretuj-ar 1
apreven-ir 77
aprim-ar 1
aprisc-ar 67
aprision-ar 1
apro-ar 1
aprob-ar 25
apront-ar 1
apropi-ar 1
apropincu-ar 1
apropincu-
arse 80
aprovech-ar 1
aprovision-ar 1
aproxim-ar 1
aprudenci-
arse 80
aprudent-
arse 80
apt-ar 1
apuchinch-ar 1
apuchinch-
arse 80
apulgar-ar 1
apulgar-arse 80
apulism-arse ... 80
apun-arse 80
apunch-ar 1
apuntal-ar 1
apunt-ar 1
apuntill-ar 1
apuñad-ar 1
apuñal-ar 1
apuñale-ar 1
apuñ-ar 1
apuñe-ar 1
apuñeg-ar 1
apuñete-ar 1
apuñusc-ar 67
apur-ar 1
apurr-ir 3
apurruñ-ar 1
apusus-arse 80
aquebraj-ar 1
aquebraz-
arse 21
aquejer-ar 1
aquejumbr-
arse 80
aquer-arse 80
aquerenci-ar 1
aqueres-ar 1
aquerid-arse 80
aquiesc-er 2,
and used in
the positions
in 45
aquiet-ar 1
aquilat-ar 1
equill-ar 1
aquintral-
arse 80
aquist-ar 1
arabiz-ar 21
arancel-ar 1
arancel-arse 80
arañ-ar 1
ar-ar 1
arbitr-ar 1
arbol-ar 1
arbole-ar 1
arbolec-er 48
arborec-er 48
arboriz-ar 21
arcabuce-ar 1
arcaiz-ar 35
arc-ar 67
archiv-ar 1
arcill-ar 1
ardale-ar 1
ard-er 2
arel-ar 1
aren-ar 1
arenc-ar 67

areng-ar 51
arf-ar 1
argamas-ar 1
argay-ar 1
argent-ar 1
argentiniz-ar 21
argoll-ar 1
argue-ar 1
arguell-arse 80
argü-ir 12
argument-ar 1
aric-ar 67
arid-arse 80
aridec-er 48
ariet-ar 1
arinc-arse 80
arisc-arse 67
arisque-ar 1
aristocratiz-ar 21
arl-ar 1
arm-ar 1
armiñ-ar 1
armoniz-ar 21
arom-ar 1
aromatiz-ar 21
arp-ar 1
arpegi-ar 1
arpi-ar 1
arpill-ar 1
arpiñ-ar 1
arpon-ar 1
arpone-ar 1
arque-ar 1
arquet-ar 1
arrabiat-ar 1
arracim-arse 80
arraig-ar 51
arraiz-ar 35
arral-ar 1
arrambl-ar 1
arrampl-ar 1
arran-arse 80
arranc-ar 67
arranch-ar 1
arranci-arse 80
arrap-ar 1
arras-ar 1
arrastr-ar 1
array-ar 1
arre-ar 1
arrebalg-ar 51
arrebañ-ar 1
arrebat-ar 1
arrebiat-ar 1
arrebol-ar 1
arreboll-arse 80
arreboz-ar 21
arrebuj-ar 1
arrebuñ-ar 1
arrecad-ar 1
arrecent-ar 53
arrechonch-arse 80
arrechunch-ar ... 1
arreci-ar 1
arrecif-ar 1
arrec-ir 4
arrec-irse 82, and used in the positions in 4
arredi-ar 1
arredil-ar 1
arredom-ar 1
arredonde-ar 1
arredr-ar 1
arregaz-ar 21
arregl-ar 1
arregost-ar 1
arreguer-ar 1
arrejac-ar 4
arrej-ar 1
arrejer-ar 1
arreling-arse 80
arrellan-arse 80
arremang-ar 51
arremanguiñ-ar 1
arremans-ar 1
arremat-ar 1
arremend-ar 1
arremet-er 2
arreming-arse 51
arremolin-ar 1
arrempuj-ar 1
arrend-ar 53
arrepanchig-arse 51
arrepas-ar 1
arrepent-ir 71
arrepent-irse ... 71
arrepist-ar 1
arrepoll-ar 1
arrequeson-arse 80
arrequint-ar 1
arrest-ar 1
arretac-arse 80
arrezag-ar 51
arri-ar 9
arriat-ar 1
arriaz-ar 21
arrib-ar 1
arrici-arse 80
arrid-ar 1
arriend-ar 1
arriesg-ar 51
arrig-irse 82, plus the changes in red in 23
arrim-ar 1
arrincon-ar 1
arriostr-ar 1
arris-ar 1
arrisc-ar 67
arriz-ar 21
arrob-ar 1
arrobin-ar 1
arrobiñ-ar 1
arroch-ar 1
arrochel-arse ... 80
arrocin-ar 1
arrodaj-arse 80
arrode-ar 1
arrodel-ar 1
arrodill-ar 1
arrodrig-ar 51
arrodrigon-ar 1
arrog-ar 51
arroj-ar 1
arroll-ar 1
arroll-arse 80
arromadiz-ar 21
arromanz-ar 21
arrom-ar 1
arromp-er 2
arron-ar 1
arronz-ar 21
arrop-ar 1
arrostr-ar 1
arroy-ar 1
arroy-arse 80
arru-ar 1
arruch-ar 1
arruf-ar 1
arrufian-arse ... 80
arrug-ar 51
arruin-ar 1
arrull-ar 1
arrum-ar 1
arrum-arse 80, and for its use regarding weather, see 45
arrumazon-arse 80
arrumb-ar 1
arrunch-arse 80
arrunfl-ar 1
arrut-ar 1
arrutin-ar 1
arterializ-ar 21
arteson-ar 1
articul-ar 1
artig-ar 51
artill-ar 1
artiz-ar 21
artuñ-ar 1
aruñ-ar 1
asac-ar 67
asaete-ar 1
asainete-ar 1
asalari-ar 1
asalmer-ar 1
asalt-ar 1
asalte-ar 1
asan-ar 1
as-ar 1
asasel-ar 1
ascend-er 2, plus the changes in red in 53
ase-ar 1
asech-ar 1
ased-ar 1
asedi-ar 1
aseglar-arse 80
asegu-ir 52
asegund-ar 1

asegur-ar ... 1
asel-arse ... 80
asemej-ar ... 1
asemill-ar ... 1
asendere-ar ... 1
asent-ar ... 53
asent-ir ... 71
aseptiz-ar ... 21
aseren-ar ... 1
aseri-arse ... 80
aserr-ar ... 53
aserre-ar ... 1
aserruch-ar ... 1
asert-ar ... 1
ases-ar ... 1
asesin-ar ... 1
asesor-ar ... 1
asest-ar 1, and alternatively, ... 53
asever-ar ... 1
asfalt-ar ... 1
asfixi-ar ... 1
asg-ar ... 1
asibil-ar ... 1
asign-ar ... 1
asiguat-arse ... 80
asil-ar ... 1
asimil-ar ... 1
asin-ar ... 1
as-ir ... 13
asist-ir ... 3
asne-ar ... 1
asobarc-ar ... 4
asobi-ar ... 1
asobin-arse ... 80
asocair-arse ... 80
asoc-ar ... 67
asoci-ar ... 1
asolan-ar ... 1
asolap-ar ... 1
asol-ar ... 25
asoldad-ar ... 1
asold-ar ... 25
asole-ar ... 1
asollam-ar ... 1
asollan-ar ... 1
asom-ar ... 1
asombr-ar ... 1
asonant-ar ... 1
ason-ar ... 25
asord-ar ... 1
asorn-ar ... 1
asoroch-arse ... 80
asoseg-ar ... 62
asotan-ar ... 1
asp-ar ... 1
aspavent-ar ... 53
aspavient-arse ... 80
aspe-ar ... 1
aspe-arse ... 80
aspere-ar ... 1
asperge-ar ... 1
asperg-er ... 23
aspergi-ar ... 1
asperj-ar ... 1
asperon-ar ... 1
aspill-ar ... 1
aspille-ar ... 1
aspir-ar ... 1
asque-ar ... 1
ast-ar ... 1
aste-ar ... 1
astill-ar ... 1
astreñ-ir ... 64
astring-ir 3, plus the changes in red in 23, plus the past participle astricto
astriñ-ir ... 17
astrolabi-ar ... 1
astrolog-ar ... 51
asubi-ar ... 1
asum-ir ... 3
asunt-ar ... 1
asur-ar ... 1
asurc-ar ... 67
asust-ar ... 1
asutil-ar ... 1
atabale-ar ... 1
atabardill-arse ... 80
atabill-ar ... 1
atabl-ar ... 1
atac-ar ... 67
atafag-ar ... 51
atagall-ar ... 1
atair-ar ... 1
ataj-ar ... 1
atalaj-ar ... 1
atalant-ar ... 1
atalay-ar ... 1
atalud-ar ... 1
ataluz-ar ... 21
atañ-er ... 14
atapial-ar ... 1
atapuz-ar ... 21
ataquiz-ar ... 21
at-ar ... 1
atarace-ar ... 1
atarant-ar ... 1
ataraz-ar ... 21
atardec-er 48, and for its use regarding weather, see ... 45
atare-ar ... 1
atarquin-ar ... 1
atarrag-ar ... 51
atarraj-ar ... 1
atarray-ar ... 1
atarrill-arse ... 80
atarug-ar ... 51
atasaj-ar ... 1
atasc-ar ... 67
atavi-ar ... 67
ate-ar ... 1
atedi-ar ... 1
atejon-arse ... 80
atemoriz-ar ... 21
atemper-ar ... 1
atenace-ar ... 1
atenaz-ar ... 21
atend-er 2, plus the changes in red in 53, plus the past participle atento
atenebr-arse 80, and for its use regarding weather, see ... 45
aten-er ... 74
atental-ar ... 1
atent-ar ... 53
atenu-ar ... 9
ateperet-arse ... 80
aterec-er ... 48
ater-ir ... 4
aternec-er ... 48
aterraj-ar ... 1
aterr-ar ... 53
aterre-ar ... 1
aterrec-er ... 48
aterrer-ar ... 1
aterrill-arse ... 80
aterriz-ar ... 21
aterron-ar ... 1
aterroriz-ar ... 21
ates-ar ... 53
atesor-ar ... 1
atest-ar 1, and alternatively, ... 53
atestigu-ar ... 7
atet-ar ... 1
atetill-ar ... 1
atez-ar ... 21
atib-ar ... 1
atiborr-ar ... 1
atiburr-ar ... 1
atiempr-ar ... 1
aties-ar ... 1
atild-ar ... 1
atilint-ar ... 1
atin-ar ... 1
atinc-ar ... 67
atincon-ar ... 1
ating-ir 3, plus the changes in red in ... 23
atip-arse ... 80
atipl-ar ... 1
atipuj-arse ... 80
atiquiz-ar ... 21
atirant-ar ... 1
atirici-arse ... 80
atisb-ar ... 1
ativ-ar ... 1
atiz-ar ... 21
atizon-ar ... 1
ato-ar ... 1
atoc-ar ... 1
atoch-ar ... 1
atocin-ar ... 1
atoj-ar ... 1
atojin-ar ... 1

atoll-ar ... 1
atollec-er ... 48
atolondr-ar ... 1
atomec-er ... 48
atom-ir ... 4
atomiz-ar ... 21
aton-ar ... 1
atond-ar ... 1
atont-ar ... 1
atontec-er ... 48
atontolin-ar ... 1
ator-ar 1, and alter-natively, ... 25
atorcaz-ar 25, plus the changes in red in ... 21
atorg-ar ... 51
atorment-ar ... 1
atornill-ar ... 1
atoroz-arse ... 21
atorozon-arse ... 80
atorr-ar ... 1
atortaj-ar ... 1
atortill-ar ... 1
atortoj-ar ... 1
atortol-ar ... 1
atortor-ar ... 1
atortuj-ar ... 1
atorzon-arse ... 80
atosig-ar ... 51
atoxic-ar ... 67
atrabaj-ar ... 1
atrabanc-ar ... 67
atrac-ar ... 67
atra-er ... 75
atrafag-ar ... 51
atragant-ar ... 1
atragant-arse ... 80
atraicion-ar ... 1
atraill-ar ... 9
atralac-arse ... 80
atramoj-ar ... 1
atramp-ar ... 1
atranc-ar ... 67
atrap-ar ... 1
atras-ar ... 1
atraves-ar ... 53
atraznal-ar ... 1

atregu-ar ... 7
atresnal-ar ... 1
atreud-ar ... 1
atrev-er ... 2
atrev-erse ... 81
atribu-ir ... 42
atribul-ar ... 1
atrill-ar ... 1
atrinc-ar ... 1
atrincher-ar ... 1
atroch-ar ... 1
atrofi-ar ... 1
atroj-ar ... 1
atron-ar 25, and for its use regarding weather, see ... 45
atronc-ar ... 1
atroner-ar ... 1
atrop-ar ... 1
atropell-ar ... 1
atropill-ar ... 1
atroz-ar ... 21
atruhan-arse ... 80
atucuñ-ar ... 1
atuf-ar ... 1
atuj-ar ... 1
atumultu-ar ... 9
atuntun-arse ... 80
atur-ar ... 1
aturbant-ar ... 1
aturbon-arse ... 80
aturd-ir ... 3
aturne-ar ... 1
aturrull-ar ... 1
aturull-ar ... 1
atus-ar ... 1
augur-ar ... 1
aull-ar ... 9
aument-ar ... 1
aun-ar ... 9
auñ-ar ... 1
aup-ar ... 9
aureol-ar ... 1
aurific-ar ... 67
auscult-ar ... 1
ausent-ar ... 1
auspici-ar ... 1
autentic-ar ... 67
autentific-ar ... 67

autocopi-ar ... 1
autografi-ar ... 9
automatiz-ar ... 21
autopsi-ar ... 1
autoriz-ar ... 21
autosuges-tion-arse ... 80
auxili-ar ... 1
avad-ar ... 1
avag-arse ... 80
avah-ar ... 1
aval-ar ... 1
avalent-ar ... 53
avaliz-ar ... 21
avall-ar ... 1
avalor-ar ... 1
avalu-ar ... 9
avanec-erse ... 48
avanz-ar ... 21
avasall-ar ... 1
avecin-ar ... 1
avecind-ar ... 1
avejanc-arse ... 67
avejent-ar ... 1
avejig-ar ... 51
avellan-ar ... 1
aven-ar ... 1
avenen-ar ... 1
aven-ir ... 77
aventaj-ar ... 1
avent-ar ... 53
aventur-ar ... 1
aver-ar ... 1
averdug-ar ... 51
avergonz-ar ... 15
averi-ar ... 9
averi-arse ... 9
averigu-ar ... 9
averrug-arse ... 51
avez-ar ... 21
avi-ar ... 9
aviej-ar ... 1
avigor-ar ... 1
avilant-arse ... 80
avillan-ar ... 1
avinagr-ar ... 1
avinz-arse ... 21
avis-ar ... 1
avisp-ar ... 1
avisped-ar ... 1
avispore-ar ... 1

avist-ar ... 1
avitol-ar ... 1
avituall-ar ... 1
aviv-ar ... 1
avizor-ar ... 1
avoc-ar ... 67
avos-ar ... 1
axegu-ar ... 1
axiomatiz-ar ... 19
aye-ar ... 1
ayerm-ar ... 1
ayud-ar ... 1
ayun-ar ... 1
ayunisar-ar ... 1
ayust-ar ... 1
azacan-arse ... 80
azacane-ar ... 1
azadon-ar ... 1
azafran-ar ... 1
azain-ar ... 1
azanj-ar ... 1
azarand-ar ... 1
azar-ar ... 1
azar-arse ... 80
azare-arse ... 80
azem-ar ... 1
azo-ar ... 1
azocal-ar ... 1
azoc-ar ... 67
azofr-ar ... 1
azog-ar ... 51
azol-ar ... 25
azolv-ar ... 1
azor-ar ... 1
azoroc-arse ... 67
azorr-ar ... 1
azorr-arse ... 80
azot-ar ... 1
azozobr-ar ... 1
azucar-ar ... 1
azufr-ar ... 1
azul-ar ... 1
azule-ar ... 1
azulej-ar ... 1
azumag-arse ... 51
azum-ar ... 1
azurron-arse ... 80
azurumb-arse ... 80
azuz-ar ... 21

b

bab-ar 1
babe-ar 1
babilone-ar 1
babose-ar 1
babuj-ar 1
babuse-ar 1
bachate-ar 1
bache-ar 1
bachille-ar 1
bachiller-ar 1
bachillere-ar 1
badaje-ar 1
badall-ar 1
badern-ar 1
badulaque-ar 1
bafane-ar 1
baf-ar 1
bafe-ar 1
bag-ar 51
bail-ar 1
bailote-ar 1
baj-ar 1
baje-ar 1
balace-ar 1
baladr-ar 1
baladre-ar 1
baladron-ar 1
baladrone-ar 1
balance-ar 1
balandrone-ar 1
balaque-ar 1
bal-ar 1
balast-ar 1
balastr-ar 1
balaustr-ar 1
balay-ar 1
balbuce-ar 1
balbuc-ir 16
balcaniz-ar 21
balcone-ar 1
bald-ar 1
balde-ar 1
baldon-ar 1
baldone-ar 1
baldos-ar 1
bale-ar 1
bali-ar 1
balit-ar 1
balite-ar 1
baliz-ar 21
ball-ar 1
ballest-ar 1
balleste-ar 1
balot-ar 1
balsam-ar 1
balsamiz-ar 21
balse-ar 1
bambale-ar 1
bambane-ar 1
bambarote-ar 1
bambe-ar 1
bambole-ar 1
bambone-ar 1
bamborde-ar 1
bambuque-ar 1
bandare-ar 1
band-arse 80
bande-ar 1
bandej-ar 1
banderille-ar 1
banderiz-ar 21
band-ir 3
bandolere-ar 1
banque-ar 1
banquete-ar 1
bañ-ar 1
baptiz-ar 21
baque-ar 1
baqueliz-ar 21
baquete-ar 1
baqui-ar 9
barahust-ar 1
baraj-ar 1
barajust-ar 1
barand-ar 1
barat-ar 1
barate-ar 1
baraust-ar 1
barb-ar 1
barbare-ar 1
barbariz-ar 21
barbasque-ar 1
barbe-ar 1
barbech-ar 1
barbolete-ar 1
barboll-ar 1
barbot-ar 1
barbote-ar 1
barbull-ar 1
barbull-ir 17
barcin-ar 1
bard-ar 1
bareque-ar 1
baritone-ar 1
barlo-ar 1
barlvente-ar 1
barniz-ar 21
barque-ar 1
barrac-arse 80
barraj-ar 1
barranque-ar 1
barraque-ar 1
barr-ar 1
barre-ar 1
barren-ar 1
barrene-ar 1
barr-er 2
barrete-ar 1
barrisc-ar 67
barrisque-ar 1
barrit-ar 1
barrunt-ar 1
bartole-ar 1
bartul-ar 1
bartule-ar 1
barull-ar 1
barzon-ar 1
barzone-ar 1
bas-ar 1
basc-ar 1
bascul-ar 1
basific-ar 1
basque-ar 1
bastante-ar 1
bast-ar 1
bastard-ar 1
bastarde-ar 1
baste-ar 1
bastec-er 48
bastere-ar 1
bastill-ar 1
bastille-ar 1
bastiment-ar 1
bastion-ar 1
bast-ir 3
bastone-ar 1
basure-ar 1
batajole-ar 1
batall-ar 1
batan-ar 1
batane-ar 1
bate-ar 1
batibole-ar 1
baticole-arse ... 80
batiport-ar 1
bat-ir 3
batoch-ar 1
batoj-ar 1
batoll-ar 1
batuc-ar 67
batuque-ar 1
bautiz-ar 21
bayoy-ar 1
bayunque-ar 1
bazuc-ar 67
bazuque-ar 1
beatific-ar 67
bebd-ar 1
beb-er 2
beberruch-ar 1
beborrete-ar 1
beborrote-ar 1
bec-ar 67
becerre-ar 1
becuadr-ar 1
bed-ar 1
bef-ar 1
bejuque-ar 1
beld-ar 53
bellaque-ar 1
bellote-ar 1
beltrane-ar 1
bembete-ar 1
bemol-ar 1
bemoliz-ar 21
bendec-ir 58, plus the regular past participle bendecido and the irregular past participle bendito
bendic-ir 58
benec-er 48
benefici-ar 1
berling-ar 51
bermeje-ar 1
bermejec-er 48
berr-ar 1
berre-ar 1

berrende-arse 80
berrinch-ar 1
berroch-ar 1
bes-ar 1
besote-ar 1
bestializ-arse ... 21
besuc-ar 67
besuque-ar 1
betume-ar 1
betuminiz-ar 1
betun-ar 1
betune-ar 1
biab-ar 1
bias-ar 1
bich-ar 1
biche-ar 1
bichofe-ar 1
bicromat-ar 1
bield-ar 1
bienaventur-ar ... 1
bienquer-er 60, plus the past participle bienquisto
bienquist-ar 1
bienviv-ir 3
bifurc-arse 67
bigarde-ar 1
bigardone-ar 1
bild-ar 1
bilm-ar 1
biloc-arse 67
bilonque-ar 1
biltrote-ar 1
bin-ar 1
biodegrad-ar 1
biografi-ar 9
birl-ar 1
birol-ar 1
birringue-ar 1
bis-ar 1
bisbis-ar 1
bisbise-ar 1
bisec-ar 67
bisegment-ar 1
bisel-ar 1
bistra-er 75
bistray-er 75
bit-ar 1
bituminiz-ar 21
bizantine-ar 1
bizarre-ar 1
bizc-ar 67
bizcoch-ar 1
bizcorne-ar 1
bizm-ar 1
bizque-ar 1
blande-ar 1
blandec-er 48
bland-ir 4
blanque-ar 1
blanquec-er 48
blasfem-ar 1
blasm-ar 1
blason-ar 1
blinc-ar 67
blind-ar 1
bloc-ar 67
bloque-ar 1
bluf-ar 1
blufe-ar 1
bobe-ar 1
bobin-ar 1
bocade-ar 1
bocarte-ar 1
boce-ar 1
bocel-ar 1
bocez-ar 21
boch-ar 1
bochinche-ar 1
bocin-ar 1
bocone-ar 1
bodegone-ar 1
bof-arse 80
bofete-ar 1
boford-ar 1
bog-ar 51
bogue-ar 1
bohord-ar 1
boicote-ar 1
boj-ar 1
boje-ar 1
bojote-ar 1
bolace-ar 1
bolcheviz-ar 21
bole-ar 1
bolere-ar 1
bolet-ar 1
bolete-ar 1
boliche-ar 1
boline-ar 1
boll-ar 1
bollici-ar 1
boll-ir 3
bolse-ar 1
bolsique-ar 1
bomb-ar 1
bombarde-ar 1
bombe-ar 1
bonderiz-ar 21
bonific-ar 67
boque-ar 1
boquete-ar 1
boraci-ar 1
borboll-ar 1
borbolle-ar 1
borbollone-ar 1
borborit-ar 1
borbot-ar 1
borbote-ar 1
bord-ar 1
borde-ar 1
bordej-ar 1
bordone-ar 1
borl-arse 80
borle-arse 80
borne-ar 1
bornegue-ar 1
borrache-ar 1
borraje-ar 1
borr-ar 1
borregue-ar 1
borrone-ar 1
bos-ar 1
boscaje-ar 1
bosquej-ar 1
boste-ar 1
bostez-ar 21
bostic-ar 67
bostone-ar 1
botacuch-ar 1
botalone-ar 1
botaniz-ar 21
bot-ar 1
botarate-ar 1
bote-ar 1
boton-ar 1
boved-ar 1
boxe-ar 1
boy-ar 1
boycote-ar 1
bozale-ar 1
brace-ar 1
bram-ar 1
brand-ar 1
brandec-er 2
bras-ar 1
brasc-ar 67
bravate-ar 1
brave-ar 1
bravi-ar 1
bravoce-ar 1
bravucone-ar 1
braz-ar 1
brazn-ar 1
bre-ar 1
brech-ar 1
breg-ar 51
bregete-ar 1
breguete-ar 1
breque-ar 1
bresc-ar 67
brete-ar 1
brez-ar 21
brib-ar 1
bribi-ar 1
bribone-ar 1
brid-ar 1
brill-ar 1
brinc-ar 67
brincole-ar 1
brind-ar 1
bris-ar 1
brisc-ar 67
briz-ar 21
brizn-ar 1
broc-ar 1
broce-arse 80
broch-ar 1
broll-ar 1
brom-ar 1
brome-ar 1
bronce-ar 1
bronque-ar 1
broquel-arse 80
brosl-ar 1
brot-ar 1
broz-ar 21
bruje-ar 1
bruj-ir 3
brujule-ar 1
brum-ar 1
bruñ-ir 17

brutaliz-ar 21
brutaliz-arse 21
brute-ar 1
bruz-ar 21
buce-ar 1
buch-ar 1
buf-ar 1
bufone-ar 1
bufone-arse 80
bufoniz-ar 21
bug-ir 3, plus the changes in red in 23
buh-ar 1
bu-ir 42
buitre-ar 1
bujarrone-ar 1
bul-ar 1
buld-ar 1
bull-ar 1
bullec-er 48
bull-ir 17
bunde-ar 1
burbuje-ar 1
bure-ar 1
buril-ar 1
burl-ar 1
burocratiz-ar 21
burraje-ar 1
burre-ar 1
busc-ar 67
buscone-ar 1
buz-ar 21

C

cabal-ar 1
cabalg-ar 51
cabaliz-ar 21
caballe-ar 1
caballere-ar 1
cabdill-ar 1
cabe-ar 1
cabece-ar 1
cabell-ar 1
cab-er 18
cabestr-ar 1
cabestre-ar 1
cabilde-ar 1
cable-ar 1
cablegrafi-ar 74
cabrafig-ar 1
cabrahig-ar 19
cabre-ar 1
cabrest-ar 1
cabreste-ar 1
cabrev-ar 1
cabrille-ar 1
cabriol-ar 1
cabriole-ar 1
cabrion-ar 1
cabruñ-ar 1
cabule-ar 1
cabz-ar 21
cacabe-ar 1
cacarañ-ar 1
cacaraque-ar 1
cacare-ar 1
cace-ar 1
cachache-ar 1
cachañ-ar 1
cachañe-ar 1
cachape-ar 1
cachaque-ar 1
cach-ar 1
cacharpe-arse 80
cacharre-ar 1
cache-ar 1
cachete-ar 1
cachiflore-ar 1
cachifol-ar 1
cachifoll-ar 1
cachilape-ar 1
cachilapi-ar 1
cachipod-ar 1
cachiporre-arse 80
cachirule-ar 1
cachonde-ar 1
cachonde-arse 80
cachorre-ar 1
cachu-ar 1
cachuche-ar 1
cachuele-ar 1
cachunc-ar 1
cachure-ar 1
cacique-ar 1
cacul-ar 1
cacule-ar 1
cadenci-ar 1
cadene-ar 1
cadmi-ar 1
caduc-ar 67
caduque-ar 1
ca-er 20
caf-ar 1
cafete-ar 1
cag-ar 51
caigü-ir 42
caimane-ar 1
cain-ar 1
cairel-ar 1
caje-ar 1
cajete-ar 1
cajone-ar 1
calabace-ar 1
calabri-ar 1
calabrot-ar 1
calace-ar 1
calafate-ar 1
calafet-ar 1
calafete-ar 1
calamon-arse 80
calamorr-ar 1
calandr-ar 1
cal-ar 1
calate-ar 1
calaver-ar 1
calavere-ar 1
calc-ar 67
calcet-ar 1
calcete-ar 1
calcific-ar 67
calcin-ar 1
calcitr-ar 1
calcografi-ar 74
calcorre-ar 1
calcul-ar 1
calde-ar 1
calec-er 48
calec-erse 48
calend-ar 1
calent-ar 53
calenture-ar 1
cal-er 2
calete-ar 1
calibr-ar 1
calich-ar 1
calific-ar 67
caligrafi-ar 74
calill-ar 1
calimb-ar 1
callant-ar 1
callape-ar 1
call-ar 1
calle-ar 1
callec-er 48
calleje-ar 1
callent-ar 1
callos-ar 1
calm-ar 1
calme-ar 1
calofri-arse 74
calomni-ar 1
caloni-ar 1
caloñ-ar 1
calor-ar 1
calosfri-arse 80
calote-ar 1
calumb-arse 80
calumni-ar 1
calv-ar 1
calvec-er 48
calz-ar 21
camandul-ar 1
camandule-ar 1
camarone-ar 1
camastre-ar 1
cambalach-ar 1
cambalache-ar 1
camb-ar 1
cambi-ar 1
cambiz-ar 21
camel-ar 1
cami-ar 1
camin-ar 1
camoch-ar 1
camod-ar 1
camorre-ar 1
camote-ar 1
campane-ar 1
campanille-ar 1
camp-ar 1
campe-ar 1
campej-ar 1
camufl-ar 1
canalete-ar 1
canaliz-ar 21
canaque-ar 1

can-ar 1
cancane-ar 1
cancel-ar 1
cancer-ar 1
canch-ar 1
canche-ar 1
cand-ar 1
candelill-ar 1
candilete-ar 1
cand-irse 82
candombe-ar 1
candongue-ar 1
cane-ar 1
canec-er 48
canec-erse 48
canfor-ar 1
cangall-ar 1
cang-ar 51
cangreje-ar 1
cangren-arse 80
canguel-ar 1
canj-ar 1
canje-ar 1
canmi-ar 1
canoniz-ar 21
cans-ar 1
cantale-ar 1
cantalete-ar 1
cant-ar 1
cante-ar 1
cantic-ar 1
cantine-ar 1
canton-ar 1
cantone-ar 1
cantone-arse 80
canturre-ar 1
canturri-ar 1
cantus-ar 1
canut-ar 1
cañ-ar 1
cañaver-ar 1
cañavere-ar 1
cañe-ar 1
cañone-ar 1
caoliniz-ar 21
capace-ar 1
capacete-ar 1
capacit-ar 1
cap-ar 1
capcion-ar 1
cape-ar 1
caperuce-ar 1
capialz-ar 21
capicul-ar 1
capirote-ar 1
capitaliz-ar 21
capitane-ar 1
capitone-ar 1
capitul-ar 1
capitule-ar 1
capol-ar 1
capon-ar 1
capone-arse 80
caporale-ar 1
capot-ar 1
capote-ar 1
caprific-ar 1
capsul-ar 1
capt-ar 1
capten-er 74
captiv-ar 1
captur-ar 1
capuce-ar 1
capuj-ar 1
capuz-ar 21
carabe-ar 1
carabin-ar 1
carabine-ar 1
carabrite-ar 1
caracole-ar 1
caracteriz-ar 21
carambol-ar 1
carambole-ar 1
caramele-ar 1
carameliz-ar 21
caramill-ar 1
carapite-ar 1
carbon-ar 1
carbonat-ar 1
carbone-ar 1
carboniz-ar 21
carbur-ar 1
carcaje-ar 1
carcav-ar 1
carcave-ar 1
carcavin-ar 1
carcel-ar 1
carcer-ar 1
carch-ar 1
carcomec-er 2
carcom-er 2
card-ar 1
cardenaliz-ar 1
carduz-ar 21
care-ar 1
carec-er 48
caren-ar 1
carg-ar 51
cargose-ar 1
cari-ar 1
caribe-ar 1
caricatur-ar 1
caricaturiz-ar 21
carillone-ar 1
carimb-ar 1
cariñ-ar 1
carle-ar 1
carmen-ar 1
carmin-ar 1
carnavale-ar 1
carne-ar 1
carnere-ar 1
carnific-arse 67
caroch-ar 1
caronch-arse 80
carpente-ar 1
carpete-ar 1
carpinte-ar 1
carpintere-ar 1
carp-ir 3
carrance-ar 1
carrañ-arse 80
carraplane-ar 1
carraspe-ar 1
carrasque-ar 1
carre-ar 1
carrej-ar 1
carrere-ar 1
carrete-ar 1
carric-ar 1
carrill-ar 1
carroce-ar 1
carroch-ar 1
carroñ-ar 1
carroz-ar 21
carruc-ar 67
cartabone-ar 1
carte-ar 1
cartele-ar 1
cartografi-ar 74
casament-ar 53
cas-ar 1
cascabele-ar 1
cascamaj-ar 1
casc-ar 67
cascare-ar 1
cascarone-ar 1
cascarrin-ar 1
cascote-ar 1
cascunde-ar 1
caseific-ar 67
caspalete-ar 1
casque-ar 1
casquine-ar 1
castañe-ar 1
castañete-ar 1
castellaniz-ar 21
castific-ar 1
castig-ar 51
castiz-ar 21
castr-ar 1
casualiz-ar 21
casuistic-ar 67
casungue-ar 1
catalaniz-ar 21
cataliz-ar 21
catalog-ar 51
catane-ar 1
catapult-ar 1
cat-ar 1
catarre-ar 1
catastr-ar 1
catat-ar 1
cate-ar 1
catedr-ar 1
catequiz-ar 21
cateteriz-ar 21
catip-ar 1
catite-ar 1
cativ-ar 1
catoliz-ar 21
catoniz-ar 21
catrine-ar 1
cauc-arse 80
cauch-ar 1
cauchut-ar 1
caucion-ar 1
caus-ar 1
cause-ar 1
caustic-ar 67
caustific-ar 1
cautel-ar 1
cauteriz-ar 21
cautiv-ar 1

coid-ar 1
coime-ar 1
coincid-ir 3
coindic-ar 1
coinquin-ar 1
coit-ar 1
coje-ar 1
colabor-ar 1
colacion-ar 1
colaps-ar 1
col-ar 1,
and alter-
natively, ... 25
colaud-ar 1
colch-ar 25
cole-ar 1
coleccion-ar 1
colect-ar 1
colectiviz-ar 21
coleg-ar 1
colegi-arse 80
coleg-ir 3,
plus the
changes
in red in 46
coleriz-ar 21
colete-ar 1
colgande-ar 1
colgandeje-ar 1
colg-ar 24
colicu-ar 74
colicuec-er 48
colid-ir 3
colig-ar 51
colig-arse 80
colim-ar 1
colind-ar 1
colision-ar 1
colite-ar 1
coll-er 2
coll-ir 3
colm-ar 1
colmat-ar 1
colmene-ar 1
colobe-ar 1
coloc-ar 67
coloniz-ar 21
color-ar 1
colore-ar 1
color-ir 4
colp-ar 1
colud-ir 3
columbe-ar 1
columbr-ar 1
columniz-ar 21
columpi-ar 1
comadre-ar 1
comale-ar 1
comalec-
erse 48
comandante-
ar 1
comand-ar 1
comandit-ar 1
comarc-ar 67
combalach-
arse 80
comb-ar 1
combat-ir 3
combin-ar 1
combr-ar 1
come-ar 1
comedi-ar 1
comed-ir 52
comed-irse 52
comend-ar 1
coment-ar 1
comentari-ar 74
comenz-ar 34
com-er 2
comercializ-
ar 21
comerci-ar 1
comet-er 2
comiche-ar 1
comine-ar 1
comique-ar 1
comis-ar 1
comisc-ar 67
comision-ar 1
comisque-ar 1
comor-ar 1
compact-ar 1
compadec-er ... 48
compadr-ar 1
compadre-ar 1
compagin-ar 1
compang-ar 51
compar-ar 1
comparec-er 48
compart-ir 1
compas-ar 1
compase-ar 1
compatibiliz-
ar 21
compel-er 2,
plus the past
participle
compulso
compendi-ar 1
compendiz-
ar 21
compenetr-ar 1
compenetr-
arse 80
compens-ar 1
compermut-ar ... 1
compet-er 2
compet-ir 52
compiad-
arse 80
compiez-ar 21
compil-ar 1
compil-ir 3
complac-er 54
complan-ar 1
complañ-ir 3
complement-
ar 1
complet-ar 1
complexion-ar ... 1
complic-ar 67
compl-ir 3
complot-ar 1
compod-ar 1
compon-er 57
componte-ar 1
comport-ar 1
comport-arse ... 80
compr-ar 1
comprend-er 2,
plus the past
participle
comprenso
comprim-ir 3,
plus the past
participle
compreso
compr-ir 3
comprob-ar 25
compromet-er ... 2
compuls-ar 1
compung-ir 3,
plus the
changes
in red in 23
compurg-ar 51
computadoriz-
ar 21
comput-ar 1
computariz-
ar 21
comulg-ar 51
comung-ar 1
comunic-ar 67
comunistiz-
ar 21
concaden-ar 1
concaten-ar 1
concaus-ar 1
concav-ar 1
conceb-ir 52
conced-er 1
concej-ar 1
concelebr-ar 1
concen-ar 1
concentr-ar 1
concepte-ar 1
conceptu-ar 74
concern-ir 3,
plus the
changes
in red in 53
concert-ar 53
conchab-ar 1
conchabe-ar 1
conch-ar 1
conchav-ar 1
conchuch-
arse 80
concienci-ar 1
concientiz-ar ... 21
concili-ar 1
concion-ar 1
concit-ar 1
conclu-ir 42,
plus the past
participle
concluso
concom-erse ... 81
concomit-ar 1
concord-ar 25
concrecion-ar 1
concret-ar 1

conculc-ar 67
concurr-ir 3
concurs-ar 1
condam-ar 1
conde-ar 1
condecend-er 2, plus the changes in red in 53
condec-ir 28
condecor-ar 1
condej-ar 1
conden-ar 1
condens-ar 1, plus the past participle condenso
condes-ar 1
condescend-er 2, plus the changes in red in 53
condex-ar 1
condicion-ar 1
condiment-ar 1
cond-ir 3
condistingu-ir 3
condolec-erse 52
condol-er 47
condol-erse 47
condon-ar 1
condongue-arse 80
conduc-ir 59
condur-ar 1
conect-ar 1
coneje-ar 1
conexion-ar 1
confabul-ar 1
confeccion-ar 1
confeder-ar 1
conferec-er 48
conferenci-ar 1
confer-ir 71
confes-ar 53, plus the past participle confeso
confi-ar 74
conficion-ar 1
confidenci-ar 1
configur-ar 1
confin-ar 1
confing-ir 3, plus the changes in red in 23
confirm-ar 1
confisc-ar 67
confit-ar 1
conflagr-ar 1
conflu-ir 42
conform-ar 1
confort-ar 1
confragu-ar 1
confratern-ar 1
confraterniz-ar 21
confric-ar 67
confront-ar 1
confu-ir 42
confund-ir 3, plus the past participle confuso
confut-ar 1
congel-ar 1
congeni-ar 1
congestion-ar 1
conglob-ar 1
conglomer-ar 1
conglori-ar 1
conglutin-ar 1
congoj-ar 1
congole-ar 1
congraci-ar 1
congratul-ar 1
congreg-ar 51
conhort-ar 1
conific-ar 1
conjetur-ar 1
conjug-ar 51
conjunt-ar 1
conjurament-ar 1
conjur-ar 1
conllev-ar 1
conllor-ar 1
conlo-ar 1
conmemor-ar 1
conmensur-ar 1
conmin-ar 1
conmiser-ar 1
conmiser-arse 80
conmocion-ar 1
conmov-er 47
conmut-ar 1
connaturaliz-ar 21
connaturaliz-arse 80
conniv-ir 3
connombr-ar 1
connot-ar 1
connumer-ar 1
conoc-er 48
conosc-er 48
conquer-ir 71
conquist-ar 1
conre-ar 1
conrein-ar 1
consacr-ar 1
consagr-ar 1
consecr-ar 1
consegr-ar 1
consegu-ir 52
consej-ar 1
consent-ir 71
conserv-ar 1
consider-ar 1
consign-ar 1
consist-ir 3
consogr-ar 25
consol-ar 25
consolid-ar 1
consonantific-ar 1
consonantiz-ar 21
conson-ar 25
conspir-ar 1
conspu-ir 42
const-ar 1
constat-ar 1
constel-ar 1
constern-ar 1
constip-ar 1
constitucion-aliz-ar 21
constitu-ir 42, plus the past participle constituto
constreñ-ir 64
constring-ir 17
constru-ir 42
constupr-ar 1
consuegr-ar 1
consult-ar 1
consum-ar 1
consum-ir 3, plus the past participle consunto
consustantiv-arse 80
contabiliz-ar 21
contact-ar 1
contagi-ar 1
contamin-ar 1
cont-ar 25
contec-er 48
contemper-ar 1
contempl-ar 1
contemporiz-ar 21
contend-er 2, plus the changes in red in 5
conten-er 74
content-ar 1, plus the past participle contento
contest-ar 1
contextu-ar 74
contingent-ar 1
continu-ar 74
cont-ir 3
contone-arse ... 80
contongue-arse 80
contorc-erse 22
contorn-ar 1
contorne-ar 1
contorsion-arse 80
contraabr-ir 3, except the past participle is contraabierto

contraafianz-
ar 21
contraatac-ar ... 67
contrabalance-
ar 1
contrabande-
ar 1
contrabat-ir 3
contrabrace-ar ... 1
contracalc-ar ... 67
contracambi-
ar 1
contrachap-ar 1
contrachape-
ar 1
contracord-
ar 25
contract-ar 1
contracuartel-
ar 1
contradec-ir 58
contraendos-
ar 1
contra-er 75,
plus the past
participle
contracto
contraescarp-
ar 1
contraesmalt-
ar 1
contraestimul-
ar 1
contrafac-er 2
contrafall-ar 1
contrafirm-ar 1
contraforj-ar 1
contragir-ar 1
contragru-ar 1
contraguiñ-ar 1
contrahac-er 41
contraherr-ar 1
contrahorod-
ar 1
contraindic-
ar 67
contra-ir 43
contral-ar 1
contralibr-ar 1
contrall-ar 1
contrallev-ar 1
contralore-ar 1
contramall-ar 1
contramand-ar ... 1
contramanifest-
ar 53
contramaniobr-
ar 1
contramarc-
ar 67
contramarch-
ar 1
contramat-ar 1
contramin-ar 1
contramurall-
ar 1
contramur-ar 1
contraorden-
ar 1
contrapas-ar 1
contrape-ar 1
contrapech-ar 1
contrapele-ar 1
contrapes-ar 1
contrapon-er 57
contraprob-
ar 25
contrapropon-
er 57
contraproyect-
ar 1
contrapugn-ar 1
contrapunt-ar 1
contrapunt-
arse 80
contrapunte-
ar 1
contrapunz-
ar 21
contrari-ar 74
contrarray-ar 1
contrarrequer-
ir 71
contrarrest-ar 1
contrar-
revolucion-ar ... 1
contrasell-ar 1
contraseñ-ar 1
contrasign-ar 1
contrast-ar 1
contrat-ar 1
contraval-ar 1
contraven-ir 78
contremec-er
48, plus the
changes
in red in 46
contribu-ir 26
contribul-ar 1
contrist-ar 1
control-ar 1
controvert-ir 71
contund-ir 3,
plus the past
participle
contuso
conturb-ar 1
contusion-ar 1
convalec-er 48
convalid-ar 1
convel-erse 81
convenc-er 5,
plus the past
participle
convicto
conven-ir 77
converg-er 23
converg-ir 3,
plus the
changes
in red in 23
convers-ar 1
convert-ir 71,
plus the past
participle
converso
convid-ar 1
conviv-ir 3
convoc-ar 67
convol-ar 25
convolv-erse 47
convoy-ar 1
convuls-ar 1
convulsion-ar 1
conyug-ar 51
coñe-arse 80
cooper-ar 1
coopt-ar 1
coordin-ar 1
cop-ar 1
cope-ar 1
copel-ar 1
copi-ar 1
copil-ar 1
copin-ar 1
cople-ar 1
copolimeriz-
arse 80
coprecipit-ar 1
coproduc-ir 13
copuch-ar 1
copul-ar 1
copul-arse 80
coque-ar 1
coquete-ar 1
coquific-ar 67
coquiz-ar 21
cor-ar 1
corbate-ar 1
corc-arse 80
corch-ar 1
corcov-ar 1
corcove-ar 1
corcus-ir 3
corde-ar 1
cordel-ar 1
core-ar 1
coreografi-ar 9
cori-ar 1
corl-ar 1
corle-ar 1
corne-ar 1
cornete-ar 1
cornific-ar 1
coron-ar 1
coroniz-ar 1
corporific-ar 67
corporiz-arse ... 21
corre-ar 1
corregent-ar 1
correg-ir 32,
plus the past
participle
correcto
correin-ar 1
correlacion-ar 1
correnci-ar 1
correnti-ar 1
corr-er 2
correspond-er 2
corretaje-ar 1
correte-ar 1
corrinche-ar 1
corrobor-ar 1

corroc-ar ... 1
corro-er ... 65
corromp-er 2, plus the past participle corrupto
corrug-ar ... 1
cors-ar ... 1
corse-ar ... 1
cortapis-ar ... 1
cort-ar ... 1
cortej-ar ... 1
cortin-ar ... 1
cortisque-ar ... 1
cortocircuit-ar ... 1
corusc-ar 67, and for its use regarding weather, see ... 45
corv-ar ... 1
corvete-ar ... 1
coscache-ar ... 1
cosc-arse ... 67
coscorrone-ar ... 1
cosech-ar ... 1
cos-er ... 2
cosete-ar ... 1
cospe-arse ... 80
cosque-ar ... 1
cosquill-ar ... 1
cosquille-ar ... 1
costal-ar ... 1
costale-arse ... 80
costane-ar ... 1
cost-ar ... 25
coste-ar ... 1
costiñ-ar ... 1
costreñ-ir ... 64
costribar ... 1
costring-ir 3, plus the changes in red in ... 23
costriñ-ir ... 17
costru-ir ... 7
costumbr-ar ... 1
costumn-ar ... 1
costur-ar ... 1
costure-ar ... 1
costurone-ar ... 1
cot-ar ... 1
cote-ar ... 1
cotej-ar ... 1
cotille-ar ... 1
cotique-ar ... 1
cotiz-ar ... 21
cotone-ar ... 1
cotorre-ar ... 1
coun-irse ... 3
coxque-ar ... 1
coyote-ar ... 1
coyund-arse ... 80
coyunde-ar ... 1
craque-ar ... 1
crascit-ar ... 1
cre-ar ... 1
crebant-ar ... 1
crecent-ar ... 1
crec-er ... 48
cre-er ... 26
crench-ar ... 1
creosot-ar ... 1
crep-ar ... 1
crepit-ar ... 1
cres-arse ... 80
cresp-ar ... 1
crest-ar ... 1
cretific-ar ... 1
crey-er ... 2
cri-ar ... 9
crib-ar ... 1
crid-ar ... 1
criminaliz-ar ... 21
crimin-ar ... 1
crin-ar ... 1
crineise-ar ... 1
crineje-ar ... 1
crism-ar ... 1
crisol-ar ... 1
crisp-ar ... 1
crisp-ir ... 3
cristaliz-ar ... 21
cristian-ar ... 1
cristianiz-ar ... 21
critic-ar ... 67
critique-ar ... 1
critiquiz-ar ... 21
croaj-ar ... 1
cro-ar ... 1
crocit-ar ... 1
crom-ar ... 1
cromat-ar ... 1
cromolitografi-ar ... 9
croniz-ar ... 1
cronometr-ar ... 1
croscit-ar ... 1
crotor-ar ... 1
crucete-ar ... 1
cruci-ar ... 1
crucific-ar ... 67
crucute-ar ... 1
cruent-ar ... 1
cruj-ir ... 3
cruz-ar ... 21
cuabe-ar ... 1
cuac-ar ... 67
cuadr-ar ... 1
cuadre-ar ... 1
cuadricul-ar ... 1
cuadrill-ar ... 1
cuadrille-ar ... 1
cuadriplic-ar ... 67
cuadruplic-ar ... 67
cuaj-ar ... 1
cualific-ar ... 67
cuanti-ar ... 9
cuantific-ar ... 67
cuaresm-ar ... 1
cuarre-ar ... 1
cuartague-ar ... 1
cuart-ar ... 1
cuarte-ar ... 1
cuartel-ar ... 1
cuartr-ar ... 1
cuatezon-ar ... 1
cuatre-ar ... 1
cuatrere-ar ... 1
cuatrodobl-ar ... 1
cuatrope-ar ... 1
cubanch-ar ... 1
cubanche-ar ... 1
cubaniz-ar ... 21
cubic-ar ... 67
cubij-ar ... 1
cubil-ar ... 1
cubilete-ar ... 1
cubr-ir 3, except the past participle is cubierto
cuc-ar ... 67
cucarache-ar ... 1
cucarre-ar ... 1
cuch-ar ... 1
cuchare-ar ... 1
cucharete-ar ... 1
cuche-ar ... 1
cuchiche-ar ... 1
cuchichi-ar ... 9
cuchill-ar ... 1
cuchuche-ar ... 1
cuchuflet-ar ... 1
cuchuflete-ar ... 1
cuchunche-ar ... 1
cucuruti-ar ... 1
cudici-ar ... 1
cued-ar ... 1
cuente-ar ... 1
cueque-ar ... 1
cuere-ar ... 1
cuerpe-ar ... 1
cuestion-ar ... 1
cuete-ar ... 1
cuete-arse ... 80
cueve-ar ... 1
cufi-ar ... 1
cuhete-ar ... 1
cuid-ar ... 1
cuit-ar ... 1
cuit-arse ... 80
cuite-ar ... 1
cuje-ar ... 1
culanque-ar ... 1
culate-ar ... 1
cule-ar ... 1
culebre-ar ... 1
culeque-ar ... 1
culinc-ar ... 1
culipande-ar ... 1
cullinc-ar ... 1
culmin-ar ... 1
culot-ar ... 1
culpabiliz-ar ... 21
culp-ar ... 1
cultiparl-ar ... 1
cultiv-ar ... 1
cultur-ar ... 1
cumbamch-ar ... 1
cumbanche-ar ... 1
cumi-ar ... 1
cumpliment-ar ... 1
cumpl-ir ... 3

cumul-ar 1
cun-ar 1
cuncune-ar 1
cund-ir 3
cune-ar 1
cunt-ir 3
cuñ-ar 1
cuprific-ar 1
cuque-ar 1
cur-ar 1
curcute-ar 1
curele-ar 1
curi-ar 1
curiose-ar 1
curr-ar 1
currel-ar 1
currucute-ar 1
currusc-ar 67
curs-ar 1
curt-ir 3
curucute-ar 1
curv-ar 1
curve-ar 1
cuscurre-ar 1
cuscute-ar 1
cus-ir 3
cusp-ar 1
cuspete-ar 1
custodi-ar 1
custr-irse 82
cutare-ar 1
cutarre-ar 1
cut-ir 3
cuzque-ar 1

d

dactilografi-ar 9
dadiv-ar 1
daguerrotip-ar ... 1
dall-ar 1
damasquin-ar 1
damn-ar 1
damn-arse 80
damnific-ar 67
danific-ar 67
dann-ar 1
danz-ar 21
danzone-ar 1
dañ-ar 1
dañific-ar 1
dañine-ar 1
dapn-ar 1
d-ar 27
dasain-ar 1
dat-ar 1
daval-ar 1
deambul-ar 1
deband-ar 1
debat-ir 3
debel-ar 1
deb-er 2
debilit-ar 1
debit-ar 1
deboc-ar 67
bebroc-ar 67
debruz-ar 21
debut-ar 1
deca-er 20
decalcific-ar 67
decalv-ar 1
decamp-ar 1
decant-ar 1
decap-ar 1
decapit-ar 1
decapsul-ar 1
decarbonat-ar 1
decarbur-ar 1
deceb-ir 3
deced-er 2
deceler-ar 1
decend-er 2, plus the changes in red in 53
decent-ar 53
decep-ar 1
decepcion-ar 1
decerc-ar 1
decern-ir 3, plus the changes in red in 53
decerrumb-ar 1
decervig-ar 1
decib-irse 82
decid-ir 3
decimaliz-ar 1
decim-ar 1
dec-ir 28
declam-ar 1
declar-ar 1
declin-ar 1
decolg-ar 25
decoll-ar 1
decolor-ar 1
decomis-ar 1
decompon-er ... 57
decontamin-ar ... 1
decor-ar 1
decorr-erse 81
decrec-er 48
decrepit-ar 1
decret-ar 1
decupl-ar 1
decuplic-ar 67
dedale-ar 1
dedic-ar 67
dedign-ar 1
dedol-ar 1
deduc-ir 59
deech-ar 1
defalc-ar 67
defam-ar 1
defec-ar 67
defeccion-ar 1
defend-er 2, plus the changes in red in 53
defenec-er 48
defens-ar 1
defer-ir 71
defes-ar 1
defi-ar 1
defin-ir 3
deflag-ar 51
deflagr-ar 1
deflegm-ar 1
deflogistic-ar ... 67
defondon-ar 1
deforest-ar 1
deform-ar 1
defosfor-ar 1
defraud-ar 1
defu-ir 42
degast-ar 1
degener-ar 1
degest-ir 3
deglut-ir 3
degoll-ar 25
degrad-ar 1
deguast-ar 1
degust-ar 1
dehend-er 2, plus the changes in red in 53
dehes-ar 1
dehort-ar 1
deific-ar 67
dej-ar 1
dejarret-ar 1
dejempl-ar 1
dejug-ar 1
delat-ar 1
delax-ar 1
delayad-ar 1
delect-ar 1
deleg-ar 51
deleit-ar 1
delej-ar 1
deletre-ar 1
delezn-arse 80
delgaz-ar 1
deliber-ar 1
delibr-ar 1
delici-arse 80
delimit-ar 1
deline-ar 1
deling-arse 80
delinqu-ir 29
delint-ar 1
delinter-ar 1
deliñ-ar 1
delir-ar 1
delong-ar 1
delud-ir 3
demacr-ar 1
demacr-arse 80
demand-ar 1
demarc-ar 67
demarr-arse 80
demasi-arse 9
demedi-ar 1
dement-ar 1
demerit-ar 1
demig-ar 1
demit-ir 3
democratiz-ar 21
demol-er 47
demonstr-ar 25

demor-ar 1
demostr-ar 25
demud-ar 1
demulc-ir 3, plus the changes in red in 46
demultiplic-ar 1
deneg-ar 62
denegrec-er 48
denegr-ir 3, and used in the positions in 45
dengue-ar 1
denigr-ar 1
denod-arse 80
denomin-ar 1
denost-ar 25
denot-ar 1
dens-ar 1
densific-ar 67
dent-ar 53
dentec-er 48
dentell-ar 1
dentelle-ar 1
dentrotra-er 75
denud-ar 1
denunci-ar 1
deñ-ar 1
depar-ar 1
depart-ir 3
depauper-ar 1
depend-er 2
depil-ar 1
deplor-ar 1
depon-er 57
deport-ar 1
depos-ar 1
deposit-ar 1
deprav-ar 1
deprec-ar 67
depreci-ar 1
depred-ar 1
deprend-er 2
deprim-ar 1
deprim-ir 3
depur-ar 1
deput-ar 1
derelinqu-ir 29
derez-ar 1
deriv-ar 1
derog-ar 51
derrab-ar 1
derraig-ar 1
derraiz-ar 21
derram-ar 1
derranc-ar 67
derranch-ar 1
derrap-ar 1
derrelinqu-ir 29, plus the past participle derrelicto
derreneg-ar 61
derreng-ar 53
derret-ir 52
derrib-ar 1
derrisc-ar 1
derroc-ar 67
derroch-ar 1
derromp-er 2
derronch-ar 1
derrostr-arse 80
derrot-ar 1
derrubi-ar 1
derru-ir 42
derrumb-ar 1
derrumbi-ar 1
desabarranc-ar 67
desabarrot-ar 1
desabastec-er 48
desabat-ir 3
desabej-ar 1
desabit-ar 1
desaboc-ar 1
desaboll-ar 1
desabollon-ar 1
desabon-ar 1
desabor-ar 1
desabord-arse 80
desaboton-ar 1
desaboved-ar 1
desaboz-ar 21
deasbraz-arse 80
desabrig-ar 51
desabrillant-ar ... 1
desabr-ir 11
desabroch-ar 1
desacalor-arse 80
desacanton-ar ... 1
desacat-ar 1
desacatarr-arse 80
desaced-ar 1
desaceit-ar 1
desacentu-ar 1
desacer-ar 1
desacerb-ar 1
desacert-ar 53
desachigu-ar 1
desachir-arse 80
desachisp-ar 1
desacidific-ar 67
desacidul-ar 1
desaclimat-ar 1
desacobard-ar ... 1
desacoll-ar 25
desacollar-ar 1
desacomod-ar ... 1
desacompañ-ar 1
desacondicion-ar 1
desaconsej-ar 1
desacopl-ar 1
desacord-ar 25
desacordon-ar ... 1
desacorral-ar 1
desacorrol-ar 1
desacostumbr-ar 1
desacot-ar 1
desacotej-ar 1
desacraliz-ar 1
desacredit-ar 1
desactiv-ar 1
desacuartel-ar ... 1
desacumul-ar 1
desacuñ-ar 1
desaderaz-ar ... 21
desaderez-ar ... 21
desadeud-ar 1
desadoquin-ar ... 1
desador-ar 1
desadormec-er 48
desadorn-ar 1
desaduj-ar 1
desadvert-ir 71
desafam-ar 1
desafe-ar 1
desafect-ar 1
desafeit-ar 1
desaferr-ar 53
desafianz-ar 21
desafi-ar 9
desaficion-ar 1
desafij-ar 1
desafil-ar 1
desafin-ar 1
desafiuci-ar 1
desafiuz-ar 21
desafor-ar 25
desaforr-ar 1
desafrances-ar 1
desafrent-ar 1
desafuci-ar 1
desagarr-ar 1
desagit-ar 1
desagot-ar 1
desagraci-ar 1
desagrad-ar 1
desagradec-er 48
desagrav-ar 1
desagravi-ar 1
desagreg-ar 51
desagri-ar 1
desagu-ar 58
desaguaz-ar 21
desaherroj-ar 1
desahij-ar 9
desahit-arse 9
desahog-ar 51
desahuci-ar 1
desahum-ar 9
desain-ar 9
desair-ar 9
desaire-ar 1
desaisl-arse 9
desajac-arse 80
desajarr-ar 1
desajust-ar 1
desalab-ar 1
desalabe-ar 1

desalag-ar ... 51
desal-ar ... 1
desalb-ar ... 1
desalbard-ar ... 1
desalbardill-ar ... 1
desalcoholiz-ar ... 21
desalegr-arse ... 80
desalent-ar ... 53
desalfiler-ar ... 1
desalfombr-ar ... 1
desalforj-ar ... 1
desalhaj-ar ... 1
desali-ar ... 9
desalin-ar ... 1
desaline-ar ... 1
desaliñ-ar ... 1
desalis-ar ... 1
desaliv-ar ... 1
desalmacen-ar ... 1
desalm-ar ... 1
desalmen-ar ... 1
desalmidon-ar ... 1
desaloj-ar ... 1
desalperch-ar ... 1
desalquil-ar ... 1
desalquitran-ar ... 1
desalter-ar ... 1
desalucin-ar ... 1
desamaner-arse ... 80
desam-ar ... 1
desamarr-ar ... 1
desamartel-ar ... 1
desamazacot-ar ... 1
desambient-ar ... 1
desamelg-ar ... 51
desamig-ar ... 51
desamist-arse ... 80
desamobl-ar ... 25
desamodorr-ar ... 1
desamojel-ar ... 1
desamold-ar ... 1
desamonton-ar ... 1
desamor-ar ... 1
desamorr-ar ... 1
desamortaj-ar ... 1
desamortec-er ... 48
desamortiz-ar ... 21
desamotin-ar ... 1
desamotin-arse ... 80
desampar-ar ... 1
desamuebl-ar ... 1
desamur-ar ... 1
desanagu-arse ... 80
desanalfabetiz-ar ... 1
desancl-ar ... 1
desancor-ar ... 1
desand-ar ... 19
desanej-arse ... 80
desanex-ar ... 1
desangr-ar ... 1
desanid-ar ... 1
desanim-ar ... 1
desantañ-arse ... 80
desanubl-ar ... 1
desanud-ar ... 1
desanzol-ar ... 25
desañ-arse ... 80
desañud-ar ... 1
desaoj-ar ... 1
desapadrin-ar ... 1
desapañ-ar ... 1
desapare-ar ... 1
desaparec-er ... 48
desaparej-ar ... 1
desaparroqui-ar ... 1
desapart-ar ... 1
desapasion-ar ... 1
desapeg-ar ... 51
desapegual-ar ... 1
desapercib-irse ... 82
desapest-ar ... 1
desapiad-arse ... 80
desapihuel-ar ... 1
desapiol-ar ... 1
desaplac-er ... 54
desaplic-ar ... 67
desaplom-ar ... 1
desapoc-ar ... 1
desapoder-ar ... 1
desapolill-ar ... 1
desaponz-ar ... 21
desaporc-ar ... 76
desaposent-ar ... 1
desaposesion-ar ... 1
desapostem-ar ... 1
desapoy-ar ... 1
desapreci-ar ... 1
desaprend-er ... 2
desaprens-ar ... 1
desapret-ar ... 53
desapretin-ar ... 1
desapr-ir ... 3
desaprisc-ar ... 1
desaprision-ar ... 1
desaprob-ar ... 25
desapropi-ar ... 1
desaprovech-ar ... 1
desapuntal-ar ... 1
desapunt-ar ... 1
desaquell-arse ... 80
desaquilat-ar ... 1
desarbol-ar ... 1
desarchiv-ar ... 1
desaren-ar ... 1
desargent-ar ... 1
desarm-ar ... 1
desarmoniz-ar ... 21
desarrabiat-ar ... 1
desarraig-ar ... 51
desarraj-ar ... 1
desarranc-arse ... 67
desarreboz-ar ... 21
desarrebuj-ar ... 1
desarregl-ar ... 1
desarrend-ar ... 53
desarrevolv-er 25, except the past participle is desarrevuelto
desarrim-ar ... 1
desarrincon-ar ... 1
desarroll-ar ... 1
desarrop-ar ... 1
desarrug-ar ... 51
desarrum-ar ... 1
desarticul-ar ... 1
desartill-ar ... 1
desarzon-ar ... 1
desas-ar ... 1
desase-ar ... 1
desasegur-ar ... 1
desasent-ar ... 53
desasfalt-ar ... 1
desasimil-ar ... 1
desas-ir ... 13
desasist-ir ... 3
desasn-ar ... 1
desasoci-ar ... 1
desasoseg-ar ... 62
desast-ar ... 1
desastill-ar ... 1
desatac-ar ... 67
desatanc-ar ... 67
desatap-ar ... 1
desat-ar ... 1
desatasc-ar ... 67
desatavi-ar ... 9
desatemoriz-ar ... 21
desatempl-arse ... 80
desatend-er 2, plus the changes in red in 53, plus the past participle desatento
desatent-ar ... 53
desater-irse ... 82
desaterr-ar ... 53
desatesor-ar ... 1
desatest-ar ... 1
desatib-ar ... 1
desatin-ar ... 1
desatoll-ar ... 1
desatolondr-ar ... 1
desatont-arse ... 80

desator-ar 1
desatornill-ar 1
desatrac-ar 67
desatra-er 75
desatraill-ar 9
desatramp-ar 1
desatranc-ar 67
desatraves-
ar 53
desatuf-arse 80
desaturd-ir 3
desatus-ar 1
desautoriz-ar ... 21
desavah-ar 1
desavasall-ar 1
desavecind-
arse 80
desaven-ir 77
desavez-ar 21
desavi-ar 9
desavis-ar 1
desayud-ar 1
desayun-ar 1
desayunt-ar 1
desayust-ar 1
desazog-ar 51
desazon-ar 1
desazucar-ar 1
desazufr-ar 1
desbab-ar 1
desbaf-arse 80
desbag-ar 51
desbalag-ar 51
desbalij-ar 1
desballest-ar 1
desbamb-
arse 80
desbanc-ar 67
desband-
arse 80
desbanz-ar 21
desbarahust-
ar 9
desbarajust-ar ... 1
desbarat-ar 1
desbaraust-ar 1
desbarb-ar 1
desbarbill-ar 1
desbard-ar 1
desbarniz-ar 21
desbarranc-
ar 67
desbarr-ar 1
desbarret-ar 1
desbarrig-ar 51
desbarrumb-
arse 80
desbast-ar 1
desbautiz-ar 21
desbeb-er 2
desbecerr-ar 1
desbenzol-ar 1
desbez-ar 21
desbinz-ar 21
desbisagr-
arse 80
desbloc-ar 67
desbloque-ar 1
desboc-ar 67
desbomb-ar 1
desbonet-
arse 80
desboquill-ar 1
desbord-ar 1
desborniz-ar 21
desboron-ar 1
desborr-ar 1
desborreg-ar 51
desbosc-ar 1
desboton-ar 1
desbrag-ar 51
desbrav-ar 1
desbrave-ar 1
desbravec-er ... 48
desbraz-arse ... 21
desbreñ-ar 1
desbrev-arse ... 80
desbrid-ar 1
desbrizn-ar 1
desbroch-ar 1
desbrot-ar 1
desbroz-ar 21
desbru-ar 9
desbruci-
arse 80
desbruj-ar 1
desbuch-ar 1
desbull-ar 1
descabal-ar 1
descabalg-ar ... 51
descabell-ar 1
descabeñ-
arse 80
descabestr-ar 1
descabez-ar 21
descrabrit-ar 1
descabull-
arse 80
descabull-
irse 17
descabuy-
arse 80
descach-ar 1
descacharr-ar 1
descachaz-ar ... 21
descacil-ar 1
descader-ar 1
descadill-ar 1
descaec-er 48
desca-er 20
descafein-ar 9
descafil-ar 1
descagaz-ar 1
descajill-arse ... 80
descalabaz-
arse 21
descalabr-ar 1
descalamin-ar ... 1
descalandraj-
ar 1
descal-ar 1
descalcañ-ar 1
descalc-ar 67
descalcific-ar ... 67
descalent-
arse 53
descalf-ar 1
descalich-
arse 80
descalific-ar 67
descalim-ar 1
descalz-ar 21
descam-ar 1
descambi-ar 1
descambur-ar 1
descamin-ar 1
descamis-ar 1
descamp-ar 1
descan-ar 1
descancel-ar 1
descans-ar 1
descant-ar 1
descante-ar 1
descanter-ar 1
descantill-ar 1
descanton-ar 1
descañ-ar 1
descañon-ar 1
descap-ar 1
descaperuz-
ar 21
descapill-ar 1
descapirot-ar 1
descapitaliz-
ar 21
descapot-ar
1, and for
its use
regarding
weather,
see 45
descapot-arse
80, and for
its use
regarding
weather,
see 45
descapuch-ar 1
descapuchon-
ar 1
descapull-ar 1
descar-arse 80
descarbonat-
ar 1
descarboniz-
ar 1
descarbur-ar 1
descarcañal-
ar 1
discard-ar 1
descarg-ar 51
descariñ-
arse 80
descarmen-ar 1
descarn-ar 1
descaroz-ar 21
descarretill-ar 1
descarri-ar 9
descarril-ar 1
descarrill-ar 1
descart-ar 1
descarter-ar 1
descartuch-ar 1
descas-ar 1

descasc-ar 67
descascar-ar 1
descascarill-ar ... 1
descascarri-ar ... 1
descasp-ar 1
descast-ar 1
descastr-ar 1
descatoliz-ar 21
descaudill-ar 1
descav-ar 1
descazarri-ar 1
desceb-ar 1
descend-er
2, plus the
changes
in red in 53
descend-ir 3
descentraliz-
ar 21
descentr-ar 1
desceñ-ir 64
descep-ar 1
descer-ar 1
descerc-ar 67
descerebr-ar 1
descerebriz-ar ... 1
descerez-ar 21
descerraj-ar 1
descerr-ar 53
descerrum-
arse 80
descervig-ar 51
deschal-ar 1
deschap-ar 1
descharch-ar 1
deschav-ar 1
deschavet-
arse 80
deschepic-ar 1
deschin-ar 1
deschupon-ar 1
descifr-ar 1
descimbr-ar 1
desciment-ar ... 53
descinch-ar 1
descing-ir 3,
plus the
changes
in red in 23
descintr-ar 1
desciviliz-ar 21
desclasific-ar ... 67
desclav-ar 1
desclavij-ar 1
descloc-ar 1
desclorur-ar 1
descluec-ar 1
descoagul-ar 1
descobaj-ar 1
descobij-ar 1
descoc-ar 67
descoc-arse 80
descoc-er 22
descocot-ar 1
descod-ar 1
descog-er 23
descogestin-
ar 1
descogoll-ar 1
descogot-ar 1
descohesion-
ar 1
descol-ar 1
descolch-ar 1
descolg-ar 24
descoll-ar 25
descolm-ar 1
descolmill-ar 1
descoloc-ar 67
descoloniz-ar ... 21
descolor-ar 1
descolor-ir 3,
and used in
the positions
in 45
descombr-ar 1
descomed-
irse 52
descom-er 2
descomong-ar ... 1
descompadr-
ar 1
descompagin-
ar 1
descompañ-ar ... 1
descompas-ar ... 1
descompas-
arse 80
descompens-
ar 1
descomplac-
er 54
descomplet-
ar 1
descompon-
er 57
descomprim-ir ... 3
descomulg-
ar 51
desconceptu-
ar 9
desconcert-
ar 53
desconchab-
ar 1
desconch-ar 1
desconchinfl-
ar 1
desconcord-
ar 25
desconect-ar 1
desconfi-ar 9
desconflaut-ar ... 1
desconform-ar ... 1
descongel-ar 1
descongestion-
ar 1
descongoj-ar 1
desconhort-ar 1
desconoc-er 48
desconsej-ar 1
desconsent-
ir 71
desconsider-
ar 1
desconsol-ar 25
descontagi-ar 1
descontamin-
ar 1
descont-ar 25
descontent-ar
1, plus the
past participle
descontento
descontinu-ar 9
descontrapes-
ar 1
descontrol-ar 1
desconven-ir ... 77
desconvent-
ir 71
desconvers-ar ... 1
desconvid-ar 1
descop-ar 1
descorazon-ar ... 1
descorch-ar 1
descord-ar 25
descorder-ar 1
descorit-ar 1
descorn-ar 25
descoron-ar 1
descorre-ar 1
descorr-er 2
descorrot-
arse 80
descortez-ar 21
descortin-ar 1
descos-er 2
descost-arse
80, plus the
changes
in red in 47
descostill-ar 1
descostr-ar 1
descot-ar 1
descotorr-ar 1
descoyunt-ar 1
descrec-er 48
descre-er 26
descrem-ar 1
descrest-ar 1
descri-ar 1
descri-arse 80
describ-ir 3,
except the
past partici-
ples are
descrito and
descripto
descrin-ar 1
descrism-ar 1
descristian-ar 1
descristianiz-
ar 21
descrucific-
ar 67
descruz-ar 21
descuacha-
rrang-arse 80
descuadern-ar ... 1
descuadr-ar 1
descuadril-
arse 80
descuadrill-

arse ... 80
descuaj-ar ... 1
descuajaring-ar ... 51
descuajering-ar ... 51
descuartel-ar ... 1
descuartiz-ar ... 21
descubr-ir 3, except the past participle is descubierto
descuer-ar ... 1
descuere-ar ... 1
descuern-ar ... 1
descuid-ar ... 1
descul-ar ... 1
desculat-ar ... 1
descumpl-ir ... 3
desd-ar ... 1
desdec-ir ... 58
desdent-ar ... 53
desdeñ-ar ... 1
desdevan-ar ... 1
desdibuj-ar ... 1
desdich-arse ... 80
desdient-ar ... 1
desdiner-ar ... 1
desdobl-ar ... 1
desdon-ar ... 1
desdoncell-ar ... 1
desdor-ar ... 1
dese-ar ... 1
deseb-ar ... 1
desec-ar ... 67
desech-ar ... 1
desedific-ar ... 67
deseduc-ar ... 67
desegu-ir ... 52
desej-arse ... 80
deselectriz-ar ... 21
desell-ar ... 1
deseman-ar ... 1
desembal-ar ... 1
desembaldos-ar ... 1
desemballest-ar ... 1
desembalsam-ar ... 1
desembals-ar ... 1
desembanast-ar ... 1
desembaraz-ar ... 21
desembarc-ar ... 67
desembarg-ar ... 51
desembarranc-ar ... 67
desembarr-ar ... 1
desembaul-ar ... 9
desembebec-erse ... 48
desembeles-arse ... 80
desembellec-er ... 48
desemblant-arse ... 80
desemboc-ar ... 67
desemboj-ar ... 1
desembols-ar ... 1
desemborrach-ar ... 1
desemborr-ar ... 1
desembosc-arse ... 67
desembot-ar ... 1
desemboz-ar ... 21
desembrag-ar ... 51
desembr-ar ... 53
desembravec-er ... 48
desembraz-ar ... 21
desembre-ar ... 1
desembriag-ar ... 51
desembrid-ar ... 1
desembroc-ar ... 67
desembroll-ar ... 1
desembroz-ar ... 21
desembruj-ar ... 1
desembrutec-er ... 48
desembuch-ar ... 1
desembud-ar ... 1
desembull-ar ... 1
desemej-ar ... 1
desempac-ar ... 67
desempach-ar ... 1
desempaj-ar ... 1
desempalag-ar ... 51
desempalm-ar ... 1
desempantan-ar ... 1
desempañ-ar ... 1
desempapel-ar ... 1
desempaquet-ar ... 1
desemparej-ar ... 1
desemparv-ar ... 1
desempast-ar ... 1
desempastel-ar ... 1
desempat-ar ... 1
desempavon-ar ... 1
desempedr-ar ... 53
desempeg-ar ... 51
desempeñ-ar ... 1
desempeor-arse ... 80
desempercud-ir ... 3
desemperez-ar ... 21
desempern-ar ... 1
desempertig-ar ... 51
desemplom-ar ... 1
desemplum-ar ... 1
desempobrec-er ... 2
desempoll-ar ... 1
desempolv-ar ... 1
desempolvor-ar ... 1
desempotr-ar ... 1
desempoz-ar ... 21
desempozoñ-ar ... 1
desempulg-ar ... 51
desempuñ-ar ... 1
desenalbard-ar ... 1
desenamor-ar ... 1
desenastr-ar ... 1
desencabalg-ar ... 51
desencab-ar ... 1
desencabestr-ar ... 1
desencaden-ar ... 1
desencaj-ar ... 1
desencajon-ar ... 1
desencalabrin-ar ... 1
desencal-ar ... 1
desencalc-ar ... 67
desencall-ar ... 1
desencamin-ar ... 1
desencanall-ar ... 1
desencandil-ar ... 1
desencant-ar ... 1
desencantar-ar ... 1
desencap-ar ... 1
desencapill-ar ... 1
desencapot-ar ... 1
desencapot-arse 80, and for its use regarding weather, see ... 45
desencaprich-ar ... 1
desencarcel-ar ... 1
desencarec-er ... 48
desencarg-ar ... 51
desencarn-ar ... 1
desencarton-ar ... 1
desencas-ar ... 1
desencasquill-ar ... 1
desencastill-ar ... 1
desencenag-

desilusion-ar 1
desimagin-ar 1
desiman-ar 1
desimant-ar 1
desimpon-er 57
desimpresion-
ar 1
desinclin-ar 1
desincorpor-ar ... 1
desincrust-ar 1
desindici-ar 1
desinfart-ar 1
desinfatu-ar 1
desinfeccion-
ar 1
desinfect-ar 1
desinficion-ar 1
desinfis-ar 1
desinflam-ar 1
desinfl-ar 1
desinquiet-ar 1
desinsacul-ar 1
desinsect-ar 1
desintegr-ar 1
desinteres-
arse 80
desintestin-ar 1
desintoxic-ar ... 67
desintub-ar 1
desinvern-ar 53
desinvert-ir 71
desiñ-ar 1
desist-ir 3
desiti-ar 1
desjarci-ar 1
desjaret-arse ... 80
desjarret-ar 1
desjet-arse 80
desjoloch-ar 1
desjuanet-ar 1
desjuard-ar 1
desjug-ar 51
desjunt-ar 1
desjuñ-ir 3
desjur-ar 1
deslabon-ar 1
deslabr-ar 1
desladrill-ar 1
deslaid-ar 1
deslam-ar 1
deslan-ar 1
deslandr-ar 1
deslard-arse 80
deslastr-ar 1
deslat-ar 1
deslateraliz-
ar 21
deslav-ar 1
deslavaz-ar 21
deslaz-ar 21
deslech-ar 1
deslechug-ar ... 51
deslechuguill-
ar 1
desle-ír 63
deslendr-ar 53
deslengu-ar 7
deslengüet-ar 1
desli-ar 9
deslig-ar 51
deslinaj-ar 1
deslin-ar 1
deslind-ar 1
desling-ar 51
desliñ-ar 1
desliz-ar 21
deslo-ar 1
deslom-ar 1
desluc-ir 3,
plus the
changes
in red in 48
deslumbr-ar 1
deslustr-ar 1
deslut-ar 1
desmadej-ar 1
desmadr-ar 1
desmadrin-
arse 80
desmagnetiz-
ar 21
desmajol-ar 25
desmalez-ar 21
desmalingr-ar 1
desmall-ar 1
desmalr-ar 1
desmam-ar 1
desmamey-ar 1
desmamon-ar 1
desmampar-ar ... 1
desman-ar 1
desman-arse ... 80
desmanch-ar 1
desmand-ar 1
desmandig-
ar 51
desmanduf-ar 1
desmane-ar 1
desmang-ar 51
desmangorre-
ar 1
desmanguill-
ar 1
desmanigu-
ar 58
desmant-ar 1
desmantec-
ar 67
desmantel-ar 1
desmantill-ar 1
desmañan-
arse 80
desmañ-ar 1
desmañ-arse ... 80
desmaquill-ar 1
desmarañ-ar 1
desmaravill-ar ... 1
desmarc-ar 67
desmarch-
arse 80
desmarid-ar 1
desmaroj-ar 1
desmarr-irse 4
desmat-ar 1
desmaterializ-
ar 21
desmaton-ar 1
desmay-ar 1
desmech-ar 1
desmechon-ar ... 1
desmed-irse 52
desmedr-ar 1
desmedul-ar 1
desmejor-ar 1
desmelancoliz-
ar 21
desmel-ar 53
desmelen-ar 1
desmembr-ar ... 53
desmemori-
arse 80
desmengu-ar ... 58
desment-ir 71
desmenude-ar ... 1
desmenuz-ar ... 21
desmeoll-ar 1
desmerec-er 48
desmerit-ar 1
desmesur-ar 1
desmezcl-ar 1
desmic-ar 67
desmigaj-ar 1
desmig-ar 51
desmilitariz-
ar 21
desmineraliz-
ar 21
desminu-ir 42
desmitific-ar 67
desmoc-ar 1
desmoch-ar 1
desmog-ar 51
desmold-ar 1
desmol-er 47
desmonetiz-
ar 21
desmont-ar 1
desmontrenc-
ar 1
desmoñ-ar 1
desmoraliz-
ar 21
desmorec-
erse 48
desmorfini-ar ... 21
desmoron-ar 1
desmost-
arse 80
desmostel-ar 1
desmostol-ar 1
desmot-ar 1
desmoviliz-ar ... 21
desmugr-ar 1
desmull-ir 17
desmultiplic-
ar 67
desmur-ar 1
desmurri-ar 1
desmutiz-ar 21
desnacionaliz-
ar 21
desnalg-ar 51
desnarcotiz-
ar 21

desnarig-ar 51
desnat-ar 1
desnaturaliz-
ar 21
desnatur-ar 1
desnazific-ar 67
desneg-ar 53
desnerv-ar 1
desnev-ar 53, and for its use regarding weather, see 45
desnicotiniz-
ar 21
desnitrific-ar 67
desnivel-ar 1
desnoblec-er ... 48
desnort-arse 80
desnuc-ar 67
desnud-ar 1
desnunc-ar 67
desnutr-irse 82
desobedec-
er 48
desoblig-ar 51
desobstru-ir 42
desoc-arse 80
desocasion-
arse 80
desocup-ar 1
desodor-ar 1
desodoriz-ar 21
desofend-
erse 81
deso-ír 49
desoj-ar 1
desol-ar 25
desolaz-ar 21
desold-ar 25
desolidariz-
arse 21
desoll-ar 25
desondr-ar 1
desonz-ar 21
desopercul-ar 1
desopil-ar 1
desopin-ar 1
desoprim-ir 3
desorbit-ar 1
desorden-ar 1
desorej-ar 1
desorganiz-
ar 21
desorient-ar 1
desorill-ar 1
desortij-ar 1
desos-ar 1, plus the changes in red in 50
desoseg-ar 62
desosific-ar 1
desospech-ar 1
desoterr-ar 53
desov-ar 1
desovill-ar 1
desoxid-ar 1
desoxigen-ar 1
despabil-ar 1
despach-ar 1
despachurr-ar 1
despag-ar 1
despaj-ar 1
despaladin-ar 1
despald-ar 1
despaldill-ar 1
despalet-ar 1
despaletill-ar 1
despalill-ar 1
despalm-ar 1
despalot-ar 1
despampan-ar ... 1
despampanill-
ar 1
despamplon-
ar 1
despan-ar 1
despanc-ar 67
despanchurr-
ar 1
despancij-ar 1
despanzurr-ar 1
despap-ar 1
desparc-ir 3, plus the changes in red in 46
despare-ar 1
desparec-er 48
despared-ar 1
desparej-ar 1
desparpaj-ar 1
desparram-ar 1
desparranc-
arse 67
desparrat-ar 1
despart-ir 3
desparv-ar 1
despas-ar 1
despasion-
arse 80
despasm-
arse 80
despast-ar 1
despatarr-ar 1
despatill-ar 1
despatri-ar 1
despaturr-ar 1
despaves-ar 1
despavon-ar 1
despavor-ir 3, and used in the positions in 45
despe-arse 80
despech-ar 1
despechug-
ar 51
despedaz-ar 21
desped-ir 52
despedr-ar 53
despedreg-ar ... 51
despeg-ar 51
despein-ar 1
despej-ar 1
despellej-ar 1
despellet-ar 1
despelot-ar 1
despelot-
arse 80
despeluc-ar 67
despeluch-ar 1
despeluz-ar 21
despeluzn-ar 1
despen-ar 1
despend-er 2
despenitenci-
ar 1
despenol-ar 1
despeñ-ar 1
despepit-ar 1
despepit-
arse 80
desper-ar 1
despercat-
arse 80
despercud-ir 3
desperdici-ar 1
desperdig-ar 51
desperec-er 48
desperec-
erse 48
desperez-ar 21
desperfeccion-
ar 1
desperfil-ar 1
desperfoll-ar 1
despernanc-
ar 67
despernanc-
arse 67
despern-ar 53
despersonaliz-
ar 21
despert-ar 53, plus the past participle despierto
despes-ar 1
despesc-ar 67
despescuez-
ar 21
despestañ-ar 1
despetrific-ar ... 67
despetronc-
arse 80
despez-ar 34
despezon-ar 1
despezuñ-
arse 80
despi-arse 80
despic-ar 67
despicaraz-
ar 21
despic-arse 80
despich-ar 1
despiez-ar 21
despil-ar 1
despilar-ar 1
despilfarr-ar 1
despilon-ar 1
despimpoll-ar 1
despinoch-ar 1

despint-ar 1
despinz-ar 21
despioj-ar 1
despist-ar 1
despistoj-
arse 80
despiton-ar 1
despizc-ar 67
desplac-er 48
desplan-ar 1
desplanch-ar 1
desplant-ar 1
desplant-
arse 80
desplat-ar 1
desplate-ar 1
desplay-ar 1
desplaz-ar 21
despleg-ar 62
despleguete-
ar 1
desplom-ar 1
desplum-ar 1
despobl-ar 25
despoetiz-ar 21
despoj-ar 1
despolariz-ar ... 21
despolitiz-ar 21
despolv-ar 1
despolvore-ar 1
despolvoriz-
ar 21
despon-er 57
desponj-ar 1
despopulariz-
ar 21
desporr-ar 1
desporrondig-
arse 51
desportill-ar 1
despos-ar 1
despose-er 70
despost-ar 1
despostill-ar 1
despotiz-ar 21
despotric-ar 67
despreci-ar 1
despredic-ar 1
desprend-er 2
desprens-ar 1
despreocup-
arse 80
despres-ar 1
desprestigi-ar 1
despretin-ar 1
despreven-ir 77
despriv-ar 1
despropi-ar 1
desproporcion-
ar 1
desprove-er 65,
plus the past
participle
desprovisto
despulg-ar 51
despul-ir 1
despull-ar 1
despulmon-
arse 80
despulp-ar 1
despuls-ar 1
despum-ar 1
despunt-ar 1,
and for its use
regarding
weather,
see 45
desquebraj-ar 1
desquebr-ar 53
desquej-ar 1
desquem-ar 1
desquer-er 60
desquici-ar 1
desquiet-ar 1
desquijar-ar 1
desquijarr-ar 1
desquijer-ar 1
desquilat-ar 1
desquilibr-ar 1
desquit-ar 1
desrabadill-ar 1
desrab-ar 1
desrabe-ar 1
desraber-ar 1
desrabill-ar 1
desrabot-ar 1
desraig-ar 1
desraiz-ar 35
desram-ar 1
desramill-ar 1
desranch-
arse 80
desranill-ar 1
desrasp-ar 1
desrastroj-ar 1
desratiz-ar 21
desray-ar 1
desrazon-ar 21
desregl-ar 1
desreling-ar 51
desriel-ar 1
desriñon-ar 1
desrisc-ar 67
desriz-ar 21
desrobl-ar 1
desrodrig-ar 51
desronch-ar 1
desroñ-ar 1
desrostr-ar 1
desrumb-ar 1
destab-ar 1
destabl-ar 1
destac-ar 67
destachon-ar 1
destacon-ar 1
destaj-ar 1
destajaz-ar 21
destall-ar 1
destalon-ar 1
destan-ar 1
destante-
arse 80
destap-ar 1
destapi-ar 1
destapon-ar 1
destar-ar 1
destarr-ar 1
destartal-ar 1
destaz-ar 21
destebrech-ar 1
destech-ar 1
destej-ar 1
destej-er 2
destel-arse 80
desteleng-ar 51
destell-ar 1
destempl-ar 1
destend-er 2,
plus the
changes
in red in 53
destent-ar 53
desteñ-ir 64
desteriliz-ar 21
destermin-ar 1
desterner-ar 1
desternill-
arse 80
desterr-ar 53
desterron-ar 1
destet-ar 1
destetill-ar 1
destetun-
arse 80
destil-ar 1
destill-ar 1
destin-ar 1
destinter-
arse 80
destiñ-ar 1
destiraniz-ar 21
destirp-ar 1
destitu-ir 42
destoc-ar 67
destocon-ar 1
destong-ar 1
destorb-ar 1
destorc-er 22
destorg-ar 77
destorm-ar 1
destorn-ar 1
destornill-ar 1
destornill-
arse 80
destornud-ar 1
destorp-ar 1
destorrent-ar 1
destorrent-
arse 80
destos-erse 81
destost-arse
80, plus the
changes
in red in 25
destoxic-ar 1
destoz-ar 21
destozol-ar 25
destrab-ar 1
destraill-ar 1
destram-ar 1
destranc-ar 67
destrast-ar 1
destrat-ar 1
destrej-ar 1

destrenz-ar 21
destrep-ar 1
destribut-ar 1
destrinc-ar 67
destrip-ar 1
destripul-ar 1
destriunf-ar 1
destriz-ar 21
destroc-ar 76
destromp-ar 1
destron-ar 1
destronc-ar 67
desronch-ar 1
destrop-ar 1
destroz-ar 21
destru-ir 42
destullec-er 48
destung-ar 51
desturb-ar 1
destus-ar 1
destustuz-ar 21
destutan-ar 1
desuard-ar 1
desubstanci-
ar 1
desuc-ar 67
desud-ar 1
desuel-ar 1
desuer-ar 1
desug-ar 51
desulfur-ar 1
desunc-ir 3,
plus the
changes
in red in 46
desunific-ar 1
desun-ir 3
desuñ-ar 1
desuñ-ir 17
desurc-ar 67
desurd-ir 3
desurt-ir 3
desus-ar 1
desustanci-ar 1
desvah-ar 1
desvain-ar 1
desva-ir 3
desval-er 2,
plus the
changes
in red in 68
desvalij-ar 1
desvalor-ar 1
desvaloriz-ar 21
desvalu-ar 9
desvanec-er 48
desvaporiz-
ar 21
desvar-ar 1
desvaret-ar 1
desvari-ar 9
desvariz-ar 21
desvas-ar 1
desvast-ar 1
desvastig-ar 51
desved-ar 1
desvel-ar 1
desveliz-ar 21
desven-ar 1
desvencij-ar 1
desvend-ar 1
desvent-ar 53
desverdec-er ... 48
desvergonz-
arse 15
desvest-ir 52
desvez-ar 21
desvi-ar 9
desviej-ar 1
desvigoriz-ar ... 21
desvincul-ar 1
desviol-ar 1
desvir-ar 1
desvirg-ar 51
desviriliz-ar 21
desvirtu-ar 9
desviscer-ar 1
desvitaliz-ar 21
desvitaminiz-
ar 21
desvitrific-ar 67
desviv-irse 82
desvolcan-
arse 80
desvolv-er
47, except
the past
participle
is desvuelto
desyem-ar 1
desyerb-ar 1
desyug-ar 51
desyunc-ir 3,
plus the
changes
in red in 46
deszafr-ar 1
deszoc-ar 67
deszulac-ar 67
deszum-ar 1
detall-ar 1
detante-arse 80
detard-ar 1
detect-ar 1
deten-er 74
detent-ar 1
deterg-er 23
deterior-ar 1
determin-ar 1
detest-ar 1
deton-ar 1
detorn-ar 1
detract-ar 1
detra-er 75
deturp-ar 1
deval-ar 1
devalu-ar 9
devan-ar 1
devane-ar 1
devast-ar 1
deved-ar 1
devel-ar 1
develiz-ar 21
deveng-ar 51
deven-ir 68
devis-ar 1
devolv-er 47,
except the
past participle
is devuelto
devor-ar 1
devot-ar 1
devov-er 2
dextriniz-ar 21
deyect-ar 1
dezm-ar 53
dezoc-ar 67
diabl-ar 1
diable-ar 1
diacon-ar 1
diaconiz-ar 21
diadem-ar 1
diafaniz-ar 21
diafragm-ar 1
diagnostic-ar ... 67
diagram-ar 1
dialis-ar 1
dializ-ar 21
dialog-ar 51
dialogiz-ar 21
diamant-ar 1
diamante-ar 1
diapent-ar 1
diatrib-ar 1
diazo-ar 1
diazot-ar 1
dibuj-ar 1
dic-ar 67
diciplin-ar 1
dictamin-ar 1
dict-ar 1
diet-ar 1
diezm-ar 1
difam-ar 1
difari-ar 1
diferec-er 48
diferenci-ar 1
difer-ir 71
dificult-ar 1
difinec-er 48
difin-ir 3
difiuci-ar 1
diflu-ir 42
difract-ar 1
difum-ar 1
difumin-ar 1
difund-ir 3,
plus the past
participle
difuso
difunte-ar 1
digerec-er 48
diger-ir 71
digest-ir 3
digitaliz-ar 21
digit-ar 1
digladi-ar 1
dign-arse 80
dignific-ar 67
digres-ar 1
digresion-ar 1
dijunte-ar 1
dilacer-ar 1
dilapid-ar 1

dilat-ar 1
diligenci-ar 1
dilori-ar 1
dilucid-ar 1
dilu-ir 42
diluvi-ar 1, and for its use regarding weather, see 45
diman-ar 1
dimidi-ar 1
dimig-ar 1
diminuec-er 48
diminu-ir 42
dim-ir 3
dimit-ir 3
dinamit-ar 1
dintel-ar 1
dinumer-ar 1
diñ-ar 1
diose-ar 1
diplom-ar 1
diptong-ar 51
diput-ar 1
diquel-ar 1
dirig-ir 3, plus the changes in red in 23
dirim-ir 3
dirradi-ar 1
dirru-ir 42
discant-ar 1
disc-ar 1
discept-ar 1
discern-er 2, plus the changes in red in 53
discern-ir 3, plus the changes in red in 53
disciplin-ar 1
discont-ar 25
discontinu-ar 9
disconven-ir 77
discord-ar 25
discrep-ar 1
discrete-ar 1
discrimin-ar 1
disculp-ar 1
discurr-ir 3
discurs-ar 1
discurse-ar 1
discut-ir 3
disec-ar 67
disemin-ar 1
disent-ir 71
diseñ-ar 1
disert-ar 1
disfam-ar 1
disform-ar 1
disforz-arse 39
disfraz-ar 21
disfrez-arse 80
disfrut-ar 1
disfum-ar 1
disfumin-ar 1
disgreg-ar 51
disgust-ar 1
disid-ir 3
disimil-ar 1
disimul-ar 1
disip-ar 1
dislacer-ar 1
disloc-ar 67
dismembr-ar 53
disminu-ir 42
disoci-ar 1
disolv-er 47, except the past participle is disuelto
dison-ar 25
dispar-ar 1
disparat-ar 1
disparate-ar 1
dispend-er 2
dispens-ar 1
dispers-ar 1
dispert-ar 53
displac-er 48
dispon-er 57
dispuntu-ar 1
disput-ar 1
distanci-ar 1
dist-ar 1
distend-er 39
distermin-ar 1
distil-ar 1
distingu-ir 30
distorsion-ar 1
distra-er 75
distribu-ir 42
disturb-ar 1
disuad-ir 3
disyunc-ir 3, plus the changes in red in 46
diuque-ar 1
divag-ar 51
divari-ar 1
divaric-ar 1
diverg-ir 3, plus the changes in red in 23
diversific-ar 67
divert-ir 71
divert-irse 71
divid-ir 3, plus the past participle diviso
divin-ar 1
diviniz-ar 21
divis-ar 1
divorci-ar 1
divulg-ar 51
dobladill-ar 1
dobl-ar 1
dobleg-ar 51
docilit-ar 1
doctor-ar 1
doctore-ar 1
doctrin-ar 1
document-ar 1
dogmatiz-ar 21
dol-ar 25
dol-er 47
dom-ar 1
domell-ar 1
domeñ-ar 1
domestic-ar 67
domicili-ar 1
domific-ar 67
domin-ar 1
don-ar 1
done-ar 1
donjuane-ar 1
doñe-ar 1
dop-ar 1
dor-ar 1
dorm-ir 31
dormit-ar 1
dosific-ar 67
dot-ar 1
dotor-ar 1
dotrin-ar 1
dovel-ar 1
drag-ar 51
dragone-ar 1
dramatiz-ar 21
drans-ar 1
drape-ar 1
dren-ar 1
dribl-ar 1
driz-ar 21
drog-ar 51
dromede-ar 1
dubd-ar 1
duch-ar 1
dud-ar 1
dulcific-ar 67
dulc-ir 3, plus the changes in red in 46
dulzor-ar 1
dulzur-ar 1
duplic-ar 67
dur-ar 1

e

ebanific-ar 1
ebaniz-ar 21
eburnific-ar 1
eccematiz-ar ... 21
ecept-ar 1
eceptu-ar 1
echacorve-ar 1
ech-ar 1
eclesiastiz-ar ... 21
eclips-ar 1
eclosion-ar 1
economiz-ar 21
eczematiz-ar ... 21
edematiz-ar 21
edict-ar 1
edific-ar 67
edit-ar 1

editorializ-ar 21
edr-ar 1
educ-ar 67
educ-ir 58
edulcor-ar 1
efectu-ar 9
efemin-ar 1
efigi-ar 1
eflorec-erse 48
efund-ir 1
egres-ar 1
egris-ar 1
egu-ar 1
eguijarr-ar 1
eguill-ar 1
ejabr-ir 1
ejarr-ar 1
ejecut-ar 1
ejecutori-ar 9
ejempl-ar 1
ejemplariz-ar ... 21
ejemplific-ar 67
ejerc-er 46
ejercit-ar 1
elabor-ar 1
elastific-ar 67
eleboriz-ar 1
electrific-ar 67
electriz-ar 21
electrocut-ar 1
electroliz-ar 21
elegatiz-ar 21
eleg-ir 32, has an additional past participle electo
element-arse ... 80
elev-ar 1
elid-ir 3
elij-ar 1
elimin-ar 1
elips-ar 1
elogi-ar 1
elote-ar 1
elucid-ar 1
elucubr-ar 1
elud-ir 3
eluvi-ar 1
eman-ar 1
emancip-ar 1
emascul-ar 1
embabuc-ar 67
embach-ar 1
embadurn-ar 1
emba-ír 33
embal-ar 1
embaldos-ar 1
emballen-ar 1
emballest-arse 80
embalsam-ar 1
embals-ar 1
embalum-ar 1
embanast-ar 1
embanc-ar 67
embanc-arse ... 67
embander-ar 1
embanquet-ar 1
embaraz-ar 21
embarb-ar 1
embarbasc-ar 67
embarbasc-arse 80
embarbec-er 48
embarbill-ar 1
embarc-ar 67
embarcen-ar 1
embarcin-ar 1
embard-ar 1
embarduñ-ar 1
embarg-ar 51
embarnec-er 48
embarniz-ar 21
embarranc-ar 67
embarr-ar 1
embarrial-arse 80
embarril-ar 1
embarriz-arse 21
embarrot-ar 1
embarrull-ar 1
embarrun-ar 1
embarull-ar 1
embas-ar 1
embast-ar 1
embastard-ar 1
embastec-er 48
embasur-ar 1
embat-irse 3
embauc-ar 67
embaul-ar 67
embay-arse 80
embaz-ar 21
embebec-er 48
embeb-er 2
embejuc-ar 67
embelec-ar 67
embeleñ-ar 1
embeles-ar 1
embellac-arse 80
embellaquec-erse 48
embellec-arse 67
embellec-er 48
embeod-ar 1
ember-ar 1
embermej-ar 1
embermejec-er 48
embermellon-ar 1
emberren-chin-arse 80
emberrinch-arse 80
embest-ir 52
embetun-ar 1
embic-ar 67
embich-arse 80
embigot-ar 1
embij-ar 1
embizarr-arse 80
embizc-ar 67
emblandec-er 48
emblanque-ar 1
emblanquec-er 48
emblematiz-ar 21
embo-ar 1
embob-ar 1
embobec-er 48
embobill-ar 1
embobin-ar 1
emboc-ar 67
embochet-ar 1
embochic-ar 1
embochin-arse 80
embochinch-ar 1
embocic-arse 80
embocin-arse 80
embod-arse 80
embodeg-ar 51
emboj-ar 1
embojot-ar 1
embol-ar 1
embolat-ar 1
embolic-ar 67
embolism-ar 1
emboll-ar 1
embols-ar 1
embolsic-ar 67
embolsific-ar 1
embon-ar 1
emboñig-ar 51
emboquill-ar 1
emborn-ar 1
emborrach-ar 1
emborr-ar 1
emborrasc-ar ... 67
emborraz-ar 21
emborric-arse 67
emborriz-ar 21
emborron-ar 1
emborrull-arse 80
emboruc-ar 1
embosc-ar 67
embosquec-er 48
embost-ar 1
embot-ar 1
embotell-ar 1
embotic-ar 67
embotic-arse ... 67
embotij-ar 1
embotin-ar 1
emboton-ar 1
emboved-ar 1
embozal-ar 1
emboz-ar 21
embracil-ar 1

empertig-ar 51
empesebr-ar 1
empesg-ar 51
empest-ar 1
empestifer-ar 1
empestill-arse 80
empetac-ar 1
empetat-ar 1
empetrenc-arse 1
empez-ar 34
empiad-ar 1
empic-ar 67
empic-arse 67
empich-arse 80
empicot-ar 1
empigüel-ar 1
empihuel-ar 1
empil-ar 1
empilch-ar 1
empilch-arse 80
empilon-ar 1
empiluch-ar 1
empin-ar 1
empingorot-ar 1
empioj-ar 1
empiol-ar 1
empip-ar 1
empip-arse 80
empit-ar 1
empiton-ar 1
empizarr-ar 1
empizc-ar 21
emplantill-ar 1
emplast-ar 1
emplastec-er 48
emplaz-ar 21
emplaz-arse 21
emple-ar 1
emplebeyec-er 48
emplegost-arse 80
emplom-ar 1
emplumaj-ar 1
emplum-ar 1
emplumec-er 48
empobrec-er 48
empoch-ar 1
empoder-ar 1
empodrec-er 48
empoj-arse 80
empolin-ar 1
empoll-ar 1
empoller-arse 80
empoltronec-erse 48
empolv-ar 1
empolvor-ar 1
empolvoriz-ar 21
emponch-arse 80
emponzoñ-ar 1
empop-ar 1
empor-ar 1
emporc-ar 76
emporret-arse 80
emporrong-arse 80
empotr-ar 1
empotrer-ar 1
empoz-ar 21
empradiz-ar 21
empr-ar 1
emprend-er 1
emprens-ar 1
emprent-ar 1
empreñ-ar 1
empresent-ar 1
emprest-ar 1
emprestill-ar 1
empretec-er 48
emprim-ar 1
emprimer-ar 1
emprim-ir 3
empring-ar 51
emprision-ar 1
empuch-ar 1
empuj-ar 1
empulg-ar 51
empunt-ar 1
empuñ-ar 1
empuñ-ir 17
empurpur-ar 1
empurr-arse 80
emputec-er 48
empuy-ar 1
emul-ar 1
emulsion-ar 1
enaceit-ar 1
enacer-ar 1
enaciy-ar 1
enaguach-ar 1
enagu-ar 1
enaguaz-ar 21
enajen-ar 1
enalbald-ar 1
enalb-ar 1
enalbard-ar 1
enalfombr-ar 1
enalmagr-ar 1
enalmen-ar 1
enalt-ar 1
enaltec-er 48
enamarillec-er 48
enamor-ar 1
enamoric-arse 67
enamorisc-arse 67
enan-arse 80
enanc-arse 67
enanch-ar 1
enangost-ar 1
enanz-ar 21
enaparej-ar 1
enarbol-ar 1
enarc-ar 67
enardec-er 48
enaren-ar 1
enarmon-ar 1
enarmor-ar 1
enarque-ar 1
enarr-ar 1
enart-ar 1
enasp-ar 1
enast-ar 1
enastil-ar 1
enastill-ar 1
encabalg-ar 51
encaball-ar 1
encab-ar 1
encabell-ar 1
encabellec-erse 48
encabestr-ar 1
encabez-ar 21
encabezon-ar 1
encabill-ar 1
encabrahig-ar 19
encabrest-ar 1
encabri-ar 9
encabrill-ar 1
encabrit-arse 80
encabron-ar 1
encabruñ-ar 1
encabull-ar 1
encabuy-ar 1
encach-ar 1
encacharr-ar 1
encach-arse 80
encachich-arse 80
encachil-arse 80
encachorr-arse 80
encad-arse 80
encaden-ar 1
encaec-er 48
encaj-ar 1
encajer-arse 80
encajet-ar 1
encajetill-ar 1
encajon-ar 1
encalabern-arse 80
encalaboz-ar 21
encalabrin-ar 1
encalambr-arse 80
encalamoc-ar 67
encalamuc-ar 67
encal-ar 1
encalat-arse 80
encalc-ar 67
encalet-ar 1
encalill-arse 80
encall-ar 1
encallec-er 48
encallejon-ar 1
encalletr-ar 1
encalm-arse 80
encalom-ar 1
encalostr-arse 80
encalv-ar 1

encalvec-er ... 48
encalz-ar ... 21
encam-ar ... 1
encamar-ar ... 1
encamb-ar ... 1
encambij-ar ... 1
encambr-ar ... 1
encambrillon-ar ... 1
encambron-ar ... 1
encambuch-ar ... 1
encamin-ar ... 1
encamis-ar ... 1
encamon-ar ... 1
encamorr-arse ... 80
encamot-arse ... 80
encampan-ar ... 1
encamp-arse ... 80
encanal-ar ... 1
encanaliz-ar ... 21
encanall-ar ... 1
encan-ar ... 1
encanast-ar ... 1
encancel-ar ... 1
encancer-arse ... 80
encanchin-arse ... 80
encanchon-ar ... 1
encandec-er ... 48
encandel-ar ... 1
encandelill-ar ... 1
encandell-ar ... 1
encandil-ar ... 1
encanec-er ... 48
encanelon-arse ... 80
encanij-ar ... 1
encanill-ar ... 1
encant-ar ... 1
encantar-ar ... 1
encantus-ar ... 1
encanut-ar ... 1
encañam-ar ... 1
encañ-ar ... 1
encañiz-ar ... 21
encañon-ar ... 1
encañut-ar ... 1
encapach-ar ... 1
encap-ar ... 1
encaparazon-ar ... 1
encapaz-ar ... 21
encaperuz-ar ... 21
encapill-ar ... 1
encapirot-ar ... 1
encapot-ar 1, and for its use regarding weather, see ... 45
encaprich-arse ... 80
encapsul-ar ... 1
encapuch-ar ... 1
encapuz-ar ... 21
encaracol-ar ... 1
encarajin-arse ... 80
encaram-ar ... 1
encaramillot-ar ... 1
encarapit-arse ... 80
encar-ar ... 1
encarcavin-ar ... 1
encarcel-ar ... 1
encard-arse ... 80
encarec-er ... 48
encarg-ar ... 51
encariñ-ar ... 1
encar-ir ... 3
encarn-ar ... 1
encarnec-er ... 48
encarniz-ar ... 21
encarp-ar ... 1
encarpet-ar ... 1
encarril-ar ... 1
encarrill-ar ... 1
encarroñ-ar ... 1
encarruj-ar ... 1
encart-ar ... 1
encarton-ar ... 1
encartuch-ar ... 1
encartul-arse ... 80
encas-ar ... 1
encascabel-ar ... 1
encasc-ar ... 67
encascot-ar ... 1
encasill-ar ... 1
encasimb-ar ... 1
encasquet-ar ... 1
encasquill-ar ... 1
encast-ar ... 1
encastill-ar ... 1
encastr-ar ... 1
encasull-ar ... 1
encatalej-ar ... 1
encativ-ar ... 1
encatus-ar ... 1
encauch-ar ... 1
encaus-ar ... 1
encaustic-ar ... 67
encaustific-ar ... 1
encauz-ar ... 21
encav-arse ... 80
encebad-ar ... 1
enceboll-ar ... 1
enceguec-er ... 48
encelaj-arse ... 80
encel-ar ... 1
enceld-ar ... 1
encell-ar ... 1
encenag-arse ... 51
encencerr-ar ... 1
encend-er 2, plus the changes in red in ... 53
encendr-ar ... 1
enceneg-arse ... 80
enceniz-ar ... 21
encens-ar ... 1
encensu-ar ... 1
encent-ar ... 53
encentr-ar ... 1
encep-ar ... 1
encer-ar ... 1
encerc-ar ... 1
encernad-ar ... 1
encerot-ar ... 1
encerr-ar ... 1
encerriz-ar ... 21
encert-ar ... 53
encesped-ar ... 1
encest-ar ... 1
encet-ar ... 1
enchalec-ar ... 67
enchamarr-ar ... 1
enchamb-ar ... 1
enchambran-ar ... 1
enchamic-ar ... 1
enchanclet-ar ... 1
enchap-ar ... 1
enchaparr-arse ... 80
enchapin-arse ... 80
enchaquet-arse ... 80
encharc-ar ... 67
encharnel-ar ... 1
encharral-arse ... 80
encharranch-ar ... 1
enchat-arse ... 80
enchauch-arse ... 80
enchavet-ar ... 1
enchepic-ar ... 1
enchic-ar ... 67
enchich-arse ... 80
enchil-ar ... 1
enchilot-arse ... 80
enchin-ar ... 1
enchinarr-ar ... 1
enchinch-ar ... 1
enchip-ar ... 1
enchiquer-ar ... 1
enchiron-ar ... 1
enchism-ar ... 1
enchisp-ar ... 1
enchiv-arse ... 80
enchocor-arse ... 80
enchoncl-arse ... 80
enchuch-ar ... 1
enchuec-ar ... 67
enchuf-ar ... 1
enchul-arse ... 80
enchulet-ar ... 1
enchullec-ar ... 67
enchumb-ar ... 1
enchut-ar ... 1
enciel-ar ... 1
enciguat-arse ... 80

encim-ar 1
encinch-ar 1
encing-ar 1
encint-ar 1
encintr-ar 1
encisc-ar 1
encism-ar 1
encit-ar 1
encizañ-ar 1
enclanch-arse 80
enclar-ar 1, and for its use regarding weather, see 45
enclaresc-er 1
enclaustr-ar 1
enclav-ar 1
enclavij-ar 1
encloc-ar 76
encloquec-er ... 67
encluc-ar 67
encluec-ar 67
encob-ar 1
encobij-ar 1
encobil-arse 80
encobr-ar 1
encocl-ar 1
encocor-ar 1
encocr-ar 1
encodill-arse ... 80
encofin-ar 1
encofr-ar 1
encog-er 23
encogoll-arse 80
encogull-ar 1
encohet-ar 1
encoj-ar 1
encol-ar 1
encolc-ar 1
encolch-ar 1
encoleriz-ar 21
encoligu-ar 1
encomend-ar ... 53
encomenz-ar ... 21
encomi-ar 1
encompadr-ar 1
encompas-ar 1
encon-ar 1
enconch-arse 80
enconfit-ar 1
encong-arse 80
enconre-ar 1
encontr-ar 25
encopet-ar 1
encorach-ar 1
encoraj-ar 1
encorajin-ar 1
encorament-ar ... 1
encor-ar 25
encoraz-ar 21
encorch-ar 1
encorchet-ar 1
encorcov-ar 1
encord-ar 25
encordel-ar 1
encordon-ar 1
encorec-er 48
encorm-ar 1
encorn-ar 25
encornud-ar 1
encoroz-ar 21
encorral-ar 1
encorre-ar 1
encorr-er 1
encorsel-ar 1
encorset-ar 1
encort-ar 1
encortin-ar 1
encoruj-arse 80
encorv-ar 1
encostal-ar 1
encost-arse 80, plus the changes in red in 25
encostr-ar 1
encov-ar 25
encovil-arse 80
encras-ar 1
encresp-ar 1
encrest-arse 80
encristal-ar 1
encrudec-er 48
encruelec-er 48
encruquill-arse 80
encruz-ar 21
encuadern-ar 1
encuadr-ar 1
encuart-ar 1
encuartel-ar 1
encuat-ar 1
encub-ar 1
encubert-ar 53
encubr-ir 3, except the past participle is encubierto
encuc-ar 67
encucuruch-arse 80
encuell-ar 1
encuend-ar 1
encuer-ar 1
encuest-ar 1
encuev-ar 1
encuit-arse 80
encuj-ar 1
encul-arse 80
enculat-ar 1
enculec-arse ... 80
enculill-arse 80
enculp-ar 1
encumbr-ar 1
encun-ar 1
encurd-arse 80
encureñ-ar 1
encurruc-arse 67
encurt-ir 3
endam-arse 80
endebl-ar 1
endech-ar 1
endehes-ar 1
endelgadec-er 48
endeliñ-ar 1
endemoni-ar 1
endent-ar 53
endentec-er 48
endeñ-arse 80
enderech-ar 1
enderez-ar 21
enderrot-ar 1
endeud-arse 80
endiabl-ar 1
endich-arse 80
endiecioch-arse 80
endient-ar 1
endilg-ar 51
endiñ-ar 1
endios-ar 1
endirg-ar 51
endit-arse 80
endobl-ar 1
endoming-ar 51
endoming-arse 51
endon-ar 1
endon-arse 80
endorm-ir 31
endors-ar 1
endos-ar 1
endosel-ar 1
endosmos-ar 1
endragon-arse 80
endrez-ar 21
endrog-arse 51
endu-ir 42
endulcec-er 48
endulc-ir 3, plus the changes in red in 23
endulz-ar 21
endulzor-ar 1
endur-ar 1
endurec-er 48
enech-ar 1
enej-ar 1
enemig-ar 1
enemist-ar 1
ener-ar 1
energiz-ar 21
eneriz-ar 21
enert-arse 80
enerv-ar 1
enfad-ar 1
enfaj-ar 1
enfajill-ar 1
enfajin-ar 1
enfald-ar 1
enfaltric-arse ... 80
enfandang-arse 80
enfang-ar 51
enfard-ar 1
enfardel-ar 1

enfarusc-
 arse 80
enfasc-ar 1
enfasti-ar 1
enfastidi-ar 1
enfatiz-ar 21
enfatu-ar 1
enfatu-arse 9
enfe-ar 1
enfebrec-er 48
enfelp-ar 1
enferm-ar 1
enfermiz-ar 21
enfermose-ar 1
enferoz-ar 21
enfervorec-er ... 48
enfervoriz-ar 21
enfest-ar 1
enfeud-ar 1
enfi-ar 1
enficion-ar 1
enfiel-ar 1
enfierec-erse ... 48
enfiest-arse 80
enfil-ar 1
enfing-ir 3,
 plus the
 changes
 in red in 23
enfistol-arse 80
enfiuz-ar 21
enflac-ar 67
enflaquec-er 48
enflat-arse 80
enflaut-ar 1
enflech-ar 1
enflor-ar 1
enflorec-er 48
enfoc-ar 67
enfog-ar 1
enfogon-ar 1
enfollin-arse 80
enfollon-ar 1
enforc-ar 67
enform-ar 1
enforn-ar 1
enforr-ar 1
enfortalec-er 48
enfortec-er 48
enfort-ir 3
enfosc-ar 67
enfot-arse 80
enfrail-ar 1
enfranj-ar 1
enfranquec-
 er 48
enfrasc-ar 67
enfrasc-arse 80
enfren-ar 1
enfrenill-ar 1
enfrent-ar 1
enfri-ar 9
enfrijol-arse 80
enfront-ar 1
enfrontil-ar 1
enfrosc-arse 67
enfuci-ar 1
enfuert-arse 80
enfuet-arse 80
enfull-ar 1
enfullin-arse 80
enfunch-ar 1
enfund-ar 1
enfuñ-arse 80
enfuñing-
 arse 80
enfurec-er 48
enfurelec-er 48
enfurgon-ar 1
enfuri-arse 80
enfurruc-
 arse 67
enfurruñ-
 arse 80
enfurrusc-
 arse 67
enfurt-ir 3
enfuruñ-arse 80
enfus-ar 1
enfusc-ar 67
enfus-ir 3
engaendr-ar 1
engaban-ar 1
engaf-ar 1
engafec-er 48
engafet-ar 1
engait-ar 1
engalabern-ar 1
engalan-ar 1
engaler-ar 1
engalg-ar 51
engali-ar 9
engalib-ar 1
engall-ar 1
engallet-ar 1
engallol-ar 1
engallot-arse ... 80
enganch-ar 1
enganduj-ar 1
engangoch-ar 1
engangren-
 arse 80
engañ-ar 1
engañil-ar 1
engañis-ar 1
engañot-ar 1
engarabat-ar 1
engarabit-ar 1
engaratus-ar 1
engarb-arse 80
engarber-ar 1
engarbull-ar 1
engarf-ar 1
engargant-ar 1
engargol-ar 1
engarigol-ar 1
engaripol-ar 1
engaripol-
 arse 80
engarit-ar 1
engarm-arse 80
engarraf-ar 1
engarr-ar 1
engarri-ar 1
engarron-ar 1
engarrot-ar 1
engarruch-ar 1
engarrull-ar 1
engarruñ-
 arse 80
engarz-ar 21
engasaj-ar 1
engas-ar 1
engasg-arse 51
engast-ar 1
engaston-ar 1
engat-ar 1
engatill-ar 1
engatuñ-arse ... 80
engatus-ar 1
engauch-ar 1
engavi-ar 1
engavilan-ar 1
engavill-ar 1
engayol-ar 1
engaz-ar 21
engaz-arse 80
engazuz-ar 21
engendr-ar 1
engent-arse 80
engeñ-ar 1
enger-ir 71
engib-ar 1
eng-ir 3,
 plus the
 changes
 in red in 23
englob-ar 1
englut-ir 3
engo-ar 1
engocet-ar 1
engod-ar 1
engol-ar 1
engolf-ar 1
engolill-ar 1
engolill-arse 80
engoll-ar 1
engollet-arse ... 80
engollip-arse ... 80
engolondrin-ar ... 1
engolosin-ar 1
engom-ar 1
engomin-ar 1
engonz-ar 21
engor-ar 25
engord-ar 1
engordec-er 48
engorgon-ar 1
engorgone-
 arse 80
engorgorit-ar 1
engorr-ar 1
engorrin-arse ... 80
engorron-
 arse 80
engot-arse 80
engozgorit-ar 1
engozn-ar 1
engraci-ar 1
engram-ar 1
engrame-ar 1
engramp-ar 1
engran-ar 1
engrand-ar 1

engrandec-er ... 48
engraner-ar 1
engranuj-
arse 80
engrap-ar 1
engras-ar 1
engrasill-ar 1
engravec-er 48
engred-ar 1
engre-ír 63
engresc-ar 67
engrif-ar 1
engrill-ar 1
engrill-arse 80
engrillet-ar 1
engrinch-
arse 80
engring-arse 51
engringol-
arse 80
engrip-arse 80
engros-ar 25
engrosec-er 48
engrud-ar 1
engrues-ar 1
engrumec-
erse 48
engruñ-ar 1
engrup-ir 3
enguach-
arse 80
enguachic-ar 1
enguachin-ar 1
enguad-ar 1
enguald-ar 1
engualdrap-ar 1
engualich-ar 1
enguanduj-
arse 80
enguangar-ar 1
enguant-ar 1
enguape-
arse 80
enguarac-
arse 80
enguaral-ar 1
enguarap-
arse 80
enguarapet-
arse 80
enguaret-
arse 80
enguasim-ar 1
enguat-ar 1
enguatus-ar 1
enguayab-
arse 80
engubi-ar 1
enguedej-ar 1
enguer-ar 1
engüer-ar 1
enguerrill-ar 1
enguerrill-
arse 80
enguijarr-ar 1
enguillot-
arse 80
enguiñ-arse 80
enguirland-ar 1
enguirnald-ar 1
enguisc-ar 67
enguitarr-
arse 80
enguizc-ar 67
enguizg-ar 51
engull-ir 17
engurr-ar 1
engurri-ar 1
engurrumin-ar ... 1
engurrum-ir 3
engurruñ-ar 1
engurruñ-ir 3
engusg-arse 51
enhacin-ar 1
enhad-ar 1
enhambrec-
er 48
enharin-ar 1
enhasti-ar 9
enhastill-ar 1
enhatij-ar 1
enhebill-ar 1
enhebr-ar 1
enhechiz-ar 21
enhen-ar 1
enherbol-ar 1
enhest-ar 53,
plus the past
participle
enhiesto
enhetr-ar 1
enhic-ar 1
enhiel-ar 1
enhil-ar 1
enhoc-ar
25, plus the
changes
in red in 67
enhollin-ar 1
enhollin-arse ... 80
enhorc-ar 67
enhorn-ar 1
enhorquet-ar 1
enhot-ar 1
enhuec-ar 67
enhuer-ar 1
enhuev-ar 1
enhumedec-
er 48
enigmatiz-ar 21
enjabeg-arse ... 51
enjabl-ar 1
enjabon-ar 1
enjaez-ar 21
enjagu-ar 7
enjalbeg-ar 51
enjalm-ar 1
enjambr-ar 1
enjamin-ar 1
enjaquim-ar 1
enjaran-arse 80
enjarci-ar 1
enjard-ar 1
enjardin-ar 1
enjaret-ar 1
enjarr-arse 80
enjarret-arse 80
enjaul-ar 1
enjeb-ar 1
enjerg-ar 51
enjer-ir 3
enjerron-ar 1
enjert-ar 1
enjic-ar 67
enjill-arse 80
enjill-irse 82
enjimelg-ar 51
enjiquer-ar 1
enjolon-arse 80
enjordan-ar 1
enjorguin-ar 1
enjorguin-
arse 80
enjorjet-ar 1
enjorquet-ar 1
enjoy-ar 1
enjoyel-ar 1
enjuag-ar 51
enjuer-ar 1
enjug-ar 51,
plus the past
participle
enjuto
enjugasc-
arse 67
enjuici-ar 1
enjunc-ar 67
enjunci-ar 1
enjur-ar 1
enjut-ar 1
enlabi-ar 1
enlaci-ar 1
enlacr-ar 1
enladrill-ar 1
enlagun-ar 1
enlaj-ar 1
enlam-ar 1
enlamin-arse ... 80
enlanch-ar 1
enlanguidec-
er 48
enlard-ar 1
enlat-ar 1
enlaz-ar 21
enlech-ar 1
enlegaj-ar 1
enlegam-ar 1
enleji-ar 9
enlenz-ar 34
enlerd-ar 1
enlig-ar 51
enlij-ar 1
enlis-ar 1
enlist-ar 1
enliston-ar 1
enlitr-arse 80
enliud-ar 1
enliz-ar 21
enllam-ar 1
enllant-ar 1
enllen-ar 1
enllentec-er 48
enlloc-ar 76
enlobreguec-

er 28
enlod-ar 1
enlodaz-ar 21
enlodocin-
arse 80
enlom-ar 1
enloquec-er 48
enlos-ar 1
enlozan-arse 80
enlozanec-er 48
enloz-ar 21
enlucern-ar 1
enluc-ir 3,
plus the
changes
in red in 48
enlustrec-er 49
enlut-ar 1
enmabit-ar 1
enmachambr-
ar 1
enmadej-ar 1
enmader-ar 1
enmadr-arse 80
enmadrastr-ar 1
enmaestr-ar 1
enmagrec-er 48
enmalec-er 48
enmalec-
erse 81
enmalet-ar 1
enmalez-
arse 21
enmall-ar 1
enmall-arse 80
enmallet-ar 1
enmang-ar 51
enmanigu-
arse 21
enmanill-ar 1
enmant-ar 1
enm-ar 1
enmarañ-ar 1
enmar-ar 1
enmarc-ar 67
enmarchit-ar 1
enmarid-ar 1
enmarillec-
erse 48
enmarom-ar 1
enmarques-ar 1

enmas-ar 1
enmascar-ar 1
enmasill-ar 1
enmat-arse 80
enmatul-ar 1
enmayen-
arse 80
enmech-ar 1
enmel-ar 53
enmelot-ar 1
enmend-ar 53
enmenz-ar 21
enmiel-ar 1
enmienz-ar 21
enmocec-er 48
enmochigu-ar 1
enmogot-
arse 80
enmohec-er 48
enmollec-er 48
enmon-arse 80
enmond-ar 1
enmonj-arse 80
enmontañ-
arse 80
enmont-ar 1
enmont-arse 80
enmonton-
arse 80
enmoñ-arse 80
enmordaz-ar 21
enmost-ar 1
enmostr-ar 25
enmot-ar 1
enmudec-er 48
enmuesc-ar 67
enmugr-ar 1
enmugrec-er 48
enmur-ar 1
enmusta-ir 3
ennat-ar 1
enneci-arse 80
ennegrec-er 48
ennoblec-er 48
ennudec-er 48
enoc-ar 1
enoj-ar 1
enojot-arse 80
enorgullec-er 48
enques-arse 80
enquici-ar 1

enquijot-arse 80
enquillotr-ar 1
enquimbr-
arse 80
enquinch-ar 1
enquiñ-ar 1
enquist-arse 80
enrab-ar 1
enrabi-ar 1
enrabiet-arse 80
enrabisc-ar 67
enrac-ar 1
enracim-arse 80
enraf-ar 1
enraigon-ar 1
enraiz-ar 35
enrajon-ar 1
enralec-er 48
enram-ar 1
enrambl-ar 1
enranci-ar 1
enrarec-er 48
enras-ar 1
enrasill-ar 1
enrastr-ar 1
enraton-arse 80
enray-ar 1
enraz-ar 21
enreci-ar 1
enred-ar 1
enrehoj-ar 1
enrejal-ar 1
enrej-ar 1
enrelig-ar 1
enresm-ar 1
enri-ar 9
enrid-ar 1
enriel-ar 1
enriend-ar 1
enrigidec-er 48
enriostr-ar 1
enripi-ar 1
enriquec-er 48
enrisc-ar 67
enristr-ar 1
enriz-ar 21
enrobin-arse 80
enrobustec-
er 48
enroc-ar 67
enroc-arse 80

enrod-ar 25
enrodel-ar 1
enrodrig-ar 51
enrodrigon-ar 1
enroj-ar 1
enrojec-er 48
enrol-ar 1
enroll-ar 1
enrolliz-ar 21
enrom-ar 1
enron-ar 1
enronch-ar 1
enronquec-er 48
enroñ-ar 1
enroñec-er 48
enros-ar 1
enrosc-ar 67
enrostr-ar 1
enrubesc-er 2
enrubi-ar 1
enrudec-er 48
enrug-ar 51
enruinec-er 48
enrul-ar 1
enrumb-ar 1
enrun-ar 1
ensaban-ar 1
ensac-ar 67
ensaler-ar 1
ensaliv-ar 1
ensalm-ar 1
ensalmor-ar 25
ensalobr-
arse 80
ensalvaj-ar 1
ensalvaj-arse 80
ensalz-ar 21
ensambenit-ar 1
ensambl-ar 1
ensanch-ar 1
ensandec-er 48
ensangost-ar 1
ensangrent-
ar 53
ensangusti-ar 1
ensani-arse 80
ensañ-ar 1
ensarment-ar 53
ensarnec-er 48
ensart-ar 1
ensat-ar 1

ensayal-ar 1
ensayal-arse 80
ensay-ar 1
ensay-arse 80
enseb-ar 1
ensec-ar 1
ensed-ar 1
ensell-ar 1
enselv-ar 1
ensen-ar 1
enseñal-ar 1
enseñ-ar 1
enseñore-ar 1
enseñore-arse 80
enser-ar 1
enseri-arse 80
enserpent-arse 80
ensil-ar 1
ensill-ar 1
ensillar-ar 1
ensilvec-erse 48
ensimism-arse 80
ensin-ar 1
ensobac-arse 80
ensobe-ar 1
ensoberbec-er 48
ensobin-arse 80
ensobr-ar 1
ensog-ar 51
ensoguill-ar 1
ensoler-ar 1
ensolv-er 47, except the past participle is ensuelto
ensombrec-er 48
ensoñ-ar 25
ensop-ar 1
ensord-ar 1
ensordec-er 48
ensort-arse 80
ensortij-ar 1
ensos-ar 1
ensotan-ar 1
ensot-arse 80
ensuavec-er 48
ensuci-ar 1
ensuegr-ar 1
ensug-ar 51
ensunch-ar 1
ensuriz-ar 21
ensuruc-arse 80
ensut-arse 80
ensuy-ar 1
entabac-ar 67
entabac-arse 67
entaban-arse 80
entabic-ar 67
entabl-ar 1
entabler-arse 80
entablill-ar 1
entalam-ar 1
entaleg-ar 51
entaling-ar 51
entall-ar 1
entallec-er 48
entalon-ar 1
entamang-arse 80
entam-ar 1
entand-ar 1
entang-arse 80
entap-ar 1
entapar-ar 1
entapec-er 48
entapi-ar 1
entapiz-ar 21
entapuj-ar 1
entaquill-ar 21
entarasc-ar 67
entarim-ar 1
entarquin-ar 1
entarr-ar 1
entarug-ar 51
entec-arse 67
entech-ar 1
entej-ar 1
entel-ar 1
entenci-ar 1
entend-er 2, plus the changes in red in 53
entenebr-ar 1
entenebrec-er 48
enter-ar 1
enterc-arse 67
enterci-ar 1
enterciopel-ar 1
enternec-er 48
enterr-ar 53
enterreg-ar 1
enterri-ar 1
enterron-ar 1
entes-ar 53
entest-ar 1
entestec-er 48
entib-ar 1
entibi-ar 1
entibiec-er 48
entichel-ar 1
entiemp-arse 80
entierr-ar 1
enties-ar 1
entigrec-erse 48
entil-ar 1
entin-ar 1
entint-ar 1
entir-ar 1
entirri-arse 80
entirs-ar 1
entis-ar 1
entiz-ar 21
entizn-ar 1
entol-ar 1
entold-ar 1, and for its use regarding weather, see 45
entomec-er 48
entomiz-ar 21
entompeat-ar 1
enton-ar 1
entonel-ar 1
entong-ar 51
entononc-ar 1
entont-ar 1
entontec-er 48
entoñ-ar 1
entopet-ar 1
entorc-arse 67
entorch-ar 1
entoril-ar 1
entorn-ar 1
entornill-ar 1
entorpec-er 48
entort-ar 25
entortij-ar 1
entosic-ar 1
entosig-ar 51
entoxic-ar 1
entrab-ar 1
entram-ar 1
entramoj-ar 1
entramp-ar 1
entrampill-ar 1
entrañ-ar 1
entrañiz-ar 21
entrapaj-ar 1
entrap-ar 1
entrapaz-ar 21
entr-ar 1
entreabr-ir 3, except the past participle is entreabierto
entreayud-arse 80
entrebol-ar 1
entrecav-ar 1
entrecerr-ar 53
entrechaz-ar 21
entrechoc-ar 67
entreclare-ar 1
entrecog-er 23
entrecom-ar 1
entrecomill-ar 1
entrecort-ar 1
entrecri-arse 9
entrecruz-ar 21
entredec-ir 58
entrederram-ar 1
entreg-ar 51
entreger-ir 71
entrejer-ir 71
entrejunt-ar 1
entrelaz-ar 21
entreline-ar 1
entrelist-ar 1
entrellev-ar 1
entreluc-ir 3, plus the changes in red in 48
entremedi-ar 1
entremes-ar 1

escuadrone-ar ... 1
escuajering-arse ... 77
escuch-ar ... 1
escuchimiz-ar ... 21
escud-ar ... 1
escudere-ar ... 1
escudill-ar ... 1
escudriñ-ar ... 1
escuezn-ar ... 1
esculc-ar ... 67
escull-ar ... 1
escull-ir ... 3
esculp-ir ... 3
escultur-ar ... 1
escup-ir ... 3
escur-ar ... 1
escurc-ar ... 1
escurec-er ... 48
escurific-ar ... 1
escurr-ir ... 3
esdrujuliz-ar ... 21
esenci-arse ... 80
esfacel-ar ... 1
esfarrap-ar ... 1
esflec-ar ... 1
esfog-ar ... 1
esfol-ar ... 1
esfoll-ar ... 1
esfornecin-ar ... 1
esforrocin-ar ... 1
esforz-ar ... 69
esfoy-ar ... 1
esfri-ar ... 1
esfum-ar ... 1
esfumin-ar ... 1
esgarabot-ar ... 1
esgarr-ar ... 1
esgatiñ-arse ... 80
esgoard-ar ... 1
esgoliz-arse ... 21
esgonz-ar ... 21
esgrafi-ar ... 9
esgrim-ir ... 3
esguardamill-ar ... 1
esguard-ar ... 1
esguaz-ar ... 21
esguil-ar ... 1
esgurrumb-ar ... 1
eslabon-ar ... 1
eslaviz-ar ... 21
esle-er ... 2
esle-ír ... 3
eslembr-arse ... 80
esling-ar ... 51
esmalt-ar ... 1
esmechud-ar ... 1
esmer-ar ... 1
esmeril-ar ... 1
esmirri-arse ... 80
esmong-ar ... 1
esmonguill-ar ... 1
esmorec-er ... 48
esmorus-arse ... 80
esmuci-arse ... 80
esmu-ir ... 42
esmuñ-ir ... 17
espabil-ar ... 1
espachurr-ar ... 1
espaci-ar ... 1
espadañ-ar ... 1
espad-ar ... 1
espadill-ar ... 1
espaladin-ar ... 1
espal-ar ... 1
espald-ar ... 1
espald-arse ... 80
espalde-ar ... 1
espaldill-ar ... 1
espaldon-ar ... 1
espaldon-arse ... 80
espaletill-ar ... 1
espalm-ar ... 1
espanc-irse 82, plus the changes in red in ... 23
espand-ir ... 3
espand-irse ... 82
espant-ar ... 1
español-ar ... 1
españole-ar ... 1
españoliz-ar ... 21
esparc-ir 3, plus the changes in red in ... 23
esparrag-ar ... 51
esparram-ar ... 1
esparranc-arse ... 67
esparru-ar ... 1
espart-ar ... 1
esparv-ar ... 1
espasm-ar ... 1
espatan-arse ... 80
espatarr-arse ... 80
espaturr-ar ... 1
espavil-ar ... 1
espavoriz-arse ... 21
espech-ar ... 1
especializ-ar ... 21
especi-ar ... 1
especific-ar ... 67
espect-ar ... 1
especul-ar ... 1
espedaz-ar ... 21
esped-irse ... 52
espej-ar ... 1
espeje-ar ... 1
espelot-arse ... 80
espeluc-ar ... 67
espelusc-ar ... 1
espeluz-ar ... 21
espeluzn-ar ... 1
esperanz-ar ... 21
esper-ar ... 1
esperdec-ir 3, plus the changes in red in ... 23
esperec-er ... 48
esperez-arse ... 21
espergur-ar ... 1
espernanc-arse ... 67
esperri-ar ... 1
espert-ar ... 1
espes-ar ... 1
espet-ar ... 1
espiant-ar ... 1
espi-ar ... 9
espich-ar ... 1
espiche-ar ... 1
espig-ar ... 51
espigue-ar ... 1
espill-ar ... 1
espin-ar ... 1
espinoch-ar ... 1
espinz-ar ... 21
espion-ar ... 1
espir-ar ... 1
espirit-ar ... 1
espiritualiz-ar ... 21
espit-ar ... 1
esplend-er ... 2
esplendor-ar ... 1
esplendore-ar ... 1
espole-ar ... 1
espoli-ar ... 1
espolin-ar ... 1
espolone-ar ... 1
espols-ar ... 1
espolvor-ar ... 1
espolvore-ar ... 1
espolvoriz-ar ... 21
esponj-ar ... 1
esponje-ar ... 1
espontane-arse ... 80
esporg-ar ... 1
esporrondig-arse ... 51
esporronding-arse ... 51
esporte-ar ... 1
espos-ar ... 1
espret-ar ... 1
esprete-ar ... 1
esprint-ar ... 1
espuel-ar ... 1
espuele-ar ... 1
espulg-ar ... 51
espul-irse ... 82
espumaj-ar ... 1
espumaje-ar ... 1
espum-ar ... 1
espumaraje-ar ... 1
espurre-ar ... 1
espurri-ar ... 9
espurr-ir ... 3
esput-ar ... 1
esquebraj-ar ... 1
esquej-ar ... 1
esquelet-ar ... 1
esqueletiz-ar ... 21
esquematiz-ar ... 21

esqui-ar 9
esquici-ar 1
esquif-ar 1
esquil-ar 1
esquilm-ar 1
esquin-ar 1
esquinz-ar 21
esquip-ar 1
esquis-ar 1
esquit-ar 1
esquiv-ar 1
estabil-ir 21
estabiliz-ar 21
estable-ar 1
establec-er 48
establ-ir 67
estabul-ar 1
estac-ar 67
estacion-ar 1
estaf-ar 1
estaj-ar 1
estaje-ar 1
estall-ar 1
estambr-ar 1
estamp-ar 1
estampill-ar 1
estanc-ar 67
estandardiz-
ar 21
estandariz-ar ... 21
estandartiz-
ar 21
estantal-ar 1
estantill-ar 1
estañ-ar 1
estaque-ar 1
estaquill-ar 1
est-ar 38
estarcicopi-ar 1
estarcigrafi-ar 1
estarc-ir 3,
plus the
changes
in red in 23
estatific-ar 67
estatiz-ar 21
estatu-ar 9
estatu-ir 42
estay-ar 1
estaz-ar 1
esteb-ar 1

estecl-ar 1
estem-ar 1
estenografi-ar 9
estenotipi-ar 1
ester-ar 1
esterc-ar 67
estercol-ar 1
estereotip-ar 1
esterific-ar 67
esteriliz-ar 21
esterill-ar 1
esteriz-ar 1
estez-ar 21
estib-ar 1
estigmatiz-ar ... 21
estil-ar 1
estiliz-ar 21
estill-ar 1
estim-ar 1
estimul-ar 1
estiomen-ar 1
estipendi-ar 1
estiptic-ar 67
estipul-ar 1
estirace-ar 1
estiraj-ar 1
estiraje-ar 1
estir-ar 1
estiraz-ar 21
estirone-ar 1
estiv-ar 1
esto-ar 1
estoc-ar 67
estof-ar 1
estoj-ar 1
estomag-ar 51
estope-ar 1
estoque-ar 1
estorb-ar 1
estorc-er 22
estord-ir 3
estornud-ar 1
estovainiz-ar 21
estov-ar 1
estoz-ar 21
estozol-ar 1
estrag-ar 51
estragol-ar 1
estrall-ar 1
estrangul-ar 1
estrapaj-ar 1

estraperle-ar 1
estrasij-arse 80
estratific-ar 4
estraz-ar 21
estrech-ar 1
estreg-ar 62
estrell-ar 1
estremec-er 48
estren-ar 1
estreñ-ir 64
estrepit-arse 80
estri-ar 9
estrib-ar 1
estric-arse 80
estricniz-ar 21
estricul-ar 1
estridul-ar 1
estrig-ar 1
estril-ar 1
estrill-ar 1
estropaje-ar 1
estrope-ar 1
estropez-ar 21
estructur-ar 1
estru-ir 42
estruj-ar 1
estrump-ir 3
estrup-ar 1
estuc-ar 67
estuch-ar 1
estudi-ar 1
estuf-ar 1
estupr-ar 1
estur-ar 1
esturdec-er 48
esturg-ar 51
esturre-ar 1
estus-ar 1
esug-ar 1
esvar-ar 1
etaling-ar 1
eterific-ar 67
eteriz-ar 21
eterniz-ar 21
etic-arse 80
etimologiz-ar ... 21
etiquet-ar 1
eufoniz-ar 21
europeiz-ar 35
evacu-ar 1
evad-ir 3

evalu-ar 9
evangeliz-ar 21
evapor-ar 1
evaporiz-ar 21
even-ir 77
evidenci-ar 1
eviscer-ar 1
evit-ar 1
evoc-ar 67
evol-ar 25
evolucion-ar 1
exacerb-ar 1
exager-ar 1
exalt-ar 1
exalz-ar 21
examin-ar 1
exardec-er 48
exasper-ar 1
exaud-ir 3
excandec-er 1
excarcel-ar 1
excardin-ar 1
excav-ar 1
exced-er 2
excepcion-ar 1
except-ar 1
exceptu-ar 9
excit-ar 1
exclam-ar 1
exclaustr-ar 1
exclu-ir 42,
plus the
past participle
excluso
excogit-ar 1
excomulg-ar 51
excori-ar 1
excorpor-ar 1
excrement-ar 1
excret-ar 1
exculp-ar 1
excursion-ar 1
excus-ar 1
execr-ar 1
exencion-ar 1
exent-ar 1
exfoli-ar 1
exhal-ar 1
exhaust-ar 1
exhered-ar 1
exhib-ir 3

exhort-ar 1
exhum-ar 1
exifore-ar 1
exig-ir 3, plus the changes in red in 16 and 7
exil-ar 1
exili-ar 1
exim-ir 3, plus the past participle exento
ex-ir 3
existim-ar 1
exist-ir 3
exond-ar 1
exoner-ar 1
exor-ar 1
exorciz-ar 21
exordi-ar 1
exord-ir 3
exorn-ar 1
expanc-irse 82, plus the changes in red in 46
expand-ir 3
expansion-arse 80
expatri-arse 9
expavec-er 48
expector-ar 1
expedient-ar 1
exped-ir 52
expedit-ar 1
expel-er 2, plus the past participle expulso
expend-er 2
expens-ar 1
experiment-ar 1
expi-ar 9
expil-ar 1
expir-ar 1
explan-ar 1
explay-ar 1
explic-ar 67
explicote-ar 1
explicote-arse 80
explor-ar 1
explosion-ar 1
explot-ar 1
expoli-ar 1
expon-er 57
export-ar 1
exprem-ir 3
expres-ar 1, plus the past participle expreso
exprim-ir 3
expropi-ar 1
expugn-ar 1
expuls-ar 1
expurg-ar 51
exquir-ir 3
exsud-ar 1
extasi-arse 9
extend-er 2, plus the changes in red in 53, plus the past participle extenso
extenu-ar 9
exterioriz-ar 21
extermin-ar 1
extern-ar 1
extingu-ir 30, plus the past participle extinto
extirp-ar 1
extorc-ar 1
extorn-ar 1
extorsion-ar 1
extract-ar 1
extra-er 75
extralimit-ar 1
extralimit-arse 80
extranjeriz-ar ... 21
extrañ-ar 1
extrapol-ar 1
extravag-ar 51
extravas-arse 80
extraven-ar 1
extravi-ar 9
extrem-ar 1
extrud-ir 3
extub-ar 1
exturb-ar 1
exuber-ar 1
exud-ar 1
exulcer-ar 1
exult-ar 1
exund-ar 1
exvincul-ar 1
eyacul-ar 1
eyect-ar 1
ezquerde-ar 1

f

fabe-ar 1
fabl-ar 1
fablistane-ar 1
fabric-ar 67
fabul-ar 1
fabuliz-ar 21
faccion-ar 1
fac-er 41
facer-ir 71
facet-ar 1
facete-ar 1
fache-ar 1
fachende-ar 1
fachose-ar 1
facilit-ar 1
factoriz-ar 21
factur-ar 1
facult-ar 1
fad-ar 1
fadig-ar 51
faen-ar 1
fafarach-ar 1
fagocit-ar 1
faite-ar 1
faj-ar 1
faje-ar 1
falag-ar 1
fal-ar 1
falcace-ar 1
falc-ar 67
falcaz-ar 1
falde-ar 1
falesc-er 2
fal-ir 3
fall-ar 1
fallec-er 48
fall-ir 3
fals-ar 1
false-ar 1
falsific-ar 67
falt-ar 1
familiariz-ar 21
fanatiz-ar 21
fandangue-ar 1
fanfarre-ar 1
fanfarrone-ar 1
fantase-ar 1
fantastic-ar 1
farabuste-ar 1
farach-ar 1
faradiz-ar 21
faramalle-ar 1
farandule-ar 1
farangue-ar 1
fard-ar 1
farfalle-ar 1
farfull-ar 1
farole-ar 1
farote-ar 1
farre-ar 1
farsante-ar 1
fars-ar 1
farse-ar 1
fart-ar 1
fascin-ar 1
fasqui-ar 1
fastidi-ar 1
fataliz-ar 1
fatig-ar 51
favorec-er 48
fazfer-ir 71
fech-ar 1
fecund-ar 1
fecundiz-ar 21
fedeg-ar 51
federaliz-ar 21
feder-ar 1
felicit-ar 1
felp-ar 1
felpe-ar 1
fem-ar 53
femenci-ar 1
feminiz-ar 1
fench-ir 52
fend-er 2, plus the changes

frez-ar 21
fric-ar 67
friccion-ar 1
frigorific-ar 67
frigoriz-ar 21
frijole-ar 1
frijoliz-ar 21
fringole-ar 1
fris-ar 1
frit-ar 1
frochigu-ar 1
frog-ar 1
frondose-ar 1
frot-ar 1
fructific-ar 67
fru-ir 42
frunc-ir 3, plus the changes in red in 23
fruñ-ir 17
frustr-ar 1
frut-ar 1
frute-ar 1
frutec-er 48
frutific-ar 1
fucil-ar 1, and for its use regarding weather, see 45
fuell-ar 1
fuete-ar 1
fuf-ar 1
fug-ar 1
fug-arse 51
fulc-ir 3, plus the changes in red in 23
fulg-ir 3, plus the changes in red in 53 and 23
fulgur-ar 1
fulgurec-er 48
fulle-ar 1
fullere-ar 1
fulmin-ar 1
fum-ar 1
fume-ar 1
fumig-ar 51
funcion-ar 1
fundament-ar 1
fund-ar 1
fundibul-ar 1
fund-ir 3
funest-ar 1
fung-ar 51
fung-ir 3, plus the changes in red in 23
fuñ-ar 1
fuñic-ar 67
furt-ar 1
fusc-ar 1
fusil-ar 1
fusion-ar 1
fustane-ar 1
fustig-ar 51
fute-arse 80
fut-irse 82
futr-arse 80
futr-ir 3
futute-ar 1
futute-arse 80

g

gabane-ar 1
gab-arse 80
gabe-ar 1
gaf-ar 1
gafe-arse 80
gague-ar 1
gaj-ar 1
galante-ar 1
galardon-ar 1
galgu-ar 1
galgue-ar 1
galib-ar 1
galim-ar 1
gall-ar 1
gallarde-ar 1
galle-ar 1
gallete-ar 1
gallof-ar 1
gallofe-ar 1
galone-ar 1
galop-ar 1
galope-ar 1
galuch-ar 1
galvaniz-ar 21
galvanotip-ar 1
gambete-ar 1
gambi-ar 1
gamit-ar 1
gamite-ar 1
gamone-ar 1
ganade-ar 1
gan-ar 1
gand-ir 3
ganduj-ar 1
gandule-ar 1
gangose-ar 1
gangren-arse 80
gangue-ar 1
ganse-ar 1
ganzu-ar 9
gañ-ir 17
gapale-ar 1
garab-ar 1
garabate-ar 1
garafate-ar 1
garafete-ar 1
garand-ar 1
garant-ir 4
garantiz-ar 21
garapiñ-ar 1
gar-ar 1
garate-ar 1
garb-ar 1
garbe-ar 1
garbill-ar 1
garce-ar 1
gard-ar 1
garete-ar 1
garfe-ar 1
garfiñ-ar 1
gargaje-ar 1
gargaliz-ar 21
gargante-ar 1
gargare-ar 1
gargariz-ar 21
garimp-ar 1
garite-ar 1
garl-ar 1
garle-ar 1
garliborle-ar 1
garnache-ar 1
garrafiñ-ar 1
garram-ar 1
garranch-ar 1
garrapate-ar 1
garrapiñ-ar 1
garr-ar 1
garrasp-ar 1
garre-ar 1
garr-ir 3
garroch-ar 1
garroche-ar 1
garrone-ar 1
garrote-ar 1
garruche-ar 1
garrul-ar 1
garsin-ar 1
garu-ar 9, and for its use regarding weather, see 45
garub-ar 1
garufe-ar 1
garug-ar 51, and used in the positions in 45
gasaj-ar 1
gasaj-arse 80
gasconiz-ar 21
gase-ar 1
gasific-ar 67
gasnache-ar 1
gaspale-ar 1
gast-ar 1
gate-ar 1
gatuñ-ar 1
gauch-ar 1
gauche-ar 1
gavi-ar 1
gavill-ar 1
gay-ar 1
gazmi-ar 1
gazn-ar 1
gaznate-ar 1
gelatinific-ar 1
gelatiniz-ar 21
gelific-ar 67
gemific-ar 67
gemin-ar 1
gemique-ar 1
gem-ir 52
generaliz-ar 21
gener-ar 1

gentiliz-ar 21
germaniz-ar 21
germific-ar 1
germin-ar 1
gerundi-ar 1
gest-ar 1
geste-ar 1
gesticul-ar 1
gestion-ar 1
get-ar 1
gib-ar 1
gigantiz-ar 21
gigue-ar 1
gilipolle-ar 1
gimoque-ar 1
gimote-ar 1
gimpl-ar 1
gingl-ar 1
gingr-ar 1
gir-ar 1
giron-ar 1
gitane-ar 1
glase-ar 1
glicer-ar 1
glicerin-ar 1
glori-ar 9
glorific-ar 67
glos-ar 1
glotone-ar 1
gluglute-ar 1
glutin-ar 1
gobern-ar 53
gofr-ar 1
golde-ar 1
gole-ar 1
golfe-ar 1
golill-ar 1
gollete-ar 1
golmaje-ar 1
golose-ar 1
golosin-ar 1
golosine-ar 1
golosme-ar 1
golpe-ar 1
golpete-ar 1
golusme-ar 1
gom-ar 1
gomorriz-ar 1
gonce-ar 1
gongoriz-ar 21
goñe-ar 1
gorbete-ar 1
gore-arse 80
gorgoj-arse 80
gorgoje-arse 80
gorgore-ar 1
gorgorite-ar 1
gorgote-ar 1
gorgue-ar 1
gorje-ar 1
gorm-ar 1
gorre-ar 1
gorrone-ar 1
goruchone-ar 1
gote-ar 1, and for its use regarding weather, see 45
gotere-ar 1, and used in the positions in 45
goz-ar 21
grab-ar 1
gracej-ar 1
grac-ir 3, plus the changes in red in 23
grad-ar 1
grade-ar 1
gradec-er 48
gradu-ar 9
grafil-ar 1
graje-ar 1
gram-ar 1
gramatiqu-er 2
granall-ar 1
gran-ar 1
grandec-er 48
grandifac-er 69
grandison-ar 25
grane-ar 1
granel-ar 1
graniz-ar 21, and for its use regarding weather, see 45
granje-ar 1
granul-ar 1
grañ-ir 17
grap-ar 1
gras-ar 1
grasin-ar 1
grat-ar 1
gratific-ar 67
gratin-ar 1
gratul-ar 1
grav-ar 1
grave-ar 1
gravit-ar 1
gray-ar 1
grazn-ar 1
grazne-ar 1
grec-ar 67
greciz-ar 21
gregaliz-ar 21
greguiz-ar 21
grete-ar 1
grib-ar 1
grid-ar 1
griet-ar 1
griet-arse 80
griete-arse 80
grif-arse 80
grill-ar 1
grill-arse 80
grillote-ar 1
grip-ar 1
gris-ar 1
grise-ar 1
grit-ar 1
gritone-ar 1
groaj-ar 1
gro-ar 1
groje-ar 1
gru-ar 9
gru-ir 42
gruj-ir 3
gruñ-ir 17
grupe-ar 1
guabine-ar 1
guacale-ar 1
guacamole-ar 1
guachache-ar 1
guachape-ar 1
guachaque-ar 1
guach-ar 1
guache-ar 1
guachi-ar 1
guachific-ar 1
guachine-ar 1
guadañ-ar 1
guadañe-ar 1
guaguare-ar 1
guaguate-ar 1
guaic-ar 1
guaique-ar 1
guait-ar 1
guaje-ar 1
gualambe-ar 1
gualardon-ar 1
gualdrape-ar 1
gualtrape-ar 1
guambi-ar 1
guame-ar 1
guanaque-ar 1
guanchaque-ar 1
guane-ar 1
guangue-ar 1
guante-ar 1
guantone-ar 1
guañ-ir 17
guape-ar 1
guaque-ar 1
guarache-ar 1
guarangue-ar 1
guarape-ar 1
guaraque-ar 1
guard-ar 1
guardarray-ar 1
guare-ar 1
guare-arse 80
guarec-er 48
guaresc-er 48
guaric-arse 80
guar-ir 3
guarism-ar 1
guarnec-er 48
guarnicion-ar 1
guarn-ir 4
guarre-ar 1
guarrey-ar 1
guase-arse 80
guasque-ar 1
guast-ar 1
guataque-ar 1
guate-ar 1
guate-arse 80
guatele-ar 1
guateque-ar 1
guatrape-ar 1

guayabe-ar 1
guay-ar 1
guayuque-ar 1
gubern-ar 1
guedej-ar 1
güelde-ar 1
guerre-ar 1
guerrile-ar 1
guerrille-ar 1
gui-ar 9
guid-ar 1
guillab-ar 1
guill-arse 80
guillotin-ar 1
guinch-ar 1
guind-ar 1
guiñ-ar 1
guiñe-ar 1
guip-ar 1
guirpiñ-ar 1
guis-ar 1
guisote-ar 1
guit-ar 1
guitarre-ar 1
guitone-ar 1
guizc-ar 67
guizg-ar 51
guizn-ar 1
gulusme-ar 1
gur-ar 1
gurbe-ar 1
gurguci-ar 1
gurr-ar 1
gurrubuce-ar 1
gurruñ-ar 1
gurrupe-ar 1
gusane-ar 1
gust-ar 1
guturaliz-ar 21
guzgue-ar 1

h

hab-ar 1
hab-er 40
habilit-ar 1
habit-ar 1
habitu-ar 9
habl-ar 1
hacend-ar 53
hac-er 41
hacer-ir 71
hach-ar 1
hache-ar 1
hacin-ar 1
had-ar 1
halag-ar 67
hal-ar 1
halcone-ar 1
halde-ar 1
hall-ar 1
hamac-ar 67
hamaque-ar 1
hambre-ar 1
handicap-ar 1
haragane-ar 1
harb-ar 1
harbull-ar 1
hargane-ar 1
harine-ar 1
harisc-arse 67
harmoniz-ar 21
harne-ar 1
harone-ar 1
harp-ar 1
harre-ar 1
hart-ar 1, plus the past participle harto
hasti-ar 9
hataj-ar 1
hate-ar 1
hazan-ar 1
hazañ-ar 1
hebet-ar 1
hebill-ar 1
hebraiz-ar 35
hechiz-ar 21
hed-er 2, plus the changes in red in 53
hedr-ar 1
hel-ar 53, and for its use regarding weather, see 45
hele-ar 1
helenistiz-ar 21
heleniz-ar 21
helitransport-ar 1
hembre-ar 1
hembrimach-ar 1
hemenci-ar 1
hemoliz-ar 21
hench-ir 52
hend-er 2, plus the changes in red in 53
hend-ir 3, plus the changes in red in 53
hene-ar 1
henific-ar 67
heñ-ir 64
hepariniz-ar 21
hepatiz-arse 80
herbaj-ar 1
herbaje-ar 1
herbal-ar 1
herb-ar 53
herbec-er 48
herbol-ar 1
herbolec-er 48
herboliz-ar 21
herboriz-ar 21
hered-ar 1
heretic-ar 1
heretiz-ar 21
her-ir 71
herman-ar 1
hermand-arse 80
hermane-ar 1
hermanec-er 48
hermose-ar 1
heroific-ar 1
herr-ar 53
herren-ar 1
herrene-ar 1
herrete-ar 1
herrumbr-ar 1
hervent-ar 53
herv-ir 71
hervoriz-arse ... 80
hesit-ar 1
hesp-irse 52
het-ar 1
heterodin-ar 1
hetic-arse 67
hibern-ar 1
hibiern-ar 1
hibometr-ar 1
hidrat-ar 1
hidrofug-ar 1
hidrogen-ar 1
hidroliz-ar 21
hidropic-arse ... 67
hidrosulfur-ar 1
hidroxil-ar 1
hidroxiliz-ar 21
hierbe-ar 1
higad-ar 1
higar-ar 1
higieniz-ar 21
hije-ar 1
hijuel-ar 1
hil-ar 1
hilvan-ar 1
himp-ar 1
himpl-ar 1
hinc-ar 67
hinch-ar 1
hinch-ir 52
hinoj-ar 1
hip-ar 1
hipe-ar 1
hiperboliz-ar 21
hiperestesi-ar 1
hiperovariz-ar 21
hipertrofi-ar 9
hipertrofi-arse 80
hipnotiz-ar 21
hiposteniz-ar ... 21
hipotec-ar 67
hipovariz-ar 21
hirm-ar 1
hirudiniz-ar 21
hiscal-ar 1
hisop-ar 1
hisope-ar 1
hispaniz-ar 21
hisp-ir 3
histori-ar 1
hit-ar 1
hocic-ar 67
hocique-ar 1

hog-ar ... 1
hojaldr-ar ... 1
hoje-ar ... 1
hojec-er ... 48
holandiz-ar ... 21
hole-ar ... 1
holg-ar ... 24
holgazane-ar ... 1
holgaz-ar ... 21
holl-ar ... 25
hollin-ar ... 1
holocaustiz-ar ... 21
hombre-ar ... 1
homenaje-ar ... 1
homici-arse ... 80
homogeneiz-ar ... 21
homogeniz-ar ... 21
homolog-ar ... 51
hond-ar ... 1
honde-ar ... 1
hondi-ar ... 1
hondon-ar ... 1
honest-ar ... 1
honor-ar ... 1
honorific-ar ... 67
honr-ar ... 1
hop-arse ... 80
hope-ar ... 1
horac-ar ... 1
horad-ar ... 1
horc-ar ... 67
horm-ar ... 1
hormej-ar ... 1
hormigue-ar ... 1
hormiguill-ar ... 1
hornague-ar ... 1
horne-ar ... 1
hornegue-ar ... 1
horquete-ar ... 1
horquill-ar ... 1
horr-ar ... 1
horre-ar ... 1
horrific-ar ... 67
horripil-ar ... 1
horroriz-ar ... 21
hosped-ar ... 1
hospitaliz-ar ... 21
hostig-ar ... 51
hostiliz-ar ... 21
hoy-ar ... 1
hoz-ar ... 21
huachafe-ar ... 1
huachape-ar ... 1
huach-ar ... 1
huaque-ar ... 1
huarac-ar ... 1
huaripampe-ar ... 1
huasque-ar ... 1
huate-ar ... 1
huate-arse ... 80
huche-ar ... 1
huelgue-ar ... 1
hueric-arse ... 80
huese-ar ... 1
hueste-ar ... 1
huev-ar ... 1
hueve-ar ... 1
huevi-ar ... 1
huilc-ar ... 1
huinch-arse ... 80
hu-ir ... 42
huisach-ar ... 1
huisache-ar ... 1
hule-ar ... 1
hulere-ar ... 1
human-ar ... 1
humaniz-ar ... 21
hum-ar ... 1
hume-ar ... 1
humect-ar ... 1
humed-ar ... 1
humedec-er ... 48
humig-ar ... 1
humili-ar ... 1
humill-ar ... 1
hund-ir ... 3
huracan-arse ... 80
hurg-ar ... 51
hurgone-ar ... 1
hurguete-ar ... 1
hurl-ar ... 1
hurone-ar ... 1
hurt-ar ... 1
husm-ar ... 1
husme-ar ... 1

i

idealiz-ar ... 21
ide-ar ... 1
identific-ar ... 67
idiotiz-ar ... 21
idolatr-ar ... 1
iet-ar ... 1
ignifug-ar ... 51
ignor-ar ... 1
igual-ar ... 1
igu-ar ... 1
ijade-ar ... 1
ilegitim-ar ... 1
ilud-ir ... 3
ilumin-ar ... 1
ilusion-ar ... 1
ilustr-ar ... 1
imagin-ar ... 1
iman-ar ... 1
imant-ar ... 1
imbric-ar ... 67
imbu-ir ... 42
imbunch-ar ... 1
imburs-ar ... 1
imit-ar ... 1
impacient-ar ... 1
impar-ir ... 3
impart-ir ... 3
impast-ar ... 3
imped-ir ... 52
impel-er ... 2
impel-ir ... 3
impend-er ... 2
imper-ar ... 1
imperfeccion-ar ... 1
imperi-ar ... 1
impermeabiliz-ar ... 21
impersonaliz-ar ... 21
impert-ir ... 71
impetr-ar ... 1
imping-ar ... 1
implant-ar ... 1
impl-ar ... 1
implic-ar 1, and alternatively, ... 67
implor-ar ... 1
impon-er ... 57
impopulariz-ar ... 21
importantiz-arse ... 21
import-ar ... 1
importun-ar ... 1
imposibilit-ar ... 1
impost-ar ... 1
imprec-ar ... 67
impregn-ar ... 1
imprem-ir ... 52
imprent-ar ... 1
impresion-ar ... 1
imprim-ar ... 1
imprim-ir 3, except the past participle is impreso
improb-ar ... 25
improper-ar ... 1
impropi-ar ... 1
improvis-ar ... 1
impugn-ar ... 1
impuls-ar ... 1
impurific-ar ... 67
imput-ar ... 1
inaugur-ar ... 1
incal-er ... 2
incamer-ar ... 1
incapacit-ar ... 1
incardin-ar ... 1
incaut-arse ... 80
incendi-ar ... 1
incens-ar ... 53
incentiv-ar ... 1
incer-ar ... 1
incest-ar ... 1
incid-ir ... 3
inciner-ar ... 1
incit-ar ... 1
inciviliz-ar ... 21
inclin-ar ... 1
inclu-ir 42, plus the past participle incluso
inco-ar 1, and used in the positions in ... 45
incomod-ar ... 1

incomunic-ar ... 67
incon-arse 80
incontr-ar 1
incordi-ar 1
incorpor-ar 1
incras-ar 1
increment-ar 1
increp-ar 1
incrimin-ar 1
incrust-ar 1
incuart-ar 1
incub-ar 1
inculc-ar 67
inculp-ar 1
incumb-ir 3, and used in the positions in 45
incumpl-ir 3
incurr-ir 3, plus the past participle incurso
incursion-ar 1
incurv-ar 1
incus-ar 1
indag-ar 51
indemniz-ar 21
independ-erse 81
independi-ar 1
independiz-ar 21
indianiz-ar 21
indic-ar 67
indici-ar 1
indigest-arse ... 80
indign-ar 1
indilg-ar 51
indin-ar 1
indisciplin-arse 80
indispon-er 57
individualiz-ar 21
individu-ar 9
induc-ir 59
indulgenci-ar 1
indult-ar 1
indur-ar 1
industrializ-ar 21
industri-ar 1
inebri-ar 1
inerv-ar 1
infam-ar 1
infart-ar 1
infatu-ar 9
infeccion-ar 1
infec-ir 52, plus the changes in red in 46
infect-ar 1
infecund-arse 80
infer-ir 71
infern-ar 53
infest-ar 1
infeud-ar 1
infibul-ar 1
inficcion-ar 1
inficion-ar 1
infiltr-ar 1
infing-ir 3, plus the changes in red in 23
infinit-ar 1
infirm-ar 1
inflam-ar 1
infl-ar 1
inflexion-arse ... 80
inflig-ir 3, plus the changes in red in 23
infling-ir 3, plus the changes in red in 23
influenci-ar 1
influ-ir 42
inform-ar 1
infravalor-ar 1
infri-ar 1
infring-ir 3, plus the changes in red in 23
infund-ir 3, plus the past participle infuso
infurt-ir 3, plus the past participle infurto
infus-ar 1
infusc-ar 67
ingeni-ar 1
inger-ir 71, plus the past participle ingerto
ingles-ar 1
inglet-ar 1
inglete-ar 1
ingres-ar 1
ingr-ir 3
ingurgit-ar 1
inhabilit-ar 1
inhabit-ar 1
inhal-ar 1
inhest-ar 53
inhi-ar 1
inhib-ir 3
inhonor-ar 1
inhum-ar 1
inici-ar 1
injer-ir 71
injert-ar 1, plus the past participle injerto
injone-ar 1
injum-ar 1
injuri-ar 1
inmaterializ-ar 21
inmerg-ir 3, plus the changes in red in 23
inmigr-ar 1
inmiscu-ir 42
inmol-ar 1
inmortaliz-ar 21
inmoviliz-ar 21
inmuniz-ar 21
inmut-ar 1
innov-ar 1
inobserv-ar 1
inocul-ar 1
inor-ar 1
inquiet-ar 1
inquin-ar 1
inquir-ir 5
insacul-ar 1
insaliv-ar 1
inscrib-ir 3, except the past participles are inscrito and inscripto
insculp-ir 3
insegu-ir 52
insensibiliz-ar 21
inser-ir 71
insert-ar 1, plus the past participle inserto
insidi-ar 1
insimul-ar 1
insinu-ar 9
insist-ir 3
insol-ar 1
insolent-ar 1
insolubiliz-ar 21
insonoriz-ar 21
inspeccion-ar 1
inspir-ar 1
instal-ar 1
inst-ar 1
instaur-ar 1
instig-ar 51
instil-ar 1
instimul-ar 1
institucionaliz-ar 21
institu-ir 42
instru-ir 42
instrument-ar 1
insubordin-ar 1
insud-ar 1
insufl-ar 1
insult-ar 1
insum-ir 3
insurreccion-ar 1
integr-ar 1
intelectualiz-

ar 21
inteligenci-
arse 80
intencion-ar 1
intens-ar 1
intensific-ar 67
intent-ar 1
intercal-ar 1
intercambi-ar 1
interced-er 2
intercept-ar 1
interclu-ir 42
intercomunic-
arse 80
interdec-ir 58
interdict-ar 1
interes-ar 1
interfer-ir 71
interfoli-ar 1
interin-ar 1
interior-arse 80
interioriz-ar 21
interline-ar 1
intermedi-ar 1
intermit-ir 3
internacionaliz-
ar 21
intern-ar 1
interpagin-ar 1
interpel-ar 1
interpol-ar 1
interpon-er 57
interprend-er 2
interpret-ar 1
interrog-ar 51
interrump-ir 3
intersec-arse ... 67
interser-ir 71
interven-ir 77
intervert-ir 71
interview-ar 1
intervist-arse ... 80
interviuv-ar 1
intest-ar 1
intim-ar 1
intimid-ar 1
intitul-ar 1
intoxic-ar 67
intranquiliz-
ar 21
intrat-ar 1
intribut-ar 1
intric-ar 67
intrig-ar 51
intrinc-ar 67
introduc-ir 59
intromet-erse ... 81
intrus-arse 80
intruse-ar 1
intub-ar 1
intu-ir 42
inund-ar 1
inutiliz-ar 21
invad-ir 3
invagin-ar 1
invalid-ar 1
invectiv-ar 1
inven-ir 77
invent-ar 1
inventari-ar 9
invern-ar 53
invert-ir 71,
plus the past
participle
inverso
investig-ar 51
invest-ir 52
inveter-arse 80
invigil-ar 1
invit-ar 1
invoc-ar 67
involucr-ar 1
inyect-ar 1
inyung-ir 3,
plus the
changes
in red in 23
inzu-ir 42
ioniz-ar 21
ir 43
ir-arse 80
iridi-ar 1
irire-ar 1
iris-ar 1
ironiz-ar 21
irradi-ar 1
irrespet-ar 1
irreverenci-ar 1
irrig-ar 51
irrit-ar 1
irrog-ar 51
irru-ir 42
irrump-ir 3
islamiz-ar 21
isomeriz-ar 21
ispe-ar 1
ispi-ar 9
istri-ar 9
italianiz-ar 21
iter-ar 1
ivern-ar 52
iz-ar 21
izquierde-ar 1

j

jabalcon-ar 1
jabalcone-ar 1
jabalon-ar 1
jabarde-ar 1
jabe-ar 1
jabel-ar 1
jabelg-ar 1
jabon-ar 1
jabone-ar 1
jabr-ir 3,
except the
past participle
is jabierto
jacale-ar 1
jacare-ar 1
jac-er 79
jacerdan-ar 1
jach-ar 1
jact-ar 1
jact-arse 80
jacul-ar 1
jade-ar 1
jadi-ar 9
jaez-ar 21
jagu-ar 1
jaharr-ar 1
jair-ar 1
jaj-ar 1
jal-ar 1
jalbeg-ar 51
jale-ar 1
jaleiz-ar 21
jall-ar 1
jalon-ar 1
jalone-ar 1
jalpac-ar 67
jamaque-ar 1
jam-ar 1
jam-arse 80
jamb-ar 1
jambr-ar 1
jamerd-ar 53
jamur-ar 1
jane-ar 1
jape-ar 1
japoniz-ar 21
japorc-ar 67
japurc-ar 67
jaque-ar 1
jaqu-ir 3
j-ar 1
jarabe-ar 1
jarane-ar 1
jarapote-ar 1
jarat-ar 1
jarb-ar 1
jarci-ar 1
jarde-ar 1
jare-ar 1
jare-arse 80
jaric-ar 67
jaring-ar 1
jaripe-ar 1
jaroch-ar 1
jarop-ar 1
jarope-ar 1
jarr-ar 1
jarre-ar 1
jarret-ar 1
jart-ar 1
jas-ar 1
jaspe-ar 1
jaspi-ar 1
jate-ar 1
jebr-ar 1
jed-ar 1
jed-er 2, plus
the changes
in red in 53
jemique-ar 1
jerarqueriz-
ar 21
jerarquiz-ar 21
jeremique-ar 1
jericople-ar 1
jerigonce-ar 1
jerigonz-ar 21

jerimique-ar 1
jering-ar 51
jerinque-ar 1
jeroglific-ar 21
jesuse-ar 1
jet-ar 1
jete-ar 1
jetend-er 2, plus the changes in red in 53
jibare-ar 1
jij-ar 1
jije-ar 1
jile-ar 1
jilipolle-ar 1
jilote-ar 1
jimelg-ar 51
jimenz-ar 34
jimique-ar 1
jimpl-ar 1
jinete-ar 1
jinquete-ar 1
jiongl-ar 1
jip-ar 1
jipate-arse 80
jipi-ar 9
jirimique-ar 1
jirpe-ar 1
jit-ar 1
jobe-ar 1
joc-ar 1
joce-ar 1
joch-ar 1
joche-ar 1
joch-er 2
jocote-ar 1
jod-er 2
jom-ar 1
jonde-ar 1
jonjab-ar 1
jonje-ar 1
jonjole-ar 1
jop-ar 1
jop-arse 80
jope-ar 1
jorc-ar 67
jorfe-ar 1
jornal-ar 1
jorob-ar 1
jorope-ar 1
jorr-ar 1
jorre-ar 1
joruche-ar 1
jorung-ar 1
jostr-ar 1
jotr-ar 1
juag-ar 51
juanche-ar 1
juane-ar 1
jubert-ar 1
jubil-ar 1
juch-ar 1
judaiz-ar 21
judg-ar 1
judi-ar 1
judic-ar 1
juergue-arse 80
jug-ar 44
juguete-ar 1
juje-ar 1
julepe-ar 1
jum-arse 80
jumentiz-ar 21
jumetre-ar 1
jun-ar 1
jung-ar 1
junt-ar 1, plus the past participle junto
juñ-ar 1
juñ-ir 17
jupi-ar 1
jupi-arse 80
jurament-ar 1
jur-ar 1
jurg-ar 1
jurguce-ar 1
juriac-ar 21
juri-arse 80
jurung-ar 1
jusmet-erse 81
just-ar 1
justici-ar 1
justific-ar 67
justipreci-ar 1
jutute-ar 1
juvenec-er 48
juzg-ar 51

k

kilometr-ar 1

l

labializ-ar 21
labiose-ar 1
labor-ar 1
labore-ar 1
labr-ar 1
lace-ar 1
lacer-ar 1
lacere-ar 1
lach-ar 1
lache-ar 1
laconiz-ar 21
lacr-ar 1
lacre-ar 1
lacrim-ar 1
lact-ar 1
lade-ar 1
ladr-ar 1
ladre-ar 1
ladrill-ar 1
ladrone-ar 1
lag-ar 1
lagare-arse 80
lagarte-ar 1
lagote-ar 1
lagrimac-er 41
lagrim-ar 1
lagrime-ar 1
laicaliz-ar 21
laiciz-ar 21
laje-ar 1
lal-ar 1
lam-ar 1
lambare-ar 1
lambe-ar 1
lamb-er 2
lambere-ar 1
lambete-ar 1
lambic-ar 1
lambisc-ar 67
lambisque-ar 1
lambruce-ar 1
lambrusque-ar ... 1
lambuce-ar 1
lament-ar 1
lam-er 2
lamin-ar 1
lamisc-ar 67
lampace-ar 1
lamp-ar 1
lampe-ar 1
lampre-ar 1
lanaplen-ar 1
lance-ar 1
lanch-ar 1, and used in the positions in 45
lancin-ar 1
lande-ar 1
langu-ar 1
languci-ar 1
languidec-er 48
lanz-ar 21
lañ-ar 1
lapach-ar 1
lapid-ar 1
lapidific-ar 67
lapiz-ar 21
laque-ar 1
lard-ar 1
larde-ar 1
larg-ar 51
larraguz-ar 21
lasc-ar 67
last-ar 1
lastim-ar 1
lastr-ar 1
lastre-ar 1
late-ar 1
lateraliz-ar 21
latigue-ar 1
latin-ar 1
latine-ar 1
latiniz-ar 21
lat-ir 3
latit-ar 1
laton-ar 1
latrocin-ar 1
lauc-ar 67
laud-ar 1
laudiniz-ar 21
laure-ar 1
lav-ar 1
lavote-ar 1
lax-ar 1
lay-ar 1

laz-ar 21
lazr-ar 1
le-ar 1
lebreje-ar 1
lech-ar 1
leche-ar 1
lechuce-ar 1
lechug-ar 1
lectit-ar 1
le-er 26
legaj-ar 1
legaliz-ar 21
leg-ar 51
legifer-ar 1
legisl-ar 1
legitim-ar 1
legr-ar 1
leij-ar 1
lej-ar 1
leld-ar 1
lembr-ar 1
lengüe-ar 1
lengüete-ar 1
lenific-ar 67
len-ir 3
leniz-ar 21
lentec-er 48
lentific-ar 67
leñ-ar 1
leñate-ar 1
leñific-ar 21
lep-ar 1
lerde-ar 1
lese-ar 1
lesion-ar 1
leste-ar 1
letific-ar 67
letre-ar 1
leud-ar 1
levant-ar 1
levant-arse 80
lev-ar 1
levig-ar 51
lexicaliz-ar 21
li-ar 9
lib-ar 1
libel-ar 1
liberaliz-ar 21
liber-ar 1
libert-ar 1
libr-ar 1
libre-ar 1
licenci-ar 1
licit-ar 1
licu-ar 9
licuec-er 48
licuefac-er 41, except the past participle is licuefacto
lidi-ar 1
liev-ar 1
lig-ar 51
liger-ar 1
ligere-ar 1
lignific-ar 67
lignific-arse 80
lij-ar 1
lileque-ar 1
lilique-ar 1
lim-ar 1
limit-ar 1
limosn-ar 1
limosne-ar 1
limpi-ar 1
lince-ar 1
linch-ar 1
lind-ar 1
line-ar 1
liofiliz-ar 21
lipid-ar 1
lipidi-ar 1
liquefac-er 41, except the past participle is liquefacido
liquid-ar 1
liquidific-ar 1
lis-ar 1
lisi-ar 1
lisonj-ar 1
lisonje-ar 1
list-ar 1
liste-ar 1
liston-ar 1
lit-ar 1
literate-ar 1
litig-ar 51
litigi-ar 1
litofotografi-ar ... 9
litografi-ar 9
liud-ar 1
lividec-er 48
lixivi-ar 1
liz-ar 21
llag-ar 51
llam-ar 1
llame-ar 1
llante-ar 1
llap-ar 1
llapihu-ar 1
llat-ir 3
llauc-ar 67
llauque-arse 80
lleg-ar 51
llen-ar 1
lleud-ar 1
llev-ar 1
llipihu-ar 1
llor-ar 1
llorique-ar 1
llorisque-ar 1
llorrit-ar 1
llostr-ar 1
llov-er 45
llovizn-ar 1, and for its use regarding weather, see 45
lo-ar 1
lobe-ar 1
lobregue-ar 1
lobreguec-er 48, and for its use regarding weather, see 45
localiz-ar 21
loc-ar 67
log-ar 51
logiz-ar 21
logr-ar 1
logre-ar 1
lom-ar 1
lombarde-ar 1
lome-ar 1
lonch-ar 1
loncote-ar 1
lonje-ar 1
loque-ar 1
los-ar 1
lote-ar 1
lotific-ar 1
lotiz-ar 21
lov-er 47
lozane-ar 1
lozanec-er 48
lu-ar 1
lubric-ar 67
lubrific-ar 67
luch-ar 1
luci-ar 1
luc-ir 3, plus the changes in red in 48
lucr-ar 1
lucubr-ar 1
ludi-ar 1
lud-ir 3
lueg-ar 51
lu-ir 42
luj-ar 1
lujuri-ar 1
lull-ir 3
lumin-ar 1
lunaniz-ar 21
lunare-ar 1
lupuliz-ar 21
luque-ar 1
lustr-ar 1
lustre-ar 1
lux-ar 1

m

macacine-ar 1
macadamiz-ar 21
macane-ar 1
macaque-ar 1
mac-ar 1
mac-arse 67
mace-ar 1
macer-ar 1
macete-ar 1
machac-ar 67
machambr-ar 1
machaque-ar 1
mach-ar 1
mach-arse 80

machasc-arse ... 67
mache-ar ... 1
machete-ar ... 1
machiembr-arse ... 80
machihembr-ar ... 1
machimbr-arse ... 80
machin-arse ... 80
machituc-ar ... 1
machone-ar ... 1
machorre-ar ... 1
machuc-ar ... 67
maciz-ar ... 21
macoll-ar ... 1
macone-ar ... 1
macoque-ar ... 1
macuje-ar ... 1
macul-ar ... 1
macurc-arse ... 80
madefact-ar ... 1
madefic-ar ... 67
mader-ar ... 1
madre-ar ... 1
madre-arse ... 80
madrug-ar ... 51
madur-ar ... 1
madurec-er ... 48
madurg-ar ... 51
maestraliz-ar ... 21
maestr-ar ... 1
maestre-ar ... 1
magadiz-ar ... 21
magance-ar ... 1
maganzone-ar ... 1
magin-ar ... 1
magnetiz-ar ... 21
magnific-ar ... 67
magost-ar ... 1
magre-ar ... 1
magrec-er ... 48
magu-arse ... 7
magul-ar ... 1
magull-ar ... 1
maher-ir ... 71
mahometiz-ar ... 21
maice-ar ... 1
maisi-ar ... 1
majade-ar ... 1
majadere-ar ... 1
maj-ar ... 1
majarete-ar ... 1
majase-ar ... 1
majenc-ar ... 1
majol-ar ... 25
malacostumbr-ar ... 1
malagor-ar ... 6
malangrin-ar ... 1
malanoch-arse ... 80
malañ-ar ... 1
malax-ar ... 1
malbarat-ar ... 1
malcas-ar ... 1
malcocin-ar ... 1
malcoloc-ar ... 1
malcom-er ... 2
malcorn-ar ... 25
malcri-ar ... 9
maldec-ir 58, plus the regular past participle maldecido and the irregular past participle maldito
maleabiliz-ar ... 21
male-ar ... 1
malefici-ar ... 1
maleiniz-ar ... 1
malemple-ar ... 1
malentend-er 2, plus the changes in red in ... 53
malete-ar ... 1
malfac-er 69, except the past participle is malfacido
malfam-ar ... 1
malgast-ar ... 1
malhay-ar ... 21
malher-ir ... 71
malhumor-ar ... 1
malici-ar ... 1
malign-ar ... 1
malingr-ar ... 1
mallad-ar ... 1
mall-ar ... 1
mallug-ar ... 1
malmari-ar ... 1
malmet-er ... 2
malmodi-ar ... 1
malogr-ar ... 1
maloje-ar ... 1
malone-ar ... 1
maloque-ar ... 1
malpar-ar ... 1
malpar-ir ... 3
malpas-ar ... 1
malple-ar ... 1
malquer-er 60, plus the past participle malquisto
malquist-ar ... 1
malrot-ar ... 1
malsin-ar ... 1
malson-ar ... 25
malt-ar ... 1
malte-ar ... 1
maltra-er ... 75
maltrat-ar ... 1
malv-ar ... 1
malvend-er ... 2
malvers-ar ... 1
malvez-ar ... 21
malviv-ir ... 3
mamante-ar ... 1
mam-ar ... 1
mamarrach-ar ... 1
mamone-ar ... 1
mamoniz-ar ... 21
mampar-ar ... 1
mamposte-ar ... 1
mampres-ar ... 1
mamuj-ar ... 1
mamull-ar ... 1
mamuse-ar ... 1
man-ar ... 1
manc-ar ... 67
mancell-ar ... 1
manch-ar ... 1
mancill-ar ... 1
mancip-ar ... 1
mancomun-ar ... 1
mancorn-ar ... 25
mancorne-ar ... 1
mand-ar ... 1
mandil-ar ... 1
mandril-ar ... 1
manduc-ar ... 67
mane-ar ... 1
manej-ar ... 1
mangane-ar ... 1
manganzone-ar ... 1
mang-ar ... 51
mang-arse ... 80
mangone-ar ... 1
mangrull-ar ... 1
manguare-ar ... 1
mangue-ar ... 1
maniat-ar ... 1
manifest-ar 53, plus the past participle manifiesto
manij-ar ... 1
maniobr-ar ... 1
manipul-ar ... 1
manipule-ar ... 1
man-ir ... 4
manjol-ar ... 1
manlev-ar ... 1
manobr-ar ... 1
manobri-ar ... 1
manoj-ar ... 1
manoje-ar ... 1
manose-ar ... 1
manote-ar ... 1
manque-ar ... 1
mansalvi-ar ... 1
mante-ar ... 1
manteca-er ... 20
manten-er ... 74
manteque-ar ... 1
mantorn-ar ... 1
manualiz-arse ... 80
manufactur-ar ... 1
manumit-ir 3, plus the past participle manumiso
manuscrib-ir 3, except the

past participle is manuscrito
manuten-er 74
many-ar 1
manzane-ar 1
mañan-ar 1
mañane-ar 1
mañe-ar 1
mañere-ar 1
mañose-ar 1
mapole-ar 1
maque-ar 1
maquete-ar 1
maquil-ar 1
maquile-ar 1
maquill-ar 1
maquin-ar 1
maquiniz-ar 21
marañ-ar 1
maraque-ar 1
maravill-ar 1
marc-ar 67
marce-ar 1, and used in the positions in 45
marcen-ar 1
marcham-ar 1
march-ar 1
marchit-ar 1, plus the past participle marchito
mare-ar 1
marg-ar 51
margen-ar 1
margin-ar 1
margom-ar 1
margull-ar 1
marid-ar 1
marimbe-ar 1
marin-ar 1
marine-ar 1
maripose-ar 1
marisc-ar 67
mariz-ar 21
mariz-arse 80
marlot-ar 1
marmitone-ar 1
marmote-ar 1
marmull-ar 1
marome-ar 1
marque-ar 1
marquet-ar 1
marramiz-ar 21
marrane-ar 1
marr-ar 1
marre-ar 1
marroj-ar 1
marrull-ar 1
marsupializ-ar 21
martaj-ar 1
martigu-ar 1
martill-ar 1
martille-ar 1
martiriz-ar 21
marulle-ar 1
masacr-ar 1
masaje-ar 1
mas-ar 1
masc-ar 67
mascar-ar 1
mascuj-ar 1
masculiniz-ar ... 21
mascull-ar 1
mase-ar 1
masill-ar 1
maste-ar 1
mastic-ar 67
mastig-ar 1
masturb-ar 1
masturb-arse ... 80
mataperre-ar 1
mat-ar 1
matasell-ar 1
mate-ar 1
materializ-ar 21
materniz-ar 1
matiz-ar 21
matone-ar 1
matrac-ar 1
matraque-ar 1
matratuc-ar 1
matrere-ar 1
matricul-ar 1
matrimoni-ar 1
matriz-ar 21
matufi-ar 1
maturrangue-ar 1
matute-ar 1
mauc-ar 1
maul-ar 9
maule-ar 1
maull-ar 9
maximiz-ar 21
may-ar 1
maye-ar 1, and used in the positions in 45
mayor-ar 1
mayordome-ar ... 1
mazamorre-ar ... 1
maz-ar 21
mazn-ar 1
mazon-ar 1
mazone-ar 1
mazorc-ar 67
me-ar 1
mecaniz-ar 21
mecanografi-ar 9
mecate-ar 1
mec-er 46
mech-ar 1
mechific-ar 67
mechone-ar 1
med-ar 1
medianiz-ar 21
medi-ar 1
mediatiz-ar 21
medicament-ar 1
medic-ar 1
medicin-ar 1
med-ir 52
medit-ar 1
medr-ar 1
meduc-ar 1
mej-er 2
mejicaniz-ar 21
mejor-ar 1
melancoliz-ar 21
mel-ar 53
melcoch-ar 1
meld-ar 1
mele-ar 1
melecin-ar 1
melen-ar 1
melg-ar 51
melific-ar 67
melindre-ar 1
melindriz-ar 21
mell-ar 1
mellor-ar 1
membr-ar 1
memor-ar 1
memoriz-ar 21
men-ar 1
menaz-ar 21
mencion-ar 1
mendig-ar 51
mendigue-ar 1
mending-ar 51
mene-ar 1
meneque-ar 1
mengu-ar 7
menor-ar 1
menore-ar 1
menorg-ar 1
menoscab-ar 1
menospreci-ar ... 1
menstru-ar 9
mensualiz-ar ... 21
mensur-ar 1
mentaliz-ar 21
ment-ar 53
ment-ir 71
menude-ar 1
menuz-ar 21
mer-ar 1
mercade-ar 1
mercance-ar 1
mercantiliz-ar 21
merc-ar 67
merce-ar 1
merced-ar 1
mercende-ar 1
merceriz-ar 21
mercurializ-ar 21
merec-er 48
merend-ar 53
merendill-ar 1
mereng-ar 51
meretric-ar 1
merit-ar 1
merm-ar 1
merode-ar 1
mes-ar 1

mescab-ar 1
mescl-ar 1
mestiz-ar 21
mestur-ar 1
mesur-ar 1
metafisique-ar ... 1
metaforiz-ar 21
metal-ar 1
metaliz-ar 21
metamorfose-
ar 1
metatiz-ar 1
meteoriz-ar 21
met-er 2
metil-ar 1
metodiz-ar 21
metrall-ar 1
metre-ar 1
metrific-ar 67
meuc-ar 67
mexicaniz-ar 21
mezcl-ar 1
mezquin-ar 1
mezuque-ar 1
miag-ar 51
miañ-ar 1
mi-ar 9
microcopi-ar 1
microfilm-ar 1
microfiltr-ar 1
microniz-ar 21
mig-ar 51
migr-ar 1
miguele-ar 1
milagre-ar 1
milimetr-ar 1
milit-ar 1
militariz-ar 21
millone-ar 1
milongue-ar 1
milpe-ar 1
mim-ar 1
mimbr-ar 1
mimbre-ar 1
mimeografi-ar ... 9
mimose-ar 1
min-ar 1
minch-ar 1
mindangue-ar 1
mine-ar 1
mineraliz-ar 21
ming-ar 51
mingone-ar 1
mingu-ar 1
mini-ar 1
miniaturiz-ar 21
minific-ar 67
minimiz-ar 21
ministr-ar 1
minor-ar 1
minut-ar 1
miñ-arse 80
miñoque-ar 1
mique-ar 1
mir-ar 1
mirific-ar 67
miristic-arse 80
mirl-ar 1
mirl-arse 80
mis-ar 1
miseñore-ar 1
misere-ar 1
mision-ar 1
mist-ar 1
mistific-ar 67
mistur-ar 1
mitay-ar 1
mitig-ar 51
mitisar-ar 1
mitote-ar 1
mitr-ar 1
mitridatiz-ar 21
mixte-ar 1
mixtific-ar 67
mixtur-ar 1
mobl-ar 25
moc-ar 67
moce-ar 1
moch-ar 1
mocion-ar 1
model-ar 1
moder-ar 1
moderniz-ar 21
modest-ar 1
modific-ar 67
modorr-ar 1
modul-ar 1
mof-ar 1
mofe-ar 1
mofle-ar 1
mofle-arse 80
mofl-ir 3
mogoll-ar 1
mogolle-ar 1
mogosi-ar 1
mohatr-ar 1
mohec-er 48
mohose-arse ... 80
moj-ar 1
mojon-ar 1
mojose-arse 80
molcajete-ar 1
mold-ar 1
molde-ar 1
moldur-ar 1
mole-ar 1
mol-er 47
molest-ar 1
molete-ar 1
molific-ar 67
molle-ar 1
mollent-ar 1
mollesc-er 2
mollic-ar 1
mollific-ar 67
molline-ar 1,
and used in
the positions
in 45
moll-ir 17
mollizn-ar 1,
and for its
use regarding
weather,
see 45
mollizne-ar 1,
and for its
use regarding
weather,
see 45
molonque-ar 1
moltur-ar 1
mome-ar 1
momific-ar 67
mond-ar 1
mone-ar 1
moned-ar 1
monede-ar 1
monetiz-ar 21
mongue-ar 1
monolog-ar 51
monopoliz-ar ... 21
monoptong-
ar 51
montadg-ar 51
montane-ar 1
montante-ar 1
mont-ar 1
montazg-ar 51
monte-ar 1
monumentaliz-
ar 21
moque-ar 1
moquete-ar 1
moquite-ar 1
moralzi-ar 21
mor-ar 1
morc-ar 67
mordent-ar 1
mord-er 47
mordic-ar 67
mordisc-ar 67
mordisque-ar 1
morete-ar 1
morf-ar 1
morfiniz-ar 21
morige-ar 1
moriger-ar 1
mor-ir 31,
except the
past participle
is muerto
mormorote-ar 1
mormull-ar 1
mormur-ar 1
moron-ar 1
morr-ar 1
morre-ar 1
morrongue-ar 1
mortaj-ar 1
mortific-ar 67
mortigu-ar 1
mosc-ar 67
moscarde-ar 1
moscone-ar 1
mosque-ar 1
mosquete-ar 1
moste-ar 1
mostr-ar 25
mostre-ar 1
mot-ar 1
mote-ar 1
motej-ar 1
motil-ar 1

motiv-ar 1
motoriz-ar 21
mov-er 47
moviliz-ar 21
mozone-ar 1
muchache-ar 1
muchigu-ar 1
mud-ar 1
muebl-ar 1
muelle-ar 1
mueque-ar 1
muergane-arse 80
muerganiz-arse 21
muesc-ar 67
mufl-ir 3
mug-ar 51
mug-ir 3, plus the changes in red in 23
mugron-ar 1
mu-ir 42
muj-ar 1
mujere-ar 1
mulab-ar 1
mulate-ar 1
mulatiz-ar 21
mulc-ar 1
mulete-ar 1
mullic-ar 67
mull-ir 17
mult-ar 1
multicopi-ar 1
multiplic-ar 67
mundane-ar 1
munde-ar 1
mundializ-ar 21
mundific-ar 67
municion-ar 1
municipaliz-ar 21
mun-ir 3
muñeque-ar 1
muñ-ir 17
muque-ar 1
muqu-ir 3
mur-ar 1
murci-ar 1
murmuje-ar 1
murmull-ar 1
murmur-ar 1
murmure-ar 1
mus-ar 1
music-ar 67
mus-irse 82
musit-ar 1
musti-arse 80
mutil-ar 1

n

nacar-ar 1
nac-er 48 has a past participle nato
nacionaliz-ar 21
nad-ar 1
nafr-ar 1
naguale-ar 1
nagualiz-ar 21
naj-ar 1
nalgue-ar 1
namor-ar 1
nance-ar 1
nane-ar 1
nant-ar 1
naquer-ar 1
narcotiz-ar 21
narigone-ar 1
narr-ar 1
nasaliz-ar 21
nast-ar 1
naturaliz-ar 21
naufrag-ar 51
naur-ar 1
nause-ar 1
navaje-ar 1
naveg-ar 51
navig-ar 1
nazare-ar 1
nebline-ar 1, and for its use regarding weather, see 45
nebuliz-ar 21
nece-ar 1
necesit-ar 1
necrosific-ar 67
neg-ar 62
negoci-ar 1
negre-ar 1
negrec-er 48
negreg-ar 51
negregue-ar 1
nej-ar 1
nembr-ar 1
neni-ar 1
nervi-ar 1
nesg-ar 51
neurotiz-ar 21
neutraliz-ar 21
neutrodin-ar 1
nev-ar 53, and for its use regarding weather, see 45
nevisc-ar 67, and for its use regarding weather, see 45
nidific-ar 67
niel-ar 1
nimb-ar 1
niñe-ar 1
niquel-ar 1
niqueliz-ar 21
nitraf-ar 1
nitr-ar 1
nitrific-ar 67
nitrogen-ar 1
nivel-ar 1
nixques-ar 1
nixquez-ar 21
noblec-er 48
noc-er 48
noc-ir 59
noctambul-ar 1
nombr-ar 1
nomin-ar 1
noque-ar 1
nordeste-ar 1
nordoveste-ar 1
normaliz-ar 21
normaniz-ar 1
norm-ar 1
noroeste-ar 1
norte-ar 1
norueste-ar 1
not-ar 1
notici-ar 1
notific-ar 67
nov-ar 1
novel-ar 1
novele-ar 1
noveliz-ar 21
novi-ar 1
nubl-ar 1, and for its use regarding weather, see 45
nuc-ir 59
nudr-ir 56
nulific-ar 1
numer-ar 1
nunci-ar 1
nutr-ir 3

ñ

ñafi-ar 1
ñafite-ar 1
ñafr-ar 1
ñam-ar 1
ñang-ar 1
ñangot-arse 80
ñangue-ar 1
ñap-ar 1
ñape-ar 1
ñarre-ar 1
ñate-ar 1
ñau-ar 1
ñeque-ar 1
ñip-ar 1
ñong-arse 80
ñongot-arse 80
ñongue-ar 1
ñoñ-ar 1
ñoñe-ar 1
ñubl-ar 1
ñusc-ar 67
ñut-ir 3

O

obcec-ar 67
obceg-ar 51
obedec-er 48
obel-ar 1
obenqui-ar 1
obisp-ar 1
obispe-ar 1
objet-ar 1
objetiv-ar 1
obl-ar 1
oblicu-ar 1
oblig-ar 51
obliter-ar 1
obnubil-ar 1
obr-ar 1
obscur-ar 1
obscurec-er
48, and for
its use
regarding
weather,
see 45
obsecr-ar 1
obsed-er 2
obsedi-ar 1
obsequi-ar 1
observ-ar 1
obsesion-ar 1
obstaculiz-ar 21
obst-ar 1
obstin-arse 80
obstruccion-ar ... 1
obstru-ir 42
obtemper-ar 1
obten-er 2
obtur-ar 1
obvi-ar 1
ocale-ar 1
ocasion-ar 1
occidentaliz-
ar 21
ocel-ar 1
och-ar 1
ochav-ar 1
ochave-ar 1
oci-ar 1
ociose-ar 1
oclu-ir 42
octav-ar 1
octave-ar 1
octuplic-ar 67
ocult-ar 1
ocup-ar 1
ocurr-ir 3
odi-ar 1
odiose-ar 1
ofend-er 2
ofens-ar 1
ofert-ar 1
oficializ-ar 21
ofici-ar 1
ofrec-er 48
ofrend-ar 1
ofusc-ar 67
o-ír 49
ojal-ar 1
oj-ar 1
oje-ar 1
ojete-ar 1
ojetill-ar 1
ojot-arse 80
ole-ar 1
ol-er 50
olete-ar 1
olfate-ar 1
oligarquiz-ar 21
olisc-ar 67
olisme-ar 1
olisque-ar 1
oliv-ar 1
oliv-arse 80
oloriz-ar 21
oloros-ar 1
olvid-ar 1
omblig-ar 1
omin-ar 1
omit-ir 3,
plus the past
participle
omiso
once-ar 1
onde-ar 1
ondison-ar 1
ondr-ar 1
ondul-ar 1
onec-er 48
onot-ar 1
opac-ar 67
opacific-ar 1
opaliz-ar 21
ope-ar 1
oper-ar 1
opil-ar 1
opil-arse 80
opin-ar 1
opon-er 57
oposit-ar 1
opres-ar 1
oprim-ir 3,
plus the past
participle
opreso
oprobi-ar 1
opsonific-ar 1
opsoniz-ar 21
opt-ar 1
optim-ar 1
optimiz-ar 21
opugn-ar 1
or-ar 1
orbay-ar 1
orden-ar 1
ordeñ-ar 1
ordin-ar 1
ore-ar 1
orec-er 48
orej-ar 1
oreje-ar 1
orfanec-er 48
orf-ar 1
organ-ar 1
organiz-ar 21
orgullec-er 48
ori-ar 1
orientaliz-ar 21
orient-ar 1
orific-ar 67
originaliz-
arse 21
origin-ar 1
orill-ar 1
orille-ar 1
orin-ar 1
orinc-ar 67
orinec-er 48
orinque-ar 1
orl-ar 1
ormej-ar 1
ornament-ar 1
orn-ar 1
orne-ar 1
oronde-ar 1
oropel-ar 1
orquest-ar 1
ortig-ar 1
ortografi-ar 9
orvall-ar 1,
and for its
use regarding
weather,
see 45
orvay-ar 1,
and for its
use regarding
weather,
see 45
orz-ar 21
os-ar 1
oscil-ar 1
oscurec-er
48, and for
its use
regarding
weather,
see 45
ose-ar 1
osific-ar 67
osl-ar 1
ostent-ar 1
ostiñ-ar 1
ot-ar 1
ote-ar 1
otil-ar 1
otoñ-ar 1
otorg-ar 51
ovacion-ar 1
oval-ar 1
ov-ar 1
overe-ar 1
ovill-ar 1
oviposit-ar 1
oxe-ar 1
oxid-ar 1
oxigen-ar 1
oxim-ar 1
ozon-ar 1
ozonific-ar 67
ozoniz-ar 21

p

pabl-ar 1
paccion-ar 1
pacent-ar 53
pac-er 48
pachamangue-ar 1
pachorre-ar 1
pachote-ar 1
pachurr-ar 1
pacific-ar 67
pact-ar 1
padec-er 48
padre-ar 1
padrine-ar 1
padrote-ar 1
paganiz-ar 21
pag-ar 51
pagin-ar 1
pair-ar 1
paire-ar 1
pait-ar 1
pajar-ar 1
pajare-ar 1
pajarole-ar 1
pajarote-ar 1
paje-ar 1
palabre-ar 1
palade-ar 1
paladin-ar 1
palangane-ar 1
palanque-ar 1
palanque-arse 80
pal-ar 1
palataliz-ar 21
palatiz-ar 21
pale-ar 1
palenque-ar 1
palete-ar 1
pali-ar 1
palidec-er 48
palique-ar 1
pallap-ar 1
pallaque-ar 1
pall-ar 1
palm-ar 1
palme-ar 1
palmete-ar 1
palmote-ar 1
palome-ar 1
palone-ar 1
palote-ar 1
palp-ar 1
palpit-ar 1
palpote-ar 1
paluche-ar 1
pampane-ar 1
pampe-ar 1
pampone-ar 1
panade-ar 1
pancreatiz-ar ... 21
pand-ar 1
pande-ar 1
panderete-ar 1
pandorgue-ar 1
pane-ar 1
panegiriz-ar 21
panele-ar 1
pang-ar 51
pangare-ar 1
pangue-ar 1
panific-ar 67
panigu-arse 80
panoj-ar 1
panque-ar 1
pantalle-ar 1
pantoc-ar 1
panuc-ar 67
papach-ar 1
papale-ar 1
papalote-ar 1
pap-ar 1
paparre-ar 1
pape-ar 1
papele-ar 1
papelete-ar 1
papeletiz-ar 21
papelone-ar 1
paporre-ar 1
papuj-arse 80
paque-ar 1
paquete-ar 1
paraboliz-ar 21
parachut-ar 1
parafin-ar 1
parafrase-ar 1
paragon-ar 1
parahus-ar 9
paralel-ar 1
paralitic-arse ... 67
paraliz-ar 21
paralogiz-ar 21
param-ar 1, and used in the positions in 45
parame-ar 1, and used in the positions in 45
parament-ar 1
parangon-ar 1
parapet-ar 1
parapet-arse 80
par-ar 1
paraus-ar 9
parcel-ar 1
parcemic-ar 1
parch-ar 1
parche-ar 1
parcializ-ar 21
parc-ir 3, plus the changes in red in 23
parde-ar 1
pare-ar 1
parec-er 48
pareje-ar 1
parific-ar 67
par-ir 3
parkeriz-ar 21
parkesiz-ar 21
parlament-ar 1
parlamente-ar 1
parl-ar 1
parlote-ar 1
parodi-ar 1
parol-ar 1
parpade-ar 1
parp-ar 1
parque-ar 1
parrafe-ar 1
parrande-ar 1
parr-ar 1
parte-ar 1
particip-ar 1
particulariz-ar 21
part-ir 3
parve-ar 1
parvific-ar 67
pasaman-ar 1
pasaport-ar 1
pasaporte-ar 1
pas-ar 1, plus the past participle paso, and for its use regarding weather, see 45
pasc-ar 67
pascone-ar 1
pase-ar 1
pasigrafi-ar 1
pasm-ar 1
pasp-ar 1
pasp-arse 80
pasquin-ar 1
past-ar 1
paste-ar 1
pastele-ar 1
pasteriz-ar 21
pasteuriz-ar 21
pastore-ar 1
pastoriz-ar 21
pastur-ar 1
patale-ar 1
patalete-ar 1
patane-ar 1
patate-arse 80
pate-ar 1
patent-ar 1
patentiz-ar 21
patin-ar 1
patiquebr-ar 53
patoche-ar 1
patoje-ar 1
patole-ar 1
patraque-ar 1
patri-ar 1
patrocin-ar 1
patrone-ar 1
patrull-ar 1
patuleque-ar 1
patull-ar 1
paul-ar 1
paus-ar 1
paut-ar 1
pave-ar 1
paviment-ar 1
pavon-ar 1

pavone-ar 1
pavorde-ar 1
payan-ar 1
payane-ar 1
pay-ar 1
payase-ar 1
peal-ar 1
pebrin-ar 1
pecane-ar 1
pec-ar 67
pechac-ar 67
pech-ar 1
peche-ar 1
pecilg-ar 51
pecore-ar 1
pect-ar 1
pedace-ar 1
pedale-ar 1
pedante-ar 1
pedaz-ar 21
ped-ir 52
pedorre-ar 1
pe-er 2
peg-ar 51
pegoste-ar 1
pegostr-ar 1
pegote-ar 1
pegunt-ar 1
pein-ar 1
peindr-ar 1
pelambr-ar 1
pel-ar 1
pele-ar 1
pelech-ar 1
peliche-ar 1
peligr-ar 1
pelizc-ar 67
pellizc-ar 67
pelote-ar 1
pelude-ar 1
peluque-ar 1
penaliz-ar 21
pen-ar 1
penc-ar 67
pendeje-ar 1
pendenci-ar 1
pend-er 2
pendone-ar 1
pendr-ar 1
penej-ar 1
peneje-ar 1
penetr-ar 1
penitenci-ar 1
pens-ar 53
pension-ar 1
pension-arse ... 70
peñ-arse 80
peñasque-ar 1
peñer-ar 1
peñisc-ar 67
peñor-ar 1
peon-ar 1
peor-ar 1
pepe-ar 1
pepen-ar 1
peptonific-ar 67
peptoniz-ar 21
peragr-ar 1
peralt-ar 1
percanz-ar 21
percat-ar 1
perch-ar 1
perche-ar 1
perchon-ar 1
perchuf-ar 1
percib-ir 3
percol-ar 1
percoll-ar 25
perconte-ar 1
percud-ir 3
percut-ir 3
perd-er 2, plus the changes in red in 53
perdig-ar 51
perdon-ar 1
perdur-ar 1
perece-ar 1
perec-er 48
peregrin-ar 1
perenniz-ar 21
perfeccion-ar 1
perfectiv-ar 1
perfil-ar 1
perfor-ar 1
perfum-ar 1
perfume-ar 1
pergeni-ar 1
pergeñ-ar 1
perhinch-ir 3
periclit-ar 1
pericote-ar 1
perifoll-ar 1
perifone-ar 1
perifrase-ar 1
perige-ar 1
periodique-ar 1
peripon-erse 57
perique-ar 1
perjudic-ar 67
perjur-ar 1
perlific-ar 67
perlong-ar 51
permanec-er 48
permit-ir 3
permut-ar 1
perne-ar 1
perniabr-ir 3, except the past participle is perniabierto
perniquebr-ar 53
pernoch-ar 1
pernoct-ar 1
pernot-ar 1
perogrulle-ar 1
peror-ar 1
peroxid-ar 1
perpas-ar 1
perpen-ar 1
perpetr-ar 1
perpetu-ar 9
perpul-ir 3
perquir-ir 5
perscrut-ar 1
persegu-ir 70
persever-ar 1
persianiz-ar 1
persign-ar 1
persist-ir 3
persog-ar 51
personaliz-ar ... 21
person-arse 80
personific-ar 67
perspir-ar 1
persuad-ir 3
pertenec-er 48
pertigue-ar 1
pertrech-ar 1
pertugue-ar 1
perturb-ar 1
peruaniz-ar 21
pervert-ir 71
perviv-ir 3
pervulg-ar 51
pes-ar 1, and used in the positions in 45
pesc-ar 67
pescoce-ar 1
pescud-ar 1
pescuece-ar 1
pesete-ar 1
pesg-ar 51
peshac-ar 67
pesi-ar 1
pespite-ar 1
pespunt-ar 1
pespunte-ar 1
pesquer-ir 71
pesquir-ir 39
pesquis-ar 1
pestañ-ar 1
pestañe-ar 1
pestiñ-ar 1
petaque-ar 1
pet-ar 1
petarde-ar 1
peticion-ar 1
petrarquiz-ar 21
petrenc-arse 67
petrific-ar 67
petrole-ar 1
peyor-ar 1
piaf-ar 1
pial-ar 1
pi-ar 9
picane-ar 1
pic-ar 67
picarde-ar 1
picariz-ar 21
picaz-ar 21
pich-arse 80
pichinch-ar 1
pichinche-ar 1
pichipar-arse ... 80
pichise-ar 1
pichisebe-ar 1
pichiside-ar 1
pichole-ar 1
pichone-ar 1
pichule-ar 1

profet-ar 1
profetiz-ar 21
profij-ar 1
proflig-ar 51
profund-ar 1
profundiz-ar 21
program-ar 1
progres-ar 1
prohib-ir 3, plus the changes in red in 9
prohij-ar 9
prolaps-arse 80
proletariz-ar 21
prolifer-ar 1
prolije-ar 1
prolog-ar 51
prologuiz-ar 21
prolong-ar 51
proman-ar 1
promedi-ar 1
promet-er 2
promiscu-ar 9
promocion-ar 1
promov-er 47
promulg-ar 51
pronostic-ar 67
prontuari-ar 1
pronunci-ar 1
propag-ar 51
propal-ar 1
propas-ar 1
propend-er 2, plus the past participle propenso
propici-ar 1
propin-ar 1
propon-er 57
proporcion-ar 1
proposit-ar 1
propugn-ar 1
propuls-ar 1
prorrate-ar 1
prorrog-ar 51
prorrump-ir 3
prosaiz-ar 21
proscrib-ir 3, except the past participles are proscrito and proscripto
prose-ar 1
prosegu-ir 70
prosific-ar 67
prospect-ar 1
prosper-ar 1
prostern-arse ... 80
prostitu-ir 42, plus the past participle prostituto
prostr-ar 1
prosupon-er 57
protagoniz-ar ... 21
proteg-er 23
protest-ar 1
protocol-ar 1
protocoliz-ar 21
provag-ar 1
provec-er 48
provech-ar 1
prove-er 22, plus the past participle provisto that is used more commonly than the regular past participle
proven-ir 77
provenzaliz-ar 21
proverbi-ar 1
providenci-ar 1
provist-ar 1
provoc-ar 67
proyect-ar 1
prudenci-ar 1
prudenci-arse 80
pu-ar 9
pubesc-er 2
public-ar 67
puch-ar 1
puchere-ar 1
pudel-ar 1
pudibundiz-arse 80
pudr-ir 56
puente-ar 1
puertafere-ar 1
puerte-ar 1
puertere-ar 1
pueste-ar 1
pugn-ar 1
puj-ar 1
pulgone-ar 1
puliment-ar 1
pul-ir 4
pulp-ar 1
pulpi-ar 1
puls-ar 1
pulse-ar 1
pulul-ar 1
pulveriz-ar 21
pun-ar 1
punch-ar 1
puncion-ar 1
pung-ir 3, plus the changes in red in 23
pun-ir 3
punn-ar 1
punque-ar 1
puntale-ar 1
punt-ar 1
punte-ar 1
puntill-ar 1
puntille-ar 1
puntualiz-ar 21
puntu-ar 9
punz-ar 21
punzon-ar 1
puñale-ar 1
pur-ar 1
pure-ar 1
purg-ar 51
purific-ar 67
purisc-ar 1
purpur-ar 1
purpure-ar 1
pusuque-ar 1
putañe-ar 1
pute-ar 1
puy-ar 1

q

quebraj-ar 1
quebraje-ar 1
quebrant-ar 1
quebr-ar 53
quebraz-arse ... 21
qued-ar 1
quej-ar 1
quejumbr-ar 1
quellotr-ar 1
quem-ar 1
quencharche-ar 1
quer-ar 1
queratiniz-ar 21
querell-arse 80
quer-er 60, plus an antiquated past participle quisto
queroch-ar 1
quese-ar 1
quess-ar 1
quichuiz-ar 21
quiet-ar 1
quijote-ar 1
quilat-ar 1
quilde-ar 1
quilific-ar 67
quill-ar 1
quillotr-ar 1
quilombe-ar 1
quilp-ar 1
quiltre-ar 1
quimbe-ar 1
quimbre-ar 1
quimere-ar 1
quimeriz-ar 21
quimific-ar 67
quin-ar 1
quinch-ar 1
quinchone-ar 1
quine-ar 1
quingue-ar 1
quinole-ar 2
quintaesenci-ar 1
quint-ar 1
quintuplic-ar 67

quiñ-ar 1
quirquinch-ar 1
quisne-ar 1
quisquill-ar 1
quisqu-irse 82
quist-arse 80
quit-ar 1
quiz-ar 21

r

rabe-ar 1
rabere-ar 1
rabi-ar 1
rabiat-ar 1
rabil-ar 1
rabiz-ar 21
rabon-ar 1
rabone-ar 1
rabose-ar 1
rabot-ar 1
rabote-ar 1
racane-ar 1
rach-ar 1
rachiz-ar 1
racim-ar 1
raciocin-ar 1
racionaliz-ar 21
racion-ar 1
radi-ar 1
radicaliz-ar 21
radic-ar 67
radioautografi-
ar 1
radiobaliz-ar 21
radiodifund-ir 3
radiodirig-ir 3,
plus the
changes
in red in 23
radiografi-ar 9
radiogui-ar 9
radiolocaliz-
ar 21
radiotelefone-
ar 1
radiotelegrafi-
ar 9
ra-er 61
rafe-ar 1
rafez-ar 21
ragu-ar 1
rahez-ar 21
raice-ar 1
raig-ar 1
raim-ar 1
raiz-ar 35
raj-ar 1
rajete-ar 1
rajuñ-ar 1
ralb-ar 1
rale-ar 1
rall-ar 1
ramaje-ar 1
ramale-ar 1
rame-ar 1
ramific-ar 67
ramone-ar 1
ranc-ar 67
rance-ar 1
ranch-ar 1
ranche-ar 1
ranci-ar 1
rancl-arse 80
rane-ar 1
ranfuñ-ar 1
rap-ar 1
rapel-ar 1
rapiñ-ar 1
rapiz-ar 21
rapose-ar 1
rapt-ar 1
rapuz-ar 21
raque-ar 1
raquiococainiz-
ar 21
raquistovainiz-
ar 21
rarefac-er 41,
except the
past participle
is rarefacto
rarific-ar 67
ras-ar 1
ras-arse 80
rascabuch-ar 1
rascabuche-ar ... 1
rascadill-ar 1
rasc-ar 67
rascol-ar 1
rascuñ-ar 1
rasg-ar 51
rasgue-ar 1
rasguñ-ar 1
rasmill-ar 1
raspahil-ar 9
rasp-ar 1
raspe-ar 1
raspone-ar 1
rasquete-ar 1
rast-ar 1
rastill-ar 1
rastrall-ar 1
rastr-ar 1
rastre-ar 1
rastrill-ar 1
rastrille-ar 1
rastroj-ar 1
rastroje-ar 1
rasur-ar 1
rate-ar 1
ratific-ar 67
ratig-ar 51
raton-ar 1
raume-ar 1
ray-ar 1
raz-ar 1
raz-arse 80
razi-ar 1
razon-ar 1
reabr-ir 3,
except the
past participle
is reabierto
reabsorb-er 2
reaccion-ar 1
reactiv-ar 1
reacuñ-ar 1
readapt-ar 1
readmit-ir 3
reafirm-ar 1
reagradec-er ... 48
reagrav-ar 1
reagrup-ar 1
reajust-ar 1
realegr-arse 80
realiz-ar 21
realquil-ar 1
realz-ar 21
ream-ar 1
reanim-ar 1
reanud-ar 1
reaparec-er 48
reaplic-ar 67
reapret-ar 53
rear-ar 1
reargü-ir 42
rearm-ar 1
reasegur-ar 1
reasent-ar 1
reasign-ar 1
reasum-ir 3
reat-ar 1
reavent-ar 53
reaviv-ar 1
rebab-arse 80
rebaj-ar 1
rebalg-ar 51
reball-ar 1
rebals-ar 1
reban-ar 1
rebane-ar 1
rebañ-ar 1
rebaque-ar 1
rebas-ar 1
rebat-ar 1
rebat-ir 3
rebautiz-ar 21
rebeb-er 2
rebel-arse 80
rebenque-ar 1
reber-ar 1
rebez-ar 21
rebin-ar 1
rebit-ar 1
reblandec-er 48
rebl-ar 1
rebobin-ar 1
reboc-ar 1
rebole-ar 1
rebomb-ar 1
reboñ-ar 1
rebord-ar 1
reborde-ar 1
reboruj-ar 1
rebos-ar 1
rebot-ar 1
reboz-ar 21
rebram-ar 1
rebrill-ar 1
rebrinc-ar 67
rebrot-ar 1
rebruñ-ir 17

rem-ar 1
remarc-ar 67
remat-ar 1
rembols-ar 1
remec-er 23
remed-ar 1
remedi-ar 1
remed-ir 52
remej-er 2
remell-ar 1
remembr-ar 53
rememor-ar 1
remend-ar 53
remene-ar 1
remes-ar 1
remet-er 2
remilg-arse 51
remilitariz-ar 21
remir-ar 1
remit-ir 3
remoj-ar 1
remol-ar 25
remolc-ar 67
remold-ar 1
remol-er 47
remolin-ar 1
remoline-ar 1
remoll-ar 25
remolone-ar 1
remond-ar 1
remont-ar 1
remor-ar 1
remord-er 47
remosque-
arse 80
remost-ar 1
remostec-
erse 48
remov-er 48
remoz-ar 21
remplaz-ar 21
rempuj-ar 1
remud-ar 1
remudi-ar 1
remug-ar 51
remull-ir 17
remuner-ar 1
remusg-ar 51
renac-er 48
rencion-ar 1
rencur-arse 80
rend-ar 1
rend-ir 52
reneg-ar 62
renegre-ar 1
reng-ar 51
rengue-ar 1
reniñ-ar 1
renombr-ar 1
renov-ar 25
renque-ar 1
rentabiliz-ar 21
rent-ar 1
renunci-ar 1
renvals-ar 1
renvid-ar 1
reñ-ir 64
reoctav-ar 1
reorden-ar 1
reorganiz-ar 21
repac-er 48
repag-ar 51
repanchig-
arse 51
repantig-arse ... 51
repapil-arse 80
repar-ar 1
repart-ir 3
repas-ar 1
repast-ar 1
repatri-ar 9
repech-ar 1
repein-ar 1
repel-ar 1
repel-er 2
repell-ar 1
repens-ar 53
repent-irse 71
repentiz-ar 21
repepen-ar 1
repercud-ir 3
repercut-ir 3
reperiquete-ar ... 1
repes-ar 1
repesc-ar 67
repet-ir 52
repic-ar 67
repicote-ar 1
repin-arse 80
repint-ar 1
repiquete-ar 1
repis-ar 1
repispe-ar 1
repizc-ar 67
replan-ar 1
replant-ar 1
replante-ar 1
replantig-
arse 80
repleg-ar 62
replet-ar 1
replic-ar 67
repobl-ar 25
repod-ar 1
repodr-ir 56
repoll-ar 1
repon-er 57
report-ar 1
reporte-ar 1
repos-ar 1
repost-ar 1
repoy-ar 1
repregunt-ar 1
reprehend-er 2
reprend-er 2
repres-ar 1
represent-ar 1
reprim-ir 3
repris-ar 1
reprob-ar 25
reproch-ar 1
reproduc-ir 59
repropi-arse 80
rept-ar 1
republicaniz-
ar 21
repuch-ar 1
repudi-ar 1
repudr-ir 56
repugn-ar 1
repuj-ar 1
repulg-ar 51
repul-ir 3
repuls-ar 1
repulul-ar 1
repunt-ar 1
repurg-ar 51
reput-ar 1
requebr-ar 53
requem-ar 1
requer-er 60
requer-ir 71
request-ar 1
requint-ar 1
requinte-ar 1
requis-ar 1
requisicion-ar 1
resab-er 66
resabi-ar 1
resac-ar 67
resal-ar 1
resalg-arse 80
resal-ir 68
resall-ar 1
resalt-ar 1
resalud-ar 1
resan-ar 1
resarc-ir 3,
plus the
changes
in red in 23
resbal-ar 1
rescald-ar 1
rescat-ar 1
rescind-ir 3
rescold-ar 1
rescolde-
arse 80
rescontr-ar 25
rescrib-ir 3,
except the
past partici-
ples are
rescrito and
rescripto
resec-ar 67
reseg-ar 62
resegu-ir 52
resell-ar 1
resembr-ar 53
resent-irse 71
reseñ-ar 1
reserv-ar 1
resfal-ar 1
resfri-ar 9
resgat-ar 1
resguard-ar 1
residenci-ar 1
resid-ir 3
resieg-ar 51
resign-ar 1
resill-ar 1
resin-ar 1
resis-ar 1

resist-ir 3
resob-ar 1
resobr-ar 1
resolg-ar 25
resoll-ar 25
resolt-arse
80, plus the
changes
in red in 25
resolv-er 47,
except the
past participle
is resuelto
reson-ar 25
resondr-ar 1
resopl-ar 1
resorb-er 2
respagil-ar 1
respahil-ar 9
respail-ar 1
respald-ar 1
respect-ar 1
respeluz-ar 21
respet-ar 1
respig-ar 51
resping-ar 51
respir-ar 1
resplandec-
er 48
respond-er 2
responsabiliz-
ar 21
responsa-
biliz-arse 21
respons-ar 1
response-ar 1
resquebraj-ar 1
resquebr-ar 53
resquem-ar 1
resquil-ar 1
resquit-ar 1
restablec-er 48
restall-ar 1
restamp-ar 1
restañ-ar 1
rest-ar 1
restaur-ar 1
restell-ar 1
resting-ar 51
restir-arse 80
restitu-ir 42
restreg-ar 62
restrell-ar 1
restrib-ar 1
restrill-ar 1
restring-ir 3,
plus the
changes
in red in 23
restriñ-ir 17
resucit-ar 1
resud-ar 1
result-ar 1,
and used in
the positions
in 45
resum-ir 3
resurg-ir 3,
plus the
changes
in red in 23
resurt-ir 3
retac-ar 67
retace-ar 1
retach-ar 1
retaj-ar 1
retall-ar 1
retallec-er 48
retaque-ar 1
ret-ar 1
retard-ar 1
retas-ar 1
retaz-ar 21
retej-ar 1
retej-er 2
retembl-ar 53
retempl-ar 1
reten-er 74
retent-ar 53
reteñ-ir 64,
plus the past
participle
retinto
retes-ar 1
retestin-ar 1
retestiñ-ar 1
retijerete-ar 1
retin-ar 1
retingl-ar 1
retintine-ar 1
retiñ-ir 17
ret-ir 52
retir-ar 1
retob-ar 1
retobe-ar 1
retoc-ar 67
retom-ar 1
retoñ-ar 1
retoñec-er 48
retoplic-ar 1
retorc-er 2,
plus the past
participle
retuerto
retorcij-ar 1
retoric-ar 67
retorn-ar 1
retortij-ar 1
retost-ar 25
retoz-ar 21
retrab-ar 1
retract-ar 1
retraduc-ir 59
retra-er 75
retranc-ar 67
retranque-ar 1
retransmit-ir 3
retras-ar 1
retrat-ar 1
retrech-ar 1
retrep-arse 80
retribu-ir 42
retrill-ar 1
retrob-ar 1
retroc-ar 25,
plus the
changes
in red in 67
retroced-er 2
retrograd-ar 1
retron-ar 25,
and for its
use regarding
weather,
see 45
retrotra-er 75
retrovacun-ar 1
retrovend-er 2
retruc-ar 67
retumb-ar 1
retund-ir 3
reunific-ar 67
reun-ir 9
reunt-ar 1
revacun-ar 1
revalid-ar 1
revalor-ar 1
revaloriz-ar 21
revalu-ar 9
reveget-ar 1
revejec-er 41
revel-ar 1
revel-er 2
reven-ar 1
revenc-er 2
revend-er 2
reven-ir 77
revent-ar 53
rev-er 78
rever-ar 1
reverber-ar 1
reverbere-ar 1
reverdec-er 48
reverenci-ar 1
revers-ar 1
revert-er 39
revert-ir 71
reves-ar 1
revest-ir 52
revez-ar 21
revid-ar 1
revigoriz-ar 21
revin-ar 1
revindic-ar 67
revir-ar 1
revis-ar 1
revist-ar 1
revitaliz-ar 21
revit-ar 1
reviv-ar 1
revivific-ar 67
reviv-ir 3
revoc-ar 67
revol-ar 25
revolc-ar 76
revole-ar 1
revolisque-ar 1
revolote-ar 1
revolte-ar 1
revolucion-ar 1
revolv-er 47,
except the
past participle
is revuelto

revot-arse 80
revuelc-ar 67
revuls-ar 1
rey-ar 1
reyert-ar 1
reyun-ar 1
rezag-ar 51
rez-ar 21
rezondr-ar 1
rezong-ar 51
rezongl-ar 1
rezum-ar 1
rezumb-ar 1
rezurc-ir 3, plus the changes in red in 23
ribete-ar 1
ridiculiz-ar 21
riel-ar 1, and for its use regarding weather, see 45
rif-ar 1
ril-ar 1
rim-ar 1
rimbomb-ar 1
ring-ar 51
ringlete-ar 1
ringuelete-ar 1
rinz-ar 21
riostr-ar 1
ripe-ar 1
ripi-ar 1
risc-ar 67
risote-ar 1
risp-ar 1
rispi-ar 1
ritm-ar 1
rivaliz-ar 21
riz-ar 21
rob-ar 1
robl-ar 1
roblon-ar 1
robor-ar 1
robr-ar 1
robustec-er 48
rocambore-ar 1
roch-ar 1
rochele-ar 1
roci-ar 9, and used in the positions in 45
rodaje-ar 1
rod-ar 25
rode-ar 1
rodrig-ar 51
ro-er 65
rog-ar 24
roguete-ar 1
roje-ar 1
rol-ar 1
rold-ar 1
role-ar 1
roll-ar 1
romadiz-arse ... 21
roman-ar 1
romance-ar 1
romane-ar 1
romaniz-ar 21
romanz-ar 21
rome-ar 1
romp-er 1, plus the past participle roto that is used more commonly than the regular past participle
ronc-ar 67
ronce-ar 1
ronch-ar 1
rond-ar 1
ronque-ar 1
ronrone-ar 1
ronz-ar 21
roñ-ar 1
ror-ar 1
rorre-ar 1
ros-ar 1, and used in the positions in 45
ros-arse 80
rosc-ar 67
rose-ar 1
roseg-ar 1
rosig-ar 51
rosm-ar 1
rosn-ar 1
rosque-ar 1
rost-ir 3
rot-ar 1
rote-ar 1
rotul-ar 1
rotur-ar 1
roy-arse 80
roz-ar 21
rozn-ar 1
ru-ar 9
rubific-ar 67
ruboriz-ar 21
rubric-ar 67
rucane-ar 1
ruc-ar 67
ruce-ar 1
ruch-ar 1
ruci-ar 1
rufiane-ar 1
rug-ar 51
rug-ir 3, plus the changes in red in 23, and used in the positions in 45
ruin-ar 1
ruji-ar 1
rul-ar 1
rumaje-ar 1
rumbanche-ar 1
rumb-ar 1
rumbe-ar 1
rumi-ar 1
rumor-ar 1
rumor-arse 80
rumore-ar 1
rumore-arse 80
rund-ir 3
runfi-ar 1
runfl-ar 1
runrune-ar 1
runrune-arse ... 80
ruñ-ar 1
ruñ-ir 3
rusent-ar 53
rusific-ar 67
rustic-ar 67
rust-ir 3
rustr-ir 3
rut-ar 1
rute-ar 1
ruti-ar 1
rutil-ar 1, and for its use regarding weather, see 45
rutr-ir 3

S

sabane-ar 1
sabatiz-ar 21
sab-er 66
sable-ar 1
sabore-ar 1
saborg-ar 51
sabote-ar 1
sabrose-ar 1
saburr-ar 1
sac-ar 67
sacarific-ar 67
sach-ar 1
saci-ar 1
sacraliz-ar 21
sacrament-ar 1
sacrific-ar 67
sacud-ir 3
saet-ar 1
saete-ar 1
saf-ar 1
sagr-ar 1
sahorn-arse 80
sahum-ar 9
sain-ar 9
sainete-ar 1
saj-ar 1
sajel-ar 1
salabarde-ar 1
sal-ar 1
salari-ar 1
salcoch-ar 1
salcochon-ar 1
sald-ar 1
sale-arse 80
saleg-ar 51
salg-ar 51
salific-ar 67
sal-ir 68
saliv-ar 1

sonsac-ar 67
sonsañ-ar 1
sonse-ar 1
sonsonete-ar 1
sonsonich-ar 1
soñ-ar 25
sopalanc-ar 67
sopape-ar 1
sopapi-ar 1
sop-ar 1
sope-ar 1
sopes-ar 1
sopete-ar 1
sopl-ar 1
soplone-ar 1
soploniz-ar 21
soport-ar 1
sopunt-ar 1
soque-ar 1
soquete-ar 1
sorb-er 2
sordec-er 48
soreraj-ar 1
sormigr-ar 1
sorn-ar 2
soroch-arse 80
sororiz-ar 21
sorprend-er 2
sorrab-ar 1
sorraj-ar 1
sorrape-ar 1
sorrasc-ar 1
sorrase-ar 1
sorreg-ar 62
sorrong-ar 51
sorrostr-ar 1
sorrostric-ar 1
sorte-ar 1
sosac-ar 67
sosañ-ar 1
soseg-ar 62
soslay-ar 1
sospech-ar 1
sospes-ar 1
sosquin-ar 1
sosten-er 74
sostitu-ir 42
sotane-ar 1
sot-ar 1
sotavent-
arse 80
sotavente-
arse 80
soterr-ar 53
sotil-arse 80
sotiliz-ar 21
sovietiz-ar 21
standardiz-ar ... 21
suavec-er 48
suavific-ar 67
suaviz-ar 21
subaliment-ar 1
subalquil-ar 1
subaltern-ar 1
subarrend-ar ... 53
subast-ar 1
subdeleg-ar 51
subdiacron-ar 1
subdistingu-
ir 30
subdivid-ir 3
subentend-er
2, plus the
changes
in red in 53
subestim-ar 1
subexpon-er 57
subflet-ar 1
subfund-ir 3
subintr-ar 1
sub-ir 3
subject-ar 1
subjetiv-ar 1
subjug-ar 1
subjuzg-ar 51
sublev-ar 1
sublim-ar 1
sublimiz-ar 21
subministr-ar 1
subordin-ar 1
subray-ar 1
subripu-ir 42
subrog-ar 51
subsan-ar 1
subscrib-ir
3, except
the past
participles
are subscrito
and
subscripto
subsegu-ir 59
subsist-ir 3
subsol-ar 25
substanci-ar 1
substantiv-ar 1
substitu-ir
42, plus the
past participle
substituto
substra-er 75
subtend-er
2, plus the
changes in
red in 53,
plus the
past participle
substituto
subtiliz-ar 21
subtitul-ar 1
subtra-er 75
subvencion-ar 1
subven-ir 77
subvert-ir 71
subyug-ar 51
succed-er 2
succion-ar 1
suced-er 2,
and for its
use regarding
weather,
see 45
sucint-arse 80
sucuche-ar 1
sucumb-ir 3
sud-ar 1
suele-ar 1
suest-ar 1
sufl-ar 1
sufoc-ar 67
sufrag-ar 51
sufr-ir 3
suger-ir 71
sugestion-ar 1
suicid-arse 80
sujet-ar 1,
plus the past
participle
sujeto
sujunc-ar 1
sulc-ar 1
sulfat-ar 1
sulfil-ar 1
sulfit-ar 1
sulfur-ar 1
sulfuriz-ar 21
sum-ar 1
sumari-ar 1
sumerg-ir 3,
plus the
changes
in red in 23
suministr-ar 1
sum-ir 3
sunch-ar 1
sunsuni-ar 1
sunt-ar 1
supedit-ar 1
superabund-ar ... 1
superaliment-
ar 1
super-ar 1
supercapitaliz-
ar 21
supercomprim-
ir 3
superentend-er
2, plus the
changes
in red in 53
superit-ar 1
superoxid-ar 1
superpon-er 57
supersatur-ar 1
supervalor-ar 1
superven-ir 77
supervis-ar 1
superviv-ir 3
supin-ar 1
supirit-ar 1
suplant-ar 1
suplic-ar 67
suplici-ar 1
supl-ir 3
supon-er 57
suport-ar 1
suposit-ar 1
suprim-ir 3,
plus the past
participle
supreso
supur-ar 1
suput-ar 1
surc-ar 67

t

trepan-ar 1
trep-ar 1
trepic-arse 80
trepid-ar 1
tresañej-ar 1
tresdobl-ar 1
tresn-ar 1
tresquil-ar 1
trezn-ar 1
triangul-ar 1
tri-ar 9
tribu-ir 42
tribul-ar 1
tribut-ar 1
tric-ar 1
tricot-ar 1
trifurc-ar 1
trifurc-arse 67
triguer-ar 1
tril-ar 1
trill-ar 1
trim-ar 1
trin-ar 1
trincafi-ar 1
trinc-ar 67
trinch-ar 1
trinche-ar 1
trintrique-ar 1
tripart-ir 3
triplic-ar 67
triptong-ar 51
tripudi-ar 1
tripul-ar 1
triquine-ar 1
tris-ar 1
tris-arse 80
trisc-ar 67
trisec-ar 67
triseccion-ar 1
tritric-ar 67
tritur-ar 1
triunf-ar 1
triz-ar 21
trobell-ar 1
troc-ar 76
troce-ar 1
troch-ar 1
troc-ir 59
trocisc-ar 67
tromp-ar 1
trompe-ar 1
trompete-ar 1
trompez-ar 34
trompic-ar 67
trompill-ar 1
tron-ar 25, and for its use regarding weather, see 45
tronc-ar 67
tronch-ar 1
troner-ar 1
tronic-ar 1
tronque-ar 1
tronz-ar 21
trope-ar 1
tropell-ar 1
tropez-ar 34
tropic-ar 1
troquel-ar 1
trot-ar 1
trote-ar 1
trotin-ar 1
trov-ar 1
troz-ar 21
truc-ar 67
truchimane-ar 1
trucid-ar 1
truf-ar 1
truhane-ar 1
trujamane-ar 1
truj-ar 1
trull-ar 1
trunc-ar 67
truntune-ar 1
trunuc-ar 67
trununc-ar 67
trunuque-ar 1
truque-ar 1
truquiñ-ar 1
tuberculiniz-ar 21
tuberculiz-ar 21
tubuliz-ar 21
tuert-ar 1
tuerte-ar 1
tuf-ar 1
tug-ar 1
tullec-er 48
tull-ir 17
tumb-ar 1
tumbe-ar 1
tumbone-ar 1
tumefac-er 41, except the past participles are tumefecho and tumefacto
tumultu-ar 9
tunante-ar 1
tun-ar 1
tun-arse 80
tunde-ar 1
tund-ir 3
tune-ar 1
tupi-ar 1
tup-ir 3
tuqui-ar 1
tur-ar 1
turb-ar 1
turbi-ar 1
turere-ar 1
turibul-ar 1
turific-ar 67
turn-ar 1
turne-ar 1
turque-arse 80
turr-ar 1
tus-ar 1
tusturr-ar 1
tute-ar 1
tutel-ar 1
tutque-ar 1
tutube-ar 1
tutubi-ar 1
tuz-ar 21

u

ubic-ar 67
uce-ar 1
ufan-arse 80
ufane-arse 80
uf-ar 1
ulcer-ar 1
ulere-ar 1
ulpe-ar 1
ultim-ar 1
ultraj-ar 1
ultralimit-ar 1
ultrapas-ar 1
ulul-ar 1
umbral-ar 1
unc-ir 3, plus the changes in red in 23
undul-ar 1
ung-ir 3, plus the changes in red in 23
unific-ar 67
uniform-ar 1
uniformiz-ar 21
unimism-ar 1
un-ir 3
unison-ar 25
universaliz-ar ... 21
univoc-arse 67
unt-ar 1
uñ-ar 1
uñate-ar 1
uñete-ar 1
uñ-ir 17
up-ar 1
uraje-ar 1
urbaje-ar 1
urbaniz-ar 21
urd-ir 3
urg-ir 3, plus the changes in red in 23, and used in the positions in 45
urraque-ar 1
us-ar 1
usucap-ir 3, and used in the positions in 45
usufructu-ar 9
usur-ar 1
usure-ar 1
usurp-ar 1
utiliz-ar 21
uvi-ar 1
uvioliz-ar 21
uze-ar 1

V

Pattern Verbs

Patterns 1-3:	Regular verbs ending in ar, er, and ir. They are non-reflexive verbs.
Patterns 4-79:	Irregular verbs ending in ar, er, and ir. They are in alphabetical order. They are non-reflexive verbs.
Patterns 80-82:	Regular verbs ending in arse, erse, and irse. They are reflexive verbs.

Subject Pronouns for Non-reflexive Verbs

Singular	Plural
yo	nosotros, nosotras
tú	vosotros, vosotras
usted (Ud.), él, ella, ello	ustedes (Uds.), ellos, ellas

Reflexive Pronouns

Singular	Plural
me	nos
te	os
se	se

Pattern 1: regular "ar" verbs.
Hablar (habl-ar, to speak) is the pattern verb.
Present part.: habl-ando Past part.: habl-ado

1
regular "ar" verbs

Singular		Plural	
Indicativo	*Subjuntivo*	*Indicativo*	*Subjuntivo*
Presente	*Presente*	*Presente*	*Presente*
habl-o	habl-e	habl-amos	habl-emos
habl-as	habl-es	habl-áis	habl-éis
habl-a	habl-e	habl-an	habl-en
Imperfecto	*Imperfecto*	*Imperfecto*	*Imperfecto*
habl-aba	habl-ara OR habl-ase	habl-ábamos	habl-áramos OR habl-ásemos
habl-abas	habl-aras OR habl-ases	habl-abais	habl-arais OR habl-aseis
habl-aba	habl-ara OR habl-ase	habl-aban	habl-aran OR habl-asen
Pretérito		*Pretérito*	
habl-é		habl-amos	
habl-aste		habl-asteis	
habl-ó		habl-aron	
Futuro	*Futuro*	*Futuro*	*Futuro*
habl-aré	habl-are	habl-aremos	habl-áremos
habl-arás	habl-ares	habl-aréis	habl-areis
habl-ará	habl-are	habl-arán	habl-aren
Potencial		*Potencial*	
habl-aría		habl-aríamos	
habl-arías		habl-aríais	
habl-aría		habl-arían	

Imperativo

Singular	*Plural*
(not used); no (not used)	habl-emos; no habl-emos
habl-a; no habl-es	habl-ad; no habl-éis
habl-e; no habl-e	habl-en; no habl-en

Make compound tenses by adding the past participle hablado to pattern 83.
Translation possibilities are at pattern 88. Conjugation tips are at pattern 89.

2
regular "er" verbs

Pattern 2: regular "er" verbs.
Comer (com-er, to eat) is the pattern verb.
Present part.: com-iendo   Past part.: com-ido

Singular		Plural	
Indicativo	*Subjuntivo*	*Indicativo*	*Subjuntivo*
Presente	*Presente*	*Presente*	*Presente*
com-o	com-a	com-emos	com-amos
com-es	com-as	com-éis	com-áis
com-e	com-a	com-en	com-an
Imperfecto	*Imperfecto*	*Imperfecto*	*Imperfecto*
com-ía	com-iera OR com-iese	com-íamos	com-iéramos OR com-iésemos
com-ías	com-ieras OR com-ieses	com-íais	com-ierais OR com-ieseis
com-ía	com-iera OR com-iese	com-ían	com-ieran OR com-iesen
Pretérito		*Pretérito*	
com-í		com-imos	
com-iste		com-isteis	
com-ió		com-ieron	
Futuro	*Futuro*	*Futuro*	*Futuro*
com-eré	com-iere	com-eremos	com-iéremos
com-erás	com-ieres	com-eréis	com-iereis
com-erá	com-iere	com-erán	com-ieren
Potencial		*Potencial*	
com-ería		com-eríamos	
com-erías		com-eríais	
com-ería		com-erían	

Imperativo

Singular	*Plural*
(not used); no (not used)	com-amos; no com-amos
com-e; no com-as	com-ed; no com-áis
com-a; no com-a	com-an; no com-an

Make compound tenses by adding the past participle comido to pattern 83.
Translation possibilities are at pattern 88. Conjugation tips are at pattern 90.

Pattern 3: regular "ir" verbs.
Vivir (viv-ir, to live) is the pattern verb.
Present part.: viv-iendo Past part.: viv-ido

3
regular "ir" verbs

Singular		*Plural*	
Indicativo	*Subjuntivo*	*Indicativo*	*Subjuntivo*
Presente	*Presente*	*Presente*	*Presente*
viv-o	viv-a	viv-imos	viv-amos
viv-es	viv-as	viv-ís	viv-áis
viv-e	viv-a	viv-en	viv-an
Imperfecto	*Imperfecto*	*Imperfecto*	*Imperfecto*
viv-ía	viv-iera OR viv-iese	viv-íamos	viv-iéramos OR viv-iésemos
viv-ías	viv-ieras OR viv-ieses	viv-íais	viv-ierais OR viv-ieseis
viv-ía	viv-iera OR viv-iese	viv-ían	viv-ieran OR viv-iesen
Pretérito		*Pretérito*	
viv-í		viv-imos	
viv-iste		viv-isteis	
viv-ió		viv-ieron	
Futuro	*Futuro*	*Futuro*	*Futuro*
viv-iré	viv-iere	viv-iremos	viv-iéremos
viv-irás	viv-ieres	viv-iréis	viv-iereis
viv-irá	viv-iere	viv-irán	viv-ieren
Potencial		*Potencial*	
viv-iría		viv-iríamos	
viv-irías		viv-iríais	
viv-iría		viv-irían	

Imperativo

Singular	*Plural*
(not used); no (not used)	viv-amos; no viv-amos
viv-e; no viv-as	viv-id; no viv-áis
viv-a; no viv-a	viv-an; no viv-an

Make compound tenses by adding the past participle vivido to pattern 83.
Translation possibilities are at pattern 88. Conjugation tips are at pattern 91.

4 abolir

Pattern 4: Some conjugations customarily are not used.
Abolir (abol-ir) (to abolish, annul) is the pattern verb.
Present participle: abol-iendo Past participle: abol-ido

Singular		*Plural*	
Indicativo	*Subjuntivo*	*Indicativo*	*Subjuntivo*
Presente	*Presente*	*Presente*	*Presente*
(not used)	(not used)	abol-imos	(not used)
(not used)	(not used)	abol-ís	(not used)
(not used)	(not used)	(not used)	(not used)
Imperfecto	*Imperfecto*	*Imperfecto*	*Imperfecto*
abol-ía	abol-iera OR abol-iese	abol-íamos	abol-iéramos OR abol-iésemos
abol-ías	abol-ieras OR abol-ieses	abol-íais	abol-ierais OR abol-ieseis
abol-ía	abol-iera OR abol-iese	abol-ían	abol-ieran OR abol-iesen
Pretérito		*Pretérito*	
abol-í		abol-imos	
abol-iste		abol-isteis	
abol-ió		abol-ieron	
Futuro	*Futuro*	*Futuro*	*Futuro*
abol-iré	abol-iere	abol-iremos	abol-iéremos
abol-irás	abol-ieres	abol-iréis	abol-iereis
abol-irá	abol-iere	abol-irán	abol-ieren
Potencial		*Potencial*	
abol-iría		abol-iríamos	
abol-irías		abol-iríais	
abol-iría		abol-irían	

Imperativo

Singular	*Plural*
(not used); no (not used)	(not used); no (not used)
(not used); no (not used)	abol-id; no abol-áis
(not used); no (not used)	(not used); no (not used)

Make compound tenses by adding the past participle abolido to pattern 83.
Translation possibilities are at pattern 88. Conjugation tips are at pattern 91.

Pattern 5: i in stem ➠ ie when stressed.
Adquirir (adquir-ir) (to acquire) is the pattern verb.
Present participle: adquir-iendo Past participle: adquir-ido

5 adquirir

Singular		Plural	
Indicativo	*Subjuntivo*	*Indicativo*	*Subjuntivo*
Presente	*Presente*	*Presente*	*Presente*
adquier-o	adquier-a	adquir-imos	adquir-amos
adquier-es	adquier-as	adquir-ís	adquir-áis
adquier-e	adquier-a	adquier-en	adquier-an
Imperfecto	*Imperfecto*	*Imperfecto*	*Imperfecto*
adquir-ía	adquir-iera OR adquir-iese	adquir-íamos	adquir-iéramos OR adquir-iésemos
adquir-ías	adquir-ieras OR adquir-ieses	adquir-íais	adquir-ierais OR adquir-ieseis
adquir-ía	adquir-iera OR adquir-iese	adquir-ían	adquir-ieran OR adquir-iesen
Pretérito		*Pretérito*	
adquir-í		adquir-imos	
adquir-iste		adquir-isteis	
adquir-ió		adquir-ieron	
Futuro	*Futuro*	*Futuro*	*Futuro*
adquir-iré	adquir-iere	adquir-iremos	adquir-iéremos
adquir-irás	adquir-ieres	adquir-iréis	adquir-iereis
adquir-irá	adquir-iere	adquir-irán	adquir-ieren
Potencial		*Potencial*	
adquir-iría		adquir-iríamos	
adquir-irías		adquir-iríais	
adquir-iría		adquir-irían	

Imperativo

Singular	Plural
(not used); no (not used)	adquir-amos; no adquir-amos
adquier-e; no adquier-as	adquir-id; no adquir-áis
adquier-a; no adquier-a	adquier-an; no adquier-an

Make compound tenses by adding the past participle adquirido to pattern 83. Translation possibilities are at pattern 88. Conjugation tips are at pattern 91.

6 agorar

Pattern 6: o ➠ üe when stressed.
Agorar (agor-ar) (to predict) is the pattern verb.
Present participle: agor-ando   Past participle: agor-ado

Singular		*Plural*	
Indicativo	*Subjuntivo*	*Indicativo*	*Subjuntivo*
Presente	*Presente*	*Presente*	*Presente*
agüer-o	agüer-e	agor-amos	agor-emos
agüer-as	agüer-es	agor-áis	agor-éis
agüer-a	agüer-e	agüer-an	agüer-en
Imperfecto	*Imperfecto*	*Imperfecto*	*Imperfecto*
agor-aba	agor-ara OR agor-ase	agor-ábamos	agor-áramos OR agor-ásemos
agor-abas	agor-aras OR agor-ases	agor-abais	agor-arais OR agor-aseis
agor-aba	agor-ara OR agor-ase	agor-aban	agor-aran OR agor-asen
Pretérito		*Pretérito*	
agor-é		agor-amos	
agor-aste		agor-asteis	
agor-ó		agor-aron	
Futuro	*Futuro*	*Futuro*	*Futuro*
agor-aré	agor-are	agor-aremos	agor-áremos
agor-arás	agor-ares	agor-aréis	agor-areis
agor-ará	agor-are	agor-arán	agor-aren
Potencial		*Potencial*	
agor-aría		agor-aríamos	
agor-arías		agor-aríais	
agor-aría		agor-arían	

Imperativo

Singular	*Plural*
(not used); no (not used)	agor-emos; no agor-emos
agüer-a; no agüer-es	agor-ad; no agor-éis
agüer-e; no agüer-e	agüer-en; no agüer-en

Make compound tenses by adding the past participle agorado to pattern 83.
Translation possibilities are at pattern 88. Conjugation tips are at pattern 89.

Pattern 7: gu ➠ gü before e to retain the gw sound.
Aguar (agu-ar) (to water, dilute, spoil, mar) is the pattern verb.
Present participle: agu-ando   Past participle: agu-ado

7 aguar

Singular		Plural	
Indicativo	*Subjuntivo*	*Indicativo*	*Subjuntivo*
Presente	*Presente*	*Presente*	*Presente*
agu-o	agü-e	agu-amos	agü-emos
agu-as	agü-es	agu-áis	agü-éis
agu-a	agü-e	agu-an	agü-en
Imperfecto	*Imperfecto*	*Imperfecto*	*Imperfecto*
agu-aba	agu-ara OR agu-ase	agu-ábamos	agu-áramos OR agu-ásemos
agu-abas	agu-aras OR agu-ases	agu-abais	agu-arais OR agu-aseis
agu-aba	agu-ara OR agu-ase	agu-aban	agu-aran OR agu-asen
Pretérito		*Pretérito*	
agü-é		agu-amos	
agu-aste		agu-asteis	
agu-ó		agu-aron	
Futuro	*Futuro*	*Futuro*	*Futuro*
agu-aré	agu-are	agu-aremos	agu-áremos
agu-arás	agu-ares	agu-aréis	agu-areis
agu-ará	agu-are	agu-arán	agu-aren
Potencial		*Potencial*	
agu-aría		agu-aríamos	
agu-arías		agu-aríais	
agu-aría		agu-arían	

Imperativo

Singular	*Plural*
(not used); no (not used)	agü-emos; no agü-emos
agu-a; no agü-es	agu-ad; no agü-éis
agü-e; no agü-e	agü-en; no agü-en

Make compound tenses by adding the past participle aguado to pattern 83.
Translation possibilities are at pattern 88. Conjugation tips are at pattern 89.

8 ahincar

Pattern 8: i ➟ í when stressed, c ➟ qu before e.
Ahincar (ahinc-ar) (to urge, press) is the pattern verb.
Present participle: ahinc-ando   Past participle: ahinc-ado

Singular		*Plural*	
Indicativo	*Subjuntivo*	*Indicativo*	*Subjuntivo*
Presente	*Presente*	*Presente*	*Presente*
ahínc-o	ahínqu-e	ahinc-amos	ahinqu-emos
ahínc-as	ahínqu-es	ahinc-áis	ahinqu-éis
ahínc-a	ahínqu-e	ahínc-an	ahínqu-en
Imperfecto	*Imperfecto*	*Imperfecto*	*Imperfecto*
ahinc-aba	ahinc-ara OR ahinc-ase	ahinc-ábamos	ahinc-áramos OR ahinc-ásemos
ahinc-abas	ahinc-aras OR ahinc-ases	ahinc-abais	ahinc-arais OR ahinc-aseis
ahinc-aba	ahinc-ara OR ahinc-ase	ahinc-aban	ahinc-aran OR ahinc-asen
Pretérito		*Pretérito*	
ahinqu-é		ahinc-amos	
ahinc-aste		ahinc-asteis	
ahinc-ó		ahinc-aron	
Futuro	*Futuro*	*Futuro*	*Futuro*
ahinc-aré	ahinc-are	ahinc-aremos	ahinc-áremos
ahinc-arás	ahinc-ares	ahinc-aréis	ahinc-areis
ahinc-ará	ahinc-are	ahinc-arán	ahinc-aren
Potencial		*Potencial*	
ahinc-aría		ahinc-aríamos	
ahinc-arías		ahinc-aríais	
ahinc-aría		ahinc-arían	

Imperativo

Singular	*Plural*
(not used); no (not used)	ahinqu-emos; no ahinqu-emos
ahínc-a; no ahínqu-es	ahinc-ad; no ahinqu-éis
ahínqu-e; no ahínqu-e	ahínqu-en; no ahínqu-en

Make compound tenses by adding the past participle ahincado to pattern 83.
Translation possibilities are at pattern 88. Conjugation tips are at pattern 89.

Pattern 9: i ➟ í, (u ➟ ú in verbs like actuar).
Airar (air-ar) (to anger, irritate) is the pattern verb.
Present participle: air-ando Past participle: air-ado

9 airar

Singular		Plural	
Indicativo	*Subjuntivo*	*Indicativo*	*Subjuntivo*
Presente	*Presente*	*Presente*	*Presente*
aír-o	aír-e	air-amos	air-emos
aír-as	aír-es	air-áis	air-éis
aír-a	aír-e	aír-an	aír-en
Imperfecto	*Imperfecto*	*Imperfecto*	*Imperfecto*
air-aba	air-ara OR air-ase	air-ábamos	air-áramos OR air-ásemos
air-abas	air-aras OR air-ases	air-abais	air-arais OR air-aseis
air-aba	air-ara OR air-ase	air-aban	air-aran OR air-asen
Pretérito		*Pretérito*	
air-é		air-amos	
air-aste		air-asteis	
air-ó		air-aron	
Futuro	*Futuro*	*Futuro*	*Futuro*
air-aré	air-are	air-aremos	air-áremos
air-arás	air-ares	air-aréis	air-areis
air-ará	air-are	air-arán	air-aren
Potencial		*Potencial*	
air-aría		air-aríamos	
air-arías		air-aríais	
air-aría		air-arían	

Imperativo

Singular	Plural
(not used); no (not used)	air-emos; no air-emos
aír-a; no aír-es	air-ad; no air-éis
aír-e; no aír-e	aír-en; no aír-en

Make compound tenses by adding the past participle airado to pattern 83.
Translation possibilities are at pattern 88. Conjugation tips are at pattern 89.

10 andar

Pattern 10: a ➠ i or ie, é ➠ e, ó ➠ o, uv is added.
Andar (and-ar) (to walk) is the pattern verb.
Present participle: and-ando   Past participle: and-ado

Singular		Plural	
Indicativo	*Subjuntivo*	*Indicativo*	*Subjuntivo*
Presente	*Presente*	*Presente*	*Presente*
and-o	and-e	and-amos	and-emos
and-as	and-es	and-áis	and-éis
and-a	and-e	and-an	and-en
Imperfecto	*Imperfecto*	*Imperfecto*	*Imperfecto*
and-aba	anduv-iera OR anduv-iese	and-ábamos	anduv-iéramos OR anduv-iésemos
and-abas	anduv-ieras OR anduv-ieses	and-abais	anduv-ierais OR anduv-ieseis
and-aba	anduv-iera OR anduv-iese	and-aban	anduv-ieran OR anduv-iesen
Pretérito		*Pretérito*	
anduv-e		anduv-imos	
anduv-iste		anduv-isteis	
anduv-o		anduv-ieron	
Futuro	*Futuro*	*Futuro*	*Futuro*
and-aré	anduv-iere	and-aremos	anduv-iéremos
and-arás	anduv-ieres	and-aréis	anduv-iereis
and-ará	anduv-iere	and-arán	anduv-ieren
Potencial		*Potencial*	
and-aría		and-aríamos	
and-arías		and-aríais	
and-aría		and-arían	

Imperativo

Singular	Plural
(not used); no (not used)	and-emos; no and-emos
and-a; no and-es	and-ad; no and-éis
and-e; no and-e	and-en; no and-en

Make compound tenses by adding the past participle andado to pattern 83.
Translation possibilities are at pattern 88. Conjugation tips are at pattern 89.

Pattern 11: Some conjugations customarily are not used.
Aplacer (aplac-er) (to please, to satisfy) is the pattern verb.
Present participle: aplac-iendo   Past participle: aplac-ido

11 aplacer

Singular		*Plural*	
Indicativo	*Subjuntivo*	*Indicativo*	*Subjuntivo*
Presente	*Presente*	*Presente*	*Presente*
(not used)	(not used)	(not used)	(not used)
(not used)	(not used)	(not used)	(not used)
aplac-e	(not used)	aplac-en	(not used)
Imperfecto	*Imperfecto*	*Imperfecto*	*Imperfecto*
(not used)	(not used) OR (not used)	(not used)	(not used) OR (not used)
(not used)	(not used) OR (not used)	(not used)	(not used) OR (not used)
aplac-ía	(not used) OR (not used)	aplac-ían	(not used) OR (not used)
Pretérito		*Pretérito*	
(not used)		(not used)	
(not used)		(not used)	
(not used)		(not used)	
Futuro	*Futuro*	*Futuro*	*Futuro*
(not used)	(not used)	(not used)	(not used)
(not used)	(not used)	(not used)	(not used)
(not used)	(not used)	(not used)	(not used)
Potencial		*Potencial*	
(not used)		(not used)	
(not used)		(not used)	
(not used)		(not used)	

Imperativo	
Singular	*Plural*
(not used); no (not used)	(not used); no (not used)
(not used); no (not used)	(not used); no (not used)
(not used); no (not used)	(not used); no (not used)

Make compound tenses by adding the past participle aplacido to pattern 83.
Translation possibilities are at pattern 88. Conjugation tips are at pattern 90.

12 argüir

Pattern 12: i ➟ y, y is added, ü ➟ u before y.
Argüir (argü-ir) (to argue) is the pattern verb.
Present participle: argu-yendo Past participle: argü-ido

Singular		Plural	
Indicativo	*Subjuntivo*	*Indicativo*	*Subjuntivo*
Presente	*Presente*	*Presente*	*Presente*
arguy-o	arguy-a	argü-imos	arguy-amos
arguy-es	arguy-as	argü-ís	arguy-áis
arguy-e	arguy-a	arguy-en	arguy-an
Imperfecto	*Imperfecto*	*Imperfecto*	*Imperfecto*
argü-ía	argu-yera OR argu-yese	argü-íamos	argu-yéramos OR argu-yésemos
argü-ías	argu-yeras OR argu-yeses	argü-íais	argu-yerais OR argu-yeseis
argü-ía	argu-yera OR argu-yese	argü-ían	argu-yeran OR argu-yesen
Pretérito		*Pretérito*	
argü-í		argü-imos	
argü-iste		argü-isteis	
argu-yó		argu-yeron	
Futuro	*Futuro*	*Futuro*	*Futuro*
argü-iré	argu-yere	argü-iremos	argu-yéremos
argü-irás	argu-yeres	argü-iréis	argu-yereis
argü-irá	argu-yere	argü-irán	argu-yeren
Potencial		*Potencial*	
argü-iría		argü-iríamos	
argü-irías		argü-iríais	
argü-iría		argü-irían	

Imperativo

Singular	*Plural*
(not used); no (not used)	arguy-amos; no arguy-amos
arguy-e; no arguy-as	argü-id; no arguy-áis
arguy-a; no arguy-a	arguy-an; no arguy-an

Make compound tenses by adding the past participle argüido to pattern 83.
Translation possibilities are at pattern 88. Conjugation tips are at pattern 91.

Pattern 13: g is added.
Asir (as-ir) (to grasp) is the pattern verb.
Present participle: as-iendo Past participle: as-ido

13
asir

Singular		Plural	
Indicativo	*Subjuntivo*	*Indicativo*	*Subjuntivo*
Presente	*Presente*	*Presente*	*Presente*
asg-o	asg-a	as-imos	asg-amos
as-es	asg-as	as-ís	asg-áis
as-e	asg-a	as-en	asg-an
Imperfecto	*Imperfecto*	*Imperfecto*	*Imperfecto*
as-ía	as-iera OR as-iese	as-íamos	as-iéramos OR as-iésemos
as-ías	as-ieras OR as-ieses	as-íais	as-ierais OR as-ieseis
as-ía	as-iera OR as-iese	as-ían	as-ieran OR as-iesen
Pretérito		*Pretérito*	
as-í		as-imos	
as-iste		as-isteis	
as-ió		as-ieron	
Futuro	*Futuro*	*Futuro*	*Futuro*
as-iré	as-iere	as-iremos	as-iéremos
as-irás	as-ieres	as-iréis	as-iereis
as-irá	as-iere	as-irán	as-ieren
Potencial		*Potencial*	
as-iría		as-iríamos	
as-irías		as-iríais	
as-iría		as-irían	

Imperativo

Singular	*Plural*
(not used); no (not used)	asg-amos; no asg-amos
as-e; no asg-as	as-id; no asg-áis
asg-a; no asg-a	asg-an; no asg-an

Make compound tenses by adding the past participle asido to pattern 83.
Translation possibilities are at pattern 88. Conjugation tips are at pattern 91.

14 atañer

Pattern 14: Some conjugations customarily are not used.
Atañer (atañ-er) (to concern) is the pattern verb.
Present participle: atañ-endo Past participle: atañ-ido

Singular		Plural	
Indicativo	*Subjuntivo*	*Indicativo*	*Subjuntivo*
Presente	*Presente*	*Presente*	*Presente*
(not used)	(not used)	(not used)	(not used)
(not used)	(not used)	(not used)	(not used)
atañ-e	atañ-a	atañ-en	atañ-an
Imperfecto	*Imperfecto*	*Imperfecto*	*Imperfecto*
(not used)	(not used) OR (not used)	(not used)	(not used) OR (not used)
(not used)	(not used) OR (not used)	(not used)	(not used) OR (not used)
atañ-ía	atañ-era OR atañ-ese	atañ-ían	atañ-eran OR atañ-esen
Pretérito		*Pretérito*	
(not used)		(not used)	
(not used)		(not used)	
atañ-ó		atañ-eron	
Futuro	*Futuro*	*Futuro*	*Futuro*
(not used)	(not used)	(not used)	(not used)
(not used)	(not used)	(not used)	(not used)
atañ-erá	atañ-ere	atañ-erán	atañ-eren
Potencial		*Potencial*	
(not used)		(not used)	
(not used)		(not used)	
atañ-ería		atañ-erían	

Imperativo

Singular	*Plural*
(not used); no (not used)	(not used); no (not used)
(not used); no (not used)	(not used); no (not used)
atañ-a; no atañ-a	atañ-an; no atañ-an

Make compound tenses by adding the past participle atañido to pattern 83.
Translation possibilities are at pattern 88. Conjugation tips are at pattern 90.

Pattern 15: o ➟ üe when stressed, z ➟ c before e.
Avergonzar (avergonz-ar) (to shame) is the pattern verb.
Present part.: avergonz-ando Past part.: avergonz-ado

15 avergonzar

Singular		Plural	
Indicativo	*Subjuntivo*	*Indicativo*	*Subjuntivo*
Presente	*Presente*	*Presente*	*Presente*
avergüenz-o	avergüenc-e	avergonz-amos	avergonc-emos
avergüenz-as	avergüenc-es	avergonz-áis	avergonc-éis
avergüenz-a	avergüenc-e	avergüenz-an	avergüenc-en
Imperfecto	*Imperfecto*	*Imperfecto*	*Imperfecto*
avergonz-aba	avergonz-ara OR avergonz-ase	avergonz-ábamos	avergonz-áramos OR avergonz-ásemos
avergonz-abas	avergonz-aras OR avergonz-ases	avergonz-abais	avergonz-arais OR avergonz-aseis
avergonz-aba	avergonz-ara OR avergonz-ase	avergonz-aban	avergonz-aran OR avergonz-asen
Pretérito		*Pretérito*	
avergonc-é		avergonz-amos	
avergonz-aste		avergonz-asteis	
avergonz-ó		avergonz-aron	
Futuro	*Futuro*	*Futuro*	*Futuro*
avergonz-aré	avergonz-are	avergonz-aremos	avergonz-áremos
avergonz-arás	avergonz-ares	avergonz-aréis	avergonz-areis
avergonz-ará	avergonz-are	avergonz-arán	avergonz-aren
Potencial		*Potencial*	
avergonz-aría		avergonz-aríamos	
avergonz-arías		avergonz-aríais	
avergonz-aría		avergonz-arían	

Imperativo

Singular	*Plural*
(not used); no (not used)	avergonc-emos; no avergonc-emos
avergüenz-a; no avergüenc-es	avergonz-ad; no avergonc-éis
avergüenc-e; no avergüenc-e	avergüenc-en; no avergüenc-en

Make compound tenses by adding the past participle avergonzado to pattern 83.
Translation possibilities are at pattern 88. Conjugation tips are at pattern 89.

16 balbucir

Pattern 16: Some conjugations customarily are not used.
Balbucir (balbuc-ir) (to stammer) is the pattern verb.
Present participle: balbuc-iendo Past participle: balbuc-ido

Singular		*Plural*	
Indicativo	*Subjuntivo*	*Indicativo*	*Subjuntivo*
Presente	*Presente*	*Presente*	*Presente*
(not used)	(not used)	balbuc-imos	(not used)
(not used)	(not used)	balbuc-ís	(not used)
(not used)	(not used)	(not used)	(not used)
Imperfecto	*Imperfecto*	*Imperfecto*	*Imperfecto*
balbuc-ía	balbuc-iera OR balbuc-iese	balbuc-íamos	balbuc-iéramos OR balbuc-iésemos
balbuc-ías	balbuc-ieras OR balbuc-ieses	balbuc-íais	balbuc-ierais OR balbuc-ieseis
balbuc-ía	balbuc-iera OR balbuc-iese	balbuc-ían	balbuc-ieran OR balbuc-iesen
Pretérito		*Pretérito*	
balbuc-í		balbuc-imos	
balbuc-iste		balbuc-isteis	
balbuc-ió		balbuc-ieron	
Futuro	*Futuro*	*Futuro*	*Futuro*
balbuc-iré	balbuc-iere	balbuc-iremos	balbuc-iéremos
balbuc-irás	balbuc-ieres	balbuc-iréis	balbuc-iereis
balbuc-irá	balbuc-iere	balbuc-irán	balbuc-ieren
Potencial		*Potencial*	
balbuc-iría		balbuc-iríamos	
balbuc-irías		balbuc-iríais	
balbuc-iría		balbuc-irían	

Imperativo	
Singular	*Plural*
(not used); no (not used)	(not used); no (not used)
(not used); no balbuz-as	(not used); no balbuz-áis
(not used); no (not used)	(not used); no (not used)

Make compound tenses by adding the past participle balbucido to pattern 83.
Translation possibilities are at pattern 88. Conjugation tips are at pattern 91.

Pattern 17: i is deleted before e or o.
Bruñir (bruñ-ir) (to polish) is the pattern verb.
Present participle: bruñ-endo   Past participle: bruñ-ido

17 bruñir

Singular Indicativo	Singular Subjuntivo	Plural Indicativo	Plural Subjuntivo
Presente	*Presente*	*Presente*	*Presente*
bruñ-o	bruñ-a	bruñ-imos	bruñ-amos
bruñ-es	bruñ-as	bruñ-ís	bruñ-áis
bruñ-e	bruñ-a	bruñ-en	bruñ-an
Imperfecto	*Imperfecto*	*Imperfecto*	*Imperfecto*
bruñ-ía	bruñ-era OR bruñ-ese	bruñ-íamos	bruñ-éramos OR bruñ-ésemos
bruñ-ías	bruñ-eras OR bruñ-eses	bruñ-íais	bruñ-erais OR bruñ-eseis
bruñ-ía	bruñ-era OR bruñ-ese	bruñ-ían	bruñ-eran OR bruñ-esen
Pretérito		*Pretérito*	
bruñ-í		bruñ-imos	
bruñ-iste		bruñ-isteis	
bruñ-ó		bruñ-eron	
Futuro	*Futuro*	*Futuro*	*Futuro*
bruñ-iré	bruñ-ere	bruñ-iremos	bruñ-éremos
bruñ-irás	bruñ-eres	bruñ-iréis	bruñ-ereis
bruñ-irá	bruñ-ere	bruñ-irán	bruñ-eren
Potencial		*Potencial*	
bruñ-iría		bruñ-iríamos	
bruñ-irías		bruñ-iríais	
bruñ-iría		bruñ-irían	

Imperativo

Singular	Plural
(not used); no (not used)	bruñ-amos; no bruñ-amos
bruñ-e; no bruñ-as	bruñ-id; no bruñ-áis
bruñ-a; no bruñ-a	bruñ-an; no bruñ-an

Make compound tenses by adding the past participle bruñido to pattern 83.
Translation possibilities are at pattern 88. Conjugation tips are at pattern 91.

18 caber

Pattern 18: a ➠ u or e, b ➠ p, c ➠ qu before e.
Caber (cab-er) (to fit, to fit into) is the pattern verb.
Present participle: cab-iendo   Past participle: cab-ido

Singular		Plural	
Indicativo	*Subjuntivo*	*Indicativo*	*Subjuntivo*
Presente	*Presente*	*Presente*	*Presente*
quep-o	quep-a	cab-emos	quep-amos
cab-es	quep-as	cab-éis	quep-áis
cab-e	quep-a	cab-en	quep-an
Imperfecto	*Imperfecto*	*Imperfecto*	*Imperfecto*
cab-ía	cup-iera OR cup-iese	cab-íamos	cup-iéramos OR cup-iésemos
cab-ías	cup-ieras OR cup-ieses	cab-íais	cup-ierais OR cup-ieseis
cab-ía	cup-iera OR cup-iese	cab-ían	cup-ieran OR cup-iesen
Pretérito		*Pretérito*	
cup-e		cup-imos	
cup-iste		cup-isteis	
cup-o		cup-ieron	
Futuro	*Futuro*	*Futuro*	*Futuro*
cab-ré	cup-iere	cab-remos	cup-iéremos
cab-rás	cup-ieres	cab-réis	cup-iereis
cab-rá	cup-iere	cab-rán	cup-ieren
Potencial		*Potencial*	
cab-ría		cab-ríamos	
cab-rías		cab-ríais	
cab-ría		cab-rían	

Imperativo

Singular	*Plural*
(not used); no (not used)	quep-amos; no quep-amos
cab-e; no quep-as	cab-ed; no quep-áis
quep-a; no quep-a	quep-an; no quep-an

Make compound tenses by adding the past participle cabido to pattern 83.
Translation possibilities are at pattern 88. Conjugation tips are at pattern 90.

Pattern 19: i ➟ í when stressed, g ➟ gu before e.
Cabrahigar (cabrahig-ar) (to pollinate, e.g., fruit trees).
Present part.: cabrahig-ando Past part.: cabrahig-ado

19 cabrahigar

Singular		Plural	
Indicativo	*Subjuntivo*	*Indicativo*	*Subjuntivo*
Presente	*Presente*	*Presente*	*Presente*
cabrahíg-o	cabrahígu-e	cabrahig-amos	cabrahigu-emos
cabrahíg-as	cabrahígu-es	cabrahig-áis	cabrahigu-éis
cabrahíg-a	cabrahígu-e	cabrahíg-an	cabrahígu-en
Imperfecto	*Imperfecto*	*Imperfecto*	*Imperfecto*
cabrahig-aba	cabrahig-ara OR cabrahig-ase	cabrahig-ábamos	cabrahig-áramos OR cabrahig-ásemos
cabrahig-abas	cabrahig-aras OR cabrahig-ases	cabrahig-abais	cabrahig-arais OR cabrahig-aseis
cabrahig-aba	cabrahig-ara OR cabrahig-ase	cabrahig-aban	cabrahig-aran OR cabrahig-asen
Pretérito		*Pretérito*	
cabrahigu-é		cabrahig-amos	
cabrahig-aste		cabrahig-asteis	
cabrahig-ó		cabrahig-aron	
Futuro	*Futuro*	*Futuro*	*Futuro*
cabrahig-aré	cabrahig-are	cabrahig-aremos	cabrahig-áremos
cabrahig-arás	cabrahig-ares	cabrahig-aréis	cabrahig-areis
cabrahig-ará	cabrahig-are	cabrahig-arán	cabrahig-aren
Potencial		*Potencial*	
cabrahig-aría		cabrahig-aríamos	
cabrahig-arías		cabrahig-aríais	
cabrahig-aría		cabrahig-arían	

Imperativo

Singular	*Plural*
(not used); no (not used)	cabrahigu-emos; no cabrahigu-emos
cabrahíg-a; no cabrahígu-es	cabrahig-ad; no cabrahigu-éis
cabrahígu-e; no cabrahígu-e	cabrahígu-en; no cabrahígu-en

Make compound tenses by adding the past participle cabrahigado to pattern 83. Translation possibilities are at pattern 88. Conjugation tips are at pattern 89.

20 caer

Pattern 20: add ig, i ➠ í or y. Similar to oír.
Caer (ca-er) (to fall, to decline) is the pattern verb.
Present participle: ca-yendo Past participle: ca-ído

Singular		Plural	
Indicativo	*Subjuntivo*	*Indicativo*	*Subjuntivo*
Presente	*Presente*	*Presente*	*Presente*
caig-o	caig-a	ca-emos	caig-amos
ca-es	caig-as	ca-éis	caig-áis
ca-e	caig-a	ca-en	caig-an
Imperfecto	*Imperfecto*	*Imperfecto*	*Imperfecto*
ca-ía	ca-yera OR ca-yese	ca-íamos	ca-yéramos OR ca-yésemos
ca-ías	ca-yeras OR ca-yeses	ca-íais	ca-yerais OR ca-yeseis
ca-ía	ca-yera OR ca-yese	ca-ían	ca-yeran OR ca-yesen
Pretérito		*Pretérito*	
ca-í		ca-ímos	
ca-íste		ca-ísteis	
ca-yó		ca-yeron	
Futuro	*Futuro*	*Futuro*	*Futuro*
ca-eré	ca-yere	ca-eremos	ca-yéremos
ca-erás	ca-yeres	ca-eréis	ca-yereis
ca-erá	ca-yere	ca-erán	ca-yeren
Potencial		*Potencial*	
ca-ería		ca-eríamos	
ca-erías		ca-eríais	
ca-ería		ca-erían	

Imperativo

Singular	*Plural*
(not used); no (not used)	caig-amos; no caig-amos
ca-e; no caig-as	ca-ed; no caig-áis
caig-a; no caig-a	caig-an; no caig-an

Make compound tenses by adding the past participle caído to pattern 83. Translation possibilities are at pattern 88. Conjugation tips are at pattern 90.

Pattern 21: z ➠ c before e to retain the s or th sound.
Cazar (caz-ar) (to hunt) is the pattern verb.
Present participle: caz-ando Past participle: caz-ado

21 cazar

Singular		Plural	
Indicativo	*Subjuntivo*	*Indicativo*	*Subjuntivo*
Presente	*Presente*	*Presente*	*Presente*
caz-o	cac-e	caz-amos	cac-emos
caz-as	cac-es	caz-áis	cac-éis
caz-a	cac-e	caz-an	cac-en
Imperfecto	*Imperfecto*	*Imperfecto*	*Imperfecto*
caz-aba	caz-ara OR caz-ase	caz-ábamos	caz-áramos OR caz-ásemos
caz-abas	caz-aras OR caz-ases	caz-abais	caz-arais OR caz-aseis
caz-aba	caz-ara OR caz-ase	caz-aban	caz-aran OR caz-asen
Pretérito		*Pretérito*	
cac-é		caz-amos	
caz-aste		caz-asteis	
caz-ó		caz-aron	
Futuro	*Futuro*	*Futuro*	*Futuro*
caz-aré	caz-are	caz-aremos	caz-áremos
caz-arás	caz-ares	caz-aréis	caz-areis
caz-ará	caz-are	caz-arán	caz-aren
Potencial		*Potencial*	
caz-aría		caz-aríamos	
caz-arías		caz-aríais	
caz-aría		caz-arían	

Imperativo

Singular	*Plural*
(not used); no (not used)	cac-emos; no cac-emos
caz-a; no cac-es	caz-ad; no cac-éis
cac-e; no cac-e	cac-en; no cac-en

Make compound tenses by adding the past participle cazado to pattern 83.
Translation possibilities are at pattern 88. Conjugation tips are at pattern 89.

22 cocer

Pattern 22: o ➠ ue when stressed, c ➠ z before a or o.
Cocer (coc-er) (to cook, boil) is the pattern verb.
Present participle: coc-iendo   Past participle: coc-ido

Singular		Plural	
Indicativo	*Subjuntivo*	*Indicativo*	*Subjuntivo*
Presente	*Presente*	*Presente*	*Presente*
cuez-o	cuez-a	coc-emos	coz-amos
cuec-es	cuez-as	coc-éis	coz-áis
cuec-e	cuez-a	cuec-en	cuez-an
Imperfecto	*Imperfecto*	*Imperfecto*	*Imperfecto*
coc-ía	coc-iera OR coc-iese	coc-íamos	coc-iéramos OR coc-iésemos
coc-ías	coc-ieras OR coc-ieses	coc-íais	coc-ierais OR coc-ieseis
coc-ía	coc-iera OR coc-iese	coc-ían	coc-ieran OR coc-iesen
Pretérito		*Pretérito*	
coc-í		coc-imos	
coc-iste		coc-isteis	
coc-ió		coc-ieron	
Futuro	*Futuro*	*Futuro*	*Futuro*
coc-eré	coc-iere	coc-eremos	coc-iéremos
coc-erás	coc-ieres	coc-eréis	coc-iereis
coc-erá	coc-iere	coc-erán	coc-ieren
Potencial		*Potencial*	
coc-ería		coc-eríamos	
coc-erías		coc-eríais	
coc-ería		coc-erían	

Imperativo

Singular	Plural
(not used); no (not used)	coz-amos; no coz-amos
cuec-e; no cuez-as	coc-ed; no coz-áis
cuez-a; no cuez-a	cuez-an; no cuez-an

Make compound tenses by adding the past participle cocido to pattern 83.
Translation possibilities are at pattern 88. Conjugation tips are at pattern 90.

Pattern 23: g ➠ j before a or o to retain the ha sound.
Coger (cog-er) (to catch, gather, collect) is the pattern verb.
Present participle: cog-iendo Past participle: cog-ido

23 coger

Singular		Plural	
Indicativo	*Subjuntivo*	*Indicativo*	*Subjuntivo*
Presente	*Presente*	*Presente*	*Presente*
coj-o	coj-a	cog-emos	coj-amos
cog-es	coj-as	cog-éis	coj-áis
cog-e	coj-a	cog-en	coj-an
Imperfecto	*Imperfecto*	*Imperfecto*	*Imperfecto*
cog-ía	cog-iera OR cog-iese	cog-íamos	cog-iéramos OR cog-iésemos
cog-ías	cog-ieras OR cog-ieses	cog-íais	cog-ierais OR cog-ieseis
cog-ía	cog-iera OR cog-iese	cog-ían	cog-ieran OR cog-iesen
Pretérito		*Pretérito*	
cog-í		cog-imos	
cog-iste		cog-isteis	
cog-ió		cog-ieron	
Futuro	*Futuro*	*Futuro*	*Futuro*
cog-eré	cog-iere	cog-eremos	cog-iéremos
cog-erás	cog-ieres	cog-eréis	cog-iereis
cog-erá	cog-iere	cog-erán	cog-ieren
Potencial		*Potencial*	
cog-ería		cog-eríamos	
cog-erías		cog-eríais	
cog-ería		cog-erían	

Imperativo

Singular	*Plural*
(not used); no (not used)	coj-amos; no coj-amos
cog-e; no coj-as	cog-ed; no coj-áis
coj-a; no coj-a	coj-an; no coj-an

Make compound tenses by adding the past participle cogido to pattern 83.
Translation possibilities are at pattern 88. Conjugation tips are at pattern 90.

24 colgar

Pattern 24: o ➠ ue when stressed, g ➠ gu before e.
Colgar (colg-ar) (to hang, to drape) is the pattern verb.
Present participle: colg-ando Past participle: colg-ado

Singular		*Plural*	
Indicativo	*Subjuntivo*	*Indicativo*	*Subjuntivo*
Presente	*Presente*	*Presente*	*Presente*
cuelg-o	cuelgu-e	colg-amos	colgu-emos
cuelg-as	cuelgu-es	colg-áis	colgu-éis
cuelg-a	cuelgu-e	cuelg-an	cuelgu-en
Imperfecto	*Imperfecto*	*Imperfecto*	*Imperfecto*
colg-aba	colg-ara OR colg-ase	colg-ábamos	colg-áramos OR colg-ásemos
colg-abas	colg-aras OR colg-ases	colg-abais	colg-arais OR colg-aseis
colg-aba	colg-ara OR colg-ase	colg-aban	colg-aran OR colg-asen
Pretérito		*Pretérito*	
colgu-é		colg-amos	
colg-aste		colg-asteis	
colg-ó		colg-aron	
Futuro	*Futuro*	*Futuro*	*Futuro*
colg-aré	colg-are	colg-aremos	colg-áremos
colg-arás	colg-ares	colg-aréis	colg-areis
colg-ará	colg-are	colg-arán	colg-aren
Potencial		*Potencial*	
colg-aría		colg-aríamos	
colg-arías		colg-aríais	
colg-aría		colg-arían	

Imperativo

Singular	*Plural*
(not used); no (not used)	colgu-emos; no colgu-emos
cuelg-a; no cuelgu-es	colg-ad; no colgu-éis
cuelgu-e; no cuelgu-e	cuelgu-en; no cuelgu-en

Make compound tenses by adding the past participle colgado to pattern 83.
Translation possibilities are at pattern 88. Conjugation tips are at pattern 89.

Pattern 25: o ➠ ue when stressed.
Contar (cont-ar) (to count) is the pattern verb.
Present participle: cont-ando   Past participle: cont-ado

25 contar

Singular		Plural	
Indicativo	*Subjuntivo*	*Indicativo*	*Subjuntivo*
Presente	*Presente*	*Presente*	*Presente*
cuent-o	cuent-e	cont-amos	cont-emos
cuent-as	cuent-es	cont-áis	cont-éis
cuent-a	cuent-e	cuent-an	cuent-en
Imperfecto	*Imperfecto*	*Imperfecto*	*Imperfecto*
cont-aba	cont-ara OR cont-ase	cont-ábamos	cont-áramos OR cont-ásemos
cont-abas	cont-aras OR cont-ases	cont-abais	cont-arais OR cont-aseis
cont-aba	cont-ara OR cont-ase	cont-aban	cont-aran OR cont-asen
Pretérito		*Pretérito*	
cont-é		cont-amos	
cont-aste		cont-asteis	
cont-ó		cont-aron	
Futuro	*Futuro*	*Futuro*	*Futuro*
cont-aré	cont-are	cont-aremos	cont-áremos
cont-arás	cont-ares	cont-aréis	cont-areis
cont-ará	cont-are	cont-arán	cont-aren
Potencial		*Potencial*	
cont-aría		cont-aríamos	
cont-arías		cont-aríais	
cont-aría		cont-arían	

Imperativo

Singular	*Plural*
(not used); no (not used)	cont-emos; no cont-emos
cuent-a; no cuent-es	cont-ad; no cont-éis
cuent-e; no cuent-e	cuent-en; no cuent-en

Make compound tenses by adding the past participle contado to pattern 83.
Translation possibilities are at pattern 88. Conjugation tips are at pattern 89.

26 creer

Pattern 26: i ➠ y or í.
Creer (cre-er) (to believe) is the pattern verb.
Present participle: cre-yendo Past participle: cre-ído

Singular		Plural	
Indicativo	*Subjuntivo*	*Indicativo*	*Subjuntivo*
Presente	*Presente*	*Presente*	*Presente*
cre-o	cre-a	cre-emos	cre-amos
cre-es	cre-as	cre-éis	cre-áis
cre-e	cre-a	cre-en	cre-an
Imperfecto	*Imperfecto*	*Imperfecto*	*Imperfecto*
cre-ía	cre-yera OR cre-yese	cre-íamos	cre-yéramos OR cre-yésemos
cre-ías	cre-yeras OR cre-yeses	cre-íais	cre-yerais OR cre-yeseis
cre-ía	cre-yera OR cre-yese	cre-ían	cre-yeran OR cre-yesen
Pretérito		*Pretérito*	
cre-í		cre-ímos	
cre-íste		cre-ísteis	
cre-yó		cre-yeron	
Futuro	*Futuro*	*Futuro*	*Futuro*
cre-eré	cre-yere	cre-eremos	cre-yéremos
cre-erás	cre-yeres	cre-eréis	cre-yereis
cre-erá	cre-yere	cre-erán	cre-yeren
Potencial		*Potencial*	
cre-ería		cre-eríamos	
cre-erías		cre-eríais	
cre-ería		cre-erían	

Imperativo

Singular	Plural
(not used); no (not used)	cre-amos; no cre-amos
cre-e; no cre-as	cre-ed; no cre-áis
cre-a; no cre-a	cre-an; no cre-an

Make compound tenses by adding the past participle creído to pattern 83.
Translation possibilities are at pattern 88. Conjugation tips are at pattern 90.

Pattern 27: a ➠ i or ie, á ➠ a, e ➠ é, é ➠ e or í, ó ➠ io, y is added.
Dar (d-ar) (to give, cause, yield) is the pattern verb.
Present participle: d-ando   Past participle: d-ado

27 dar

Singular		*Plural*	
Indicativo	*Subjuntivo*	*Indicativo*	*Subjuntivo*
Presente	*Presente*	*Presente*	*Presente*
d-oy	d-é	d-amos	d-emos
d-as	d-es	d-ais	d-eis
d-a	d-é	d-an	d-en
Imperfecto	*Imperfecto*	*Imperfecto*	*Imperfecto*
d-aba	d-iera OR d-iese	d-ábamos	d-iéramos OR d-iésemos
d-abas	d-ieras OR d-ieses	d-abais	d-ierais OR d-ieseis
d-aba	d-iera OR d-iese	d-aban	d-ieran OR d-iesen
Pretérito		*Pretérito*	
d-í		d-imos	
d-iste		d-istems	
d-io		d-ieron	
Futuro	*Futuro*	*Futuro*	*Futuro*
d-aré	d-iere	d-aremos	d-iéremos
d-arás	d-ieres	d-aréis	d-iereis
d-ará	d-iere	d-arán	d-ieren
Potencial		*Potencial*	
d-aría		d-aríamos	
d-arías		d-aríais	
d-aría		d-arían	

Imperativo

Singular	*Plural*
(not used); no (not used)	d-emos; no d-emos
d-a; no d-es	d-ad; no d-eis
d-é; no d-é	d-en; no d-en

Make compound tenses by adding the past participle dado to pattern 83.
Translation possibilities are at pattern 88. Conjugation tips are at pattern 89.

28 decir

Pattern 28: e ➠ i, c ➠ g or j, plus other changes.
Decir (dec-ir) (to say, tell, talk) is the pattern verb.
Present participle: dic-iendo Past participle: dic-ho

Singular		Plural	
Indicativo	*Subjuntivo*	*Indicativo*	*Subjuntivo*
Presente	*Presente*	*Presente*	*Presente*
dig-o	dig-a	dec-imos	dig-amos
dic-es	dig-as	dec-ís	dig-áis
dic-e	dig-a	dic-en	dig-an
Imperfecto	*Imperfecto*	*Imperfecto*	*Imperfecto*
dec-ía	dij-era OR dij-ese	dec-íamos	dij-éramos OR dij-ésemos
dec-ías	dij-eras OR dij-eses	dec-íais	dij-erais OR dij-eseis
dec-ía	dij-era OR dij-ese	dec-ían	dij-eran OR dij-esen
Pretérito		*Pretérito*	
dij-e		dij-imos	
dij-iste		dij-isteis	
dij-o		dij-eron	
Futuro	*Futuro*	*Futuro*	*Futuro*
d-iré	dij-ere	d-iremos	dij-éremos
d-irás	dij-eres	d-iréis	dij-ereis
d-irá	dij-ere	d-irán	dij-eren
Potencial		*Potencial*	
d-iría		d-iríamos	
d-irías		d-iríais	
d-iría		d-irían	

Imperativo

Singular	Plural
(not used); no (not used)	dig-amos; no dig-amos
d-i; no dig-as	dec-id; no dig-áis
dig-a; no dig-a	dig-an; no dig-an

Make compound tenses by adding the past participle dicho to pattern 83.
Translation possibilities are at pattern 88. Conjugation tips are at pattern 91.

Pattern 29: qu ➟ c before a or o to retain the k sound.
Delinquir (delinqu-ir) (to be delinquent) is the pattern verb.
Present part.: delinqu-iendo   Past part.: delinqu-ido

29 delinquir

Singular		Plural	
Indicativo	*Subjuntivo*	*Indicativo*	*Subjuntivo*
Presente	*Presente*	*Presente*	*Presente*
delinc-o	delinc-a	delinqu-imos	delinc-amos
delinqu-es	delinc-as	delinqu-ís	delinc-áis
delinqu-e	delinc-a	delinqu-en	delinc-an
Imperfecto	*Imperfecto*	*Imperfecto*	*Imperfecto*
delinqu-ía	delinqu-iera OR delinqu-iese	delinqu-íamos	delinqu-iéramos OR delinqu-iésemos
delinqu-ías	delinqu-ieras OR delinqu-ieses	delinqu-íais	delinqu-ierais OR delinqu-ieseis
delinqu-ía	delinqu-iera OR delinqu-iese	delinqu-ían	delinqu-ieran OR delinqu-iesen
Pretérito		*Pretérito*	
delinqu-í		delinqu-imos	
delinqu-iste		delinqu-isteis	
delinqu-ió		delinqu-ieron	
Futuro	*Futuro*	*Futuro*	*Futuro*
delinqu-iré	delinqu-iere	delinqu-iremos	delinqu-iéremos
delinqu-irás	delinqu-ieres	delinqu-iréis	delinqu-iereis
delinqu-irá	delinqu-iere	delinqu-irán	delinqu-ieren
Potencial		*Potencial*	
delinqu-iría		delinqu-iríamos	
delinqu-irías		delinqu-iríais	
delinqu-iría		delinqu-irían	

Imperativo

Singular	*Plural*
(not used); no (not used)	delinc-amos; no delinc-amos
delinqu-e; no delinc-as	delinqu-id; no delinc-áis
delinc-a; no delinc-a	delinc-an; no delinc-an

Make compound tenses by adding the past participle delinquido to pattern 83. Translation possibilities are at pattern 88. Conjugation tips are at pattern 91.

30 distinguir

Pattern 30: gu ➠ g before a or o to retain the hard g sound. Distinguir (distingu-ir) (to distinguish) is the pattern verb.
Present part.: distingu-iendo Past part.: distingu-ido

Singular		Plural	
Indicativo	*Subjuntivo*	*Indicativo*	*Subjuntivo*
Presente	*Presente*	*Presente*	*Presente*
disting-o	disting-a	distingu-imos	disting-amos
distingu-es	disting-as	distingu-ís	disting-áis
distingu-e	disting-a	distingu-en	disting-an
Imperfecto	*Imperfecto*	*Imperfecto*	*Imperfecto*
distingu-ía	distingu-iera OR distingu-iese	distingu-íamos	distingu-iéramos OR distingu-iésemos
distingu-ías	distingu-ieras OR distingu-ieses	distingu-íais	distingu-ierais OR distingu-ieseis
distingu-ía	distingu-iera OR distingu-iese	distingu-ían	distingu-ieran OR distingu-iesen
Pretérito		*Pretérito*	
distingu-í		distingu-imos	
distingu-iste		distingu-isteis	
distingu-ió		distingu-ieron	
Futuro	*Futuro*	*Futuro*	*Futuro*
distingu-iré	distingu-iere	distingu-iremos	distingu-iéremos
distingu-irás	distingu-ieres	distingu-iréis	distingu-iereis
distingu-irá	distingu-iere	distingu-irán	distingu-ieren
Potencial		*Potencial*	
distingu-iría		distingu-iríamos	
distingu-irías		distingu-iríais	
distingu-iría		distingu-irían	

Imperativo

Singular	Plural
(not used); no (not used)	disting-amos; no disting-amos
distingu-e; no disting-as	distingu-id; no disting-áis
disting-a; no disting-a	disting-an; no disting-an

Make compound tenses by adding the past participle distinguido to pattern 83. Translation possibilities are at pattern 88. Conjugation tips are at pattern 91.

Pattern 31: o ➡ ue or u.
Dormir (dorm-ir) (to sleep) is the pattern verb.
Present participle: durm-iendo Past participle: dorm-ido

31 dormir

Singular		Plural	
Indicativo	*Subjuntivo*	*Indicativo*	*Subjuntivo*
Presente	*Presente*	*Presente*	*Presente*
duerm-o	duerm-a	dorm-imos	durm-amos
duerm-es	duerm-as	dorm-ís	durm-áis
duerm-e	duerm-a	duerm-en	duerm-an
Imperfecto	*Imperfecto*	*Imperfecto*	*Imperfecto*
dorm-ía	durm-iera OR durm-iese	dorm-íamos	durm-iéramos OR durm-iésemos
dorm-ías	durm-ieras OR durm-ieses	dorm-íais	durm-ierais OR durm-ieseis
dorm-ía	durm-iera OR durm-iese	dorm-ían	durm-ieran OR durm-iesen
Pretérito		*Pretérito*	
dorm-í		dorm-imos	
dorm-iste		dom-isteis	
durm-ió		durm-ieron	
Futuro	*Futuro*	*Futuro*	*Futuro*
dorm-iré	durm-iere	dorm-iremos	durm-iéremos
dorm-irás	durm-ieres	dorm-iréis	durm-iereis
dorm-irá	durm-iere	dorm-irán	durm-ieren
Potencial		*Potencial*	
dorm-iría		dorm-iríamos	
dorm-irías		dorm-iríais	
dorm-iría		dorm-irían	

Imperativo

Singular	*Plural*
(not used); no (not used)	durm-amos; no durm-amos
duerm-e; no duerm-as	dorm-id; no durm-áis
duerm-a; no duerm-a	duerm-an; no duerm-an

Make compound tenses by adding the past participle dormido to pattern 83.
Translation possibilities are at pattern 88. Conjugation tips are at pattern 91.

32 elegir

Pattern 32: e ➠ i, g ➠ j, plus past participle electo.
Elegir (eleg-ir) (to elect) is the pattern verb.
Present participle: elig-iendo Past participle: eleg-ido

Singular		Plural	
Indicativo	*Subjuntivo*	*Indicativo*	*Subjuntivo*
Presente	*Presente*	*Presente*	*Presente*
elij-o	elij-a	eleg-imos	elij-amos
elig-es	elij-as	eleg-ís	elij-áis
elig-e	elij-a	elig-en	elij-an
Imperfecto	*Imperfecto*	*Imperfecto*	*Imperfecto*
eleg-ía	elig-iera OR elig-iese	eleg-íamos	elig-iéramos OR elig-iésemos
eleg-ías	elig-ieras OR elig-ieses	eleg-íais	elig-ierais OR elig-ieseis
eleg-ía	elig-iera OR elig-iese	eleg-ían	elig-ieran OR elig-iesen
Pretérito		*Pretérito*	
eleg-í		eleg-imos	
eleg-iste		eleg-isteis	
elig-ió		elig-ieron	
Futuro	*Futuro*	*Futuro*	*Futuro*
eleg-iré	elig-iere	eleg-iremos	elig-iéremos
eleg-irás	elig-ieres	eleg-iréis	elig-iereis
eleg-irá	elig-iere	eleg-irán	elig-ieren
Potencial		*Potencial*	
eleg-iría		eleg-iríamos	
eleg-irías		eleg-iríais	
eleg-iría		eleg-irían	

Imperativo

Singular	Plural
(not used); no (not used)	elij-amos; no elij-amos
elig-e; no elij-as	eleg-id; no elij-áis
elij-a; no elij-a	elij-an; no elij-an

Make compound tenses by adding the past participle elegido to pattern 83.
Translation possibilities are at pattern 88. Conjugation tips are at pattern 91.

Pattern 33: Some conjugations customarily are not used.
Embaír (emba-ír) (to deceive, trick) is the pattern verb.
Present participle: emba-yendo   Past participle: emba-ído

33 embaír

Singular		Plural	
Indicativo	*Subjuntivo*	*Indicativo*	*Subjuntivo*
Presente	*Presente*	*Presente*	*Presente*
(not used)	(not used)	emba-ímos	(not used)
(not used)	(not used)	emba-ís	(not used)
(not used)	(not used)	(not used)	(not used)
Imperfecto	*Imperfecto*	*Imperfecto*	*Imperfecto*
emba-ía	emba-yera OR emba-yese	emba-íamos	emba-yéramos OR emba-yésemos
emba-ías	emba-yeras OR emba-yeses	emba-íais	emba-yerais OR emba-yeseis
emba-ía	emba-yera OR emba-yese	emba-ían	emba-yeran OR emba-yesen
Pretérito		*Pretérito*	
emba-í		emba-ímos	
emba-íste		emba-ísteis	
emba-yó		emba-yeron	
Futuro	*Futuro*	*Futuro*	*Futuro*
emba-iré	emba-yere	emba-iremos	emba-yéremos
emba-irás	emba-yeres	emba-iréis	emba-yereis
emba-irá	emba-yere	emba-irán	emba-yeren
Potencial		*Potencial*	
emba-iría		emba-iríamos	
emba-irías		emba-iríais	
emba-iría		emba-irían	

Imperativo

Singular	*Plural*
(not used); no (not used)	(not used); no (not used)
(not used); no (not used)	emba-id; no (not used)
(not used); no (not used)	(not used); no (not used)

Make compound tenses by adding the past participle embaído to pattern 83.
Translation possibilities are at pattern 88. Conjugation tips are at pattern 91.

34 empezar

Pattern 34: e in stem ➠ ie when stressed, z ➠ c before e.
Empezar (empez-ar) (to begin) is the pattern verb.
Present participle: empez-ando   Past participle: empez-ado

Singular		Plural	
Indicativo	*Subjuntivo*	*Indicativo*	*Subjuntivo*
Presente	*Presente*	*Presente*	*Presente*
empiez-o	empiec-e	empez-amos	empec-emos
empiez-as	empiec-es	empez-áis	empec-éis
empiez-a	empiec-e	empiez-an	empiec-en
Imperfecto	*Imperfecto*	*Imperfecto*	*Imperfecto*
empez-aba	empez-ara OR empez-ase	empez-ábamos	empez-áramos OR empez-ásemos
empez-abas	empez-aras OR empez-ases	empez-abais	empez-arais OR empez-aseis
empez-aba	empez-ara OR empez-ase	empez-aban	empez-aran OR empez-asen
Pretérito		*Pretérito*	
empec-é		empez-amos	
empez-aste		empez-asteis	
empez-ó		empez-aron	
Futuro	*Futuro*	*Futuro*	*Futuro*
empez-aré	empez-are	empez-aremos	empez-áremos
empez-arás	empez-ares	empez-aréis	empez-areis
empez-ará	empez-are	empez-arán	empez-aren
Potencial		*Potencial*	
empez-aría		empez-aríamos	
empez-arías		empez-aríais	
empez-aría		empez-arían	

Imperativo

Singular	Plural
(not used); no (not used)	empec-emos; no empec-emos
empiez-a; no empiec-es	empez-ad; no empec-éis
empiec-e; no empice-e	empiec-en; no empiec-en

Make compound tenses by adding the past participle empezado to pattern 83.
Translation possibilities are at pattern 88. Conjugation tips are at pattern 89.

Pattern 35: i ➠ í when stressed, z ➠ c before e.
Enraizar (enraiz-ar) (to grow roots, take root) is the pattern verb.
Present participle: enraiz-ando Past participle: enraiz-ado

35 enraizar

Singular		Plural	
Indicativo	*Subjuntivo*	*Indicativo*	*Subjuntivo*
Presente	*Presente*	*Presente*	*Presente*
enraíz-o	enraíc-e	enraiz-amos	enraic-emos
enraíz-as	enraíc-es	enraiz-áis	enraic-éis
enraíz-a	enraíc-e	enraíz-an	enraíc-en
Imperfecto	*Imperfecto*	*Imperfecto*	*Imperfecto*
enraiz-aba	enraiz-ara OR enraiz-ase	enraiz-ábamos	enraiz-áramos OR enraiz-ásemos
enraiz-abas	enraiz-aras OR enraiz-ases	enraiz-abais	enraiz-arais OR enraiz-aseis
enraiz-aba	enraiz-ara OR enraiz-ase	enraiz-aban	enraiz-aran OR enraiz-asen
Pretérito		*Pretérito*	
enraic-é		enraiz-amos	
enraiz-aste		enraiz-asteis	
enraiz-ó		enraiz-aron	
Futuro	*Futuro*	*Futuro*	*Futuro*
enraiz-aré	enraiz-are	enraiz-aremos	enraiz-áremos
enraiz-arás	enraiz-ares	enraiz-aréis	enraiz-areis
enraiz-ará	enraiz-are	enraiz-arán	enraiz-aren
Potencial		*Potencial*	
enraiz-aría		enraiz-aríamos	
enraiz-arías		enraiz-aríais	
enraiz-aría		enraiz-arían	

Imperativo

Singular	*Plural*
(not used); no (not used)	enraic-emos; no enraic-emos
enraíz-a; no enraíc-es	enraiz-ad; no enraic-éis
enraíc-e; no enraíc-e	enraíc-en; no enraíc-en

Make compound tenses by adding the past participle enraizado to pattern 83.
Translation possibilities are at pattern 88. Conjugation tips are at pattern 89.

36 erguir

Pattern 36: e ➠ i, gu ➠ g, y is added.
Erguir (ergu-ir) (to be erect) is the pattern verb.
Present participle: irgu-iendo   Past participle: ergu-ido

Singular		Plural	
Indicativo	*Subjuntivo*	*Indicativo*	*Subjuntivo*
Presente	*Presente*	*Presente*	*Presente*
irg-o, yerg-o	irg-a, yerg-a	ergu-imos	irg-amos, yerg-amos
irgu-es, yergu-es	irg-as, yerg-as	ergu-ís	irg-áis, yerg-áis
irgu-e, yergu-e	irg-a, yerg-a	irgu-en, yergu-en	irg-an, yerg-an
Imperfecto	*Imperfecto*	*Imperfecto*	*Imperfecto*
ergu-ía	irgu-iera OR irgu-iese	ergu-íamos	irgu-iéramos OR irgu-iésemos
ergu-ías	irgu-ieras OR irgu-ieses	ergu-íais	irgu-ierais OR irgu-ieseis
ergu-ía	irgu-iera OR irgu-iese	ergu-ían	irgu-ieran OR irgu-iesen
Pretérito		*Pretérito*	
ergu-í		ergu-imos	
ergu-iste		ergu-isteis	
irgu-ió		irgu-ieron	
Futuro	*Futuro*	*Futuro*	*Futuro*
ergu-iré	irgu-iere	ergu-iremos	irgu-iéremos
ergu-irás	irgu-ieres	ergu-iréis	irgu-iereis
ergu-irá	irgu-iere	ergu-irán	irgu-ieren
Potencial		*Potencial*	
ergu-iría		ergu-iríamos	
ergu-irías		ergu-iríais	
ergu-iría		ergu-irían	

Imperativo

Singular	Plural
(not used); no (not used)	irg-amos, yerg-amos; no irg-amos, no yerg-amos
irgu-e, yergu-e; no irg-as, no yerg-as	ergu-id; no irg-áis, no yerg-áis
irg-a, yerg-a; no irg-a, no yerg-a	irg-an, yerg-an; no irg-an, no yerg-an

Make compound tenses by adding the past participle erguido to pattern 83.
Translation possibilities are at pattern 88. Conjugation tips are at pattern 91.

Pattern 37: y is added before e in stem when e is stressed.
Errar (err-ar) (to be wrong or mistaken) is the pattern verb.
Present participle: err-ando   Past participle: err-ado

37 errar

Singular		Plural	
Indicativo	*Subjuntivo*	*Indicativo*	*Subjuntivo*
Presente	*Presente*	*Presente*	*Presente*
yerr-o	yerr-e	err-amos	err-emos
yerr-as	yerr-es	err-áis	err-éis
yerr-a	yerr-e	yerr-an	yerr-en
Imperfecto	*Imperfecto*	*Imperfecto*	*Imperfecto*
err-aba	err-ara OR err-ase	err-ábamos	err-áramos OR err-ásemos
err-abas	err-aras OR err-ases	err-abais	err-arais OR err-aseis
err-aba	err-ara OR err-ase	err-aban	err-aran OR err-asen
Pretérito		*Pretérito*	
err-é		err-amos	
err-aste		err-asteis	
err-ó		err-aron	
Futuro	*Futuro*	*Futuro*	*Futuro*
err-aré	err-are	err-aremos	err-áremos
err-arás	err-ares	err-aréis	err-areis
err-ará	err-are	err-arán	err-aren
Potencial		*Potencial*	
err-aría		err-aríamos	
err-arías		err-aríais	
err-aría		err-arían	

Imperativo

Singular	*Plural*
(not used); no (not used)	err-emos; no err-emos
yerr-a; no yerr-es	err-ad; no err-éis
yerr-e; no yerr-e	yerr-en; no yerr-en

Make compound tenses by adding the past participle errado to pattern 83.
Translation possibilities are at pattern 88. Conjugation tips are at pattern 89.

38 estar

Pattern 38: a ➟ i or ie, é ➟ e, ó ➟ o, add y, add uv, + accents.
Estar (est-ar) (to be, to stand) (an auxiliary verb) is the pattern verb.
Present participle: est-ando   Past participle: est-ado

Singular		*Plural*	
Indicativo	*Subjuntivo*	*Indicativo*	*Subjuntivo*
Presente	*Presente*	*Presente*	*Presente*
est-oy	est-é	est-amos	est-emos
est-ás	est-és	est-áis	est-éis
est-á	est-é	est-án	est-én
Imperfecto	*Imperfecto*	*Imperfecto*	*Imperfecto*
est-aba	estuv-iera OR estuv-iese	est-ábamos	estuv-iéramos OR estuv-iésemos
est-abas	estuv-ieras OR estuv-ieses	est-abais	estuv-ierais OR estuv-ieseis
est-aba	estuv-iera OR estuv-iese	est-aban	estuv-ieran OR estuv-iesen
Pretérito		*Pretérito*	
estuv-e		estuv-imos	
estuv-iste		estuv-isteis	
estuv-o		estuv-ieron	
Futuro	*Futuro*	*Futuro*	*Futuro*
est-aré	estuv-iere	est-aremos	estuv-iéremos
est-arás	estuv-ieres	est-aréis	estuv-iereis
est-ará	estuv-iere	est-arán	estuv-ieren
Potencial		*Potencial*	
est-aría		est-aríamos	
est-arías		est-aríais	
est-aría		est-arían	

Imperativo

Singular	*Plural*
(not used); no (not used)	est-emos; no est-emos
est-á; no est-és	est-ad; no est-éis
est-é; no est-é	est-én; no est-én

Make compound tenses by adding the past participle estado to pattern 83.
Translation possibilities are at pattern 88. Conjugation tips are at pattern 89.

Pattern 39: o ➠ ue when stressed, z ➠ c before e.
Forzar (forz-ar) (to force) is the pattern verb.
Present participle: forz-ando   Past participle: forz-ado

39 forzar

Singular		Plural	
Indicativo	*Subjuntivo*	*Indicativo*	*Subjuntivo*
Presente	*Presente*	*Presente*	*Presente*
fuerz-o	fuerc-e	forz-amos	forc-emos
fuerz-as	fuerc-es	forz-áis	forc-éis
fuerz-a	fuerc-e	fuerz-an	fuerc-en
Imperfecto	*Imperfecto*	*Imperfecto*	*Imperfecto*
forz-aba	forz-ara OR forz-ase	forz-ábamos	forz-áramos OR forz-ásemos
forz-abas	forz-aras OR forz-ases	forz-abais	forz-arais OR forz-aseis
forz-aba	forz-ara OR forz-ase	forz-aban	forz-aran OR forz-asen
Pretérito		*Pretérito*	
forc-é		forz-amos	
forz-aste		forz-asteis	
forz-ó		forz-aron	
Futuro	*Futuro*	*Futuro*	*Futuro*
forz-aré	forz-are	forz-aremos	forz-áremos
forz-arás	forz-ares	forz-aréis	forz-areis
forz-ará	forz-are	forz-arán	forz-aren
Potencial		*Potencial*	
forz-aría		forz-aríamos	
forz-arías		forz-aríais	
forz-aría		forz-arían	

Imperativo

Singular	*Plural*
(not used); no (not used)	forc-emos; no forc-emos
fuerz-a; no fuerc-es	forz-ad; no forc-éis
fuerc-e; no fuerc-e	fuerc-en; no fuerc-en

Make compound tenses by adding the past participle forzado at pattern 83. Translation possibilities are at pattern 88. Conjugation tips are at pattern 89.

40 haber

Pattern 40: a ➠ e or u, e ➠ a, o ➠ e, b ➠ y, delete a, e and b.
Haber (hab-er) (to have) (an auxilary verb) is the pattern verb.
Present participle: hab-iendo   Past participle: hab-ido

Singular		Plural	
Indicativo	*Subjuntivo*	*Indicativo*	*Subjuntivo*
Presente	*Presente*	*Presente*	*Presente*
h-e	hay-a	h-emos	hay-amos
h-as	hay-as	hab-éis	hay-áis
h-a, ha-y[1]	hay-a	ha-n	hay-an
Imperfecto	*Imperfecto*	*Imperfecto*	*Imperfecto*
hab-ía	hub-iera OR hub-iese	hab-íamos	hub-iéramos OR hub-iésemos
hab-ías	hub-ieras OR hub-ieses	hab-íais	hub-ierais OR hub-ieseis
hab-ía	hub-iera OR hub-iese	hab-ían	hub-ieran OR hub-iesen
Pretérito		*Pretérito*	
hub-e		hub-imos	
hub-iste		hub-isteis	
hub-o		hub-ieron	
Futuro	*Futuro*	*Futuro*	*Futuro*
hab-ré	hub-iere	hab-remos	hub-iéremos
hab-rás	hub-ieres	hab-réis	hub-iereis
hab-rá	hub-iere	hab-rán	hub-ieren
Potencial		*Potencial*	
hab-ría		hab-ríamos	
hab-rías		hab-ríais	
hab-ría		hab-rían	

Imperativo

Singular	*Plural*
(not used); no (not used)	hay-amos; no hay-amos
h-é or h-e; no hay-as	hab-ed; no hay-áis
hay-a; no hay-a	hay-an; no hay-an

Make compound tenses by adding the past participle habido to pattern 83.
Translation possibilities are at pattern 88. Conjugation tips are at pattern 90.
[1]When using the impersonal, the third person singular form is hay.

Pattern 41: a ➠ i, c ➠ g or z, delete c or e, irregular past participle.
Hacer (hac-er) (to make, to do) is the pattern verb.
Present participle: hac-iendo Past participle: hec-ho

41 hacer

Singular		Plural	
Indicativo	*Subjuntivo*	*Indicativo*	*Subjuntivo*
Presente	*Presente*	*Presente*	*Presente*
hag-o	hag-a	hac-emos	hag-amos
hac-es	hag-as	hac-éis	hag-áis
hac-e	hag-a	hac-en	hag-an
Imperfecto	*Imperfecto*	*Imperfecto*	*Imperfecto*
hac-ía	hic-iera OR hic-iese	hac-íamos	hic-iéramos OR hic-iésemos
hac-ías	hic-ieras OR hic-ieses	hac-íais	hic-ierais OR hic-ieseis
hac-ía	hic-iera OR hic-iese	hac-ían	hic-ieran OR hic-iesen
Pretérito		*Pretérito*	
hic-e		hic-imos	
hic-iste		hic-isteis	
hiz-o		hic-ieron	
Futuro	*Futuro*	*Futuro*	*Futuro*
ha-ré	hic-iere	ha-remos	hic-iéremos
ha-rás	hic-ieres	ha-réis	hic-iereis
ha-rá	hic-iere	ha-rán	hic-ieren
Potencial		*Potencial*	
ha-ría		ha-ríamos	
ha-rías		ha-ríais	
ha-ría		ha-rían	

Imperativo

Singular	*Plural*
(not used); no (not used)	hag-amos; no hag-amos
haz; no hag-as	hac-ed; no hag-áis
hag-a; no hag-a	hag-an; no hag-an

Make compound tenses by adding the past participle hecho to pattern 83.
Translation possibilities are at pattern 88. Conjugation tips are at pattern 90.

42 huir

Pattern 42: i ➠ y, y is added.
Huir (hu-ir) (to flee, avoid, shun) is the pattern verb.
Present participle: hu-yendo Past participle: hu-ido

Singular		Plural	
Indicativo	*Subjuntivo*	*Indicativo*	*Subjuntivo*
Presente	*Presente*	*Presente*	*Presente*
huy-o	huy-a	hu-imos	huy-amos
huy-es	huy-as	hu-ís	huy-áis
huy-e	huy-a	huy-en	huy-an
Imperfecto	*Imperfecto*	*Imperfecto*	*Imperfecto*
hu-ía	hu-yera OR hu-yese	hu-íamos	hu-yéramos OR hu-yésemos
hu-ías	hu-yeras OR hu-yeses	hu-íais	hu-yerais OR hu-yeseis
hu-ía	hu-yera OR hu-yese	hu-ían	hu-yeran OR hu-yesen
Pretérito		*Pretérito*	
hu-í		hu-imos	
hu-iste		hu-isteis	
hu-yó		hu-yeron	
Futuro	*Futuro*	*Futuro*	*Futuro*
hu-iré	hu-yere	hu-iremos	hu-yéremos
hu-irás	hu-yeres	hu-iréis	hu-yereis
hu-irá	hu-yere	hu-irán	hu-yeren
Potencial		*Potencial*	
hu-iría		hu-iríamos	
hu-irías		hu-iríais	
hu-iría		hu-irían	

Imperativo

Singular	Plural
(not used); no (not used)	huy-amos; no huy-amos
huy-e; no huy-as	hu-id; no huy-áis
huy-a; no huy-a	huy-an; no huy-an

Make compound tenses by adding the past participle huido to pattern 83.
Translation possibilities are at pattern 88. Conjugation tips are at pattern 91.

Pattern 43: v, va, vay, ib, and fu are roots, plus other changes.
Ir (ir) (to go) is the pattern verb.
Present participle: yendo   Past participle: ido

43
ir

Singular		Plural	
Indicativo	*Subjuntivo*	*Indicativo*	*Subjuntivo*
Presente	*Presente*	*Presente*	*Presente*
v-oy	vay-a	va-mos	vay-amos
v-as	vay-as	va-is	vay-áis
v-a	vay-a	va-n	vay-an
Imperfecto	*Imperfecto*	*Imperfecto*	*Imperfecto*
ib-a	fu-era OR fu-ese	íb-amos	fu-éramos OR fu-ésemos
ib-as	fu-eras OR fu-eses	ib-ais	fu-erais OR fu-eseis
ib-a	fu-era OR fu-ese	ib-an	fu-eran OR fu-esen
Pretérito		*Pretérito*	
fu-i		fu-imos	
fu-iste		fu-isteis	
fu-e		fu-eron	
Futuro	*Futuro*	*Futuro*	*Futuro*
iré	fu-ere	iremos	fu-éremos
irás	fu-eres	iréis	fu-ereis
irá	fu-ere	irán	fu-eren
Potencial		*Potencial*	
iría		iríamos	
irías		iríais	
iría		irían	

Imperativo

Singular	Plural
(not used); no (not used)	v-amos or vay-amos; no vay-amos
v-e; no vay-as	id; no vay-áis
vay-a; no vay-a	vay-an; no vay-an

Make compound tenses by adding the past participle ido to pattern 83.
Translation possibilities are at pattern 88. Conjugation tips are at pattern 91.

44 jugar

Pattern 44: u ➟ ue when stressed, g ➟ gu before e.
Jugar (jug-ar) (to play, gamble, risk) is the pattern verb.
Present participle: jug-ando   Past participle: jug-ado

Singular		Plural	
Indicativo	*Subjuntivo*	*Indicativo*	*Subjuntivo*
Presente	*Presente*	*Presente*	*Presente*
jueg-o	juegu-e	jug-amos	jugu-emos
jueg-as	juegu-es	jug-áis	jugu-éis
jueg-a	juegu-e	jueg-an	juegu-en
Imperfecto	*Imperfecto*	*Imperfecto*	*Imperfecto*
jug-aba	jug-ara OR jug-ase	jug-ábamos	jug-áramos OR jug-ásemos
jug-abas	jug-aras OR jug-ases	jug-abais	jug-arais OR jug-aseis
jug-aba	jug-ara OR jug-ase	jug-aban	jug-aran OR jug-asen
Pretérito		*Pretérito*	
jugu-é		jug-amos	
jug-aste		jug-asteis	
jug-ó		jug-aron	
Futuro	*Futuro*	*Futuro*	*Futuro*
jug-aré	jug-are	jug-aremos	jug-áremos
jug-arás	jug-ares	jug-aréis	jug-areis
jug-ará	jug-are	jug-arán	jug-aren
Potencial		*Potencial*	
jug-aría		jug-aríamos	
jug-arías		jug-aríais	
jug-aría		jug-arían	

Imperativo

Singular	*Plural*
(not used); no (not used)	jugu-emos; no jugu-emos
jueg-a; no juegu-es	jug-ad; no jugu-éis
juegu-e; no juegu-e	juegu-en; no juegu-en

Make compound tenses by adding the past participle jugado to pattern 83. Translation possibilities are at pattern 88. Conjugation tips are at pattern 89.

Pattern 45: Some conjugations customarily are not used.
Llover (llov-er) (to rain, leak) is the pattern verb.
Present participle: llov-iendo Past participle: llov-ido

45 llover

Singular		Plural	
Indicativo	*Subjuntivo*	*Indicativo*	*Subjuntivo*
Presente	*Presente*	*Presente*	*Presente*
(not used)	(not used)	(not used)	(not used)
(not used)	(not used)	(not used)	(not used)
lluev-e (or está lloviendo)	lluev-a	(not used)	(not used)
Imperfecto	*Imperfecto*	*Imperfecto*	*Imperfecto*
(not used)	(not used) OR (not used)	(not used)	(not used) OR (not used)
(not used)	(not used) OR (not used)	(not used)	(not used) OR (not used)
llov-ía (or estaba lloviendo)	llov-iera OR llov-iese	(not used)	(not used) OR (not used)
Pretérito		*Pretérito*	
(not used)		(not used)	
(not used)		(not used)	
llov-ió		(not used)	
Futuro	*Futuro*	*Futuro*	*Futuro*
(not used)	(not used)	(not used)	(not used)
(not used)	(not used)	(not used)	(not used)
llov-erá	(not used)	(not used)	(not used)
Potencial		*Potencial*	
(not used)		(not used)	
(not used)		(not used)	
llov-ería		(not used)	

Imperativo

Singular	Plural
(not used); no (not used)	(not used); no (not used)
(not used); no (not used)	(not used); no (not used)
¡Que lluev-a! (Let it rain!); no (not used)	(not used); no (not used)

Make compound tenses by adding the past participle llovido to pattern 83.
Translation possibilities are at pattern 88. Conjugation tips are at pattern 90.

46 mecer

Pattern 46: c ➠ z before a or o to retain the s or th sound.
Mecer (mec-er) (to rock, swing, stir) is the pattern verb.
Present participle: mec-iendo Past participle: mec-ido

Singular		Plural	
Indicativo	*Subjuntivo*	*Indicativo*	*Subjuntivo*
Presente	*Presente*	*Presente*	*Presente*
mez-o	mez-a	mec-emos	mez-amos
mec-es	mez-as	mec-éis	mez-áis
mec-e	mez-a	mec-en	mez-an
Imperfecto	*Imperfecto*	*Imperfecto*	*Imperfecto*
mec-ía	mec-iera OR mec-iese	mec-íamos	mec-iéramos OR mec-iésemos
mec-ías	mec-ieras OR mec-ieses	mec-íais	mec-ierais OR mec-ieseis
mec-ía	mec-iera OR mec-iese	mec-ían	mec-ieran OR mec-iesen
Pretérito		*Pretérito*	
mec-í		mec-imos	
mec-iste		mec-isteis	
mec-ió		mec-ieron	
Futuro	*Futuro*	*Futuro*	*Futuro*
mec-eré	mec-iere	mec-eremos	mec-iéremos
mec-erás	mec-ieres	mec-eréis	mec-iereis
mec-erá	mec-iere	mec-erán	mec-ieren
Potencial		*Potencial*	
mec-ería		mec-eríamos	
mec-erías		mec-eríais	
mec-ería		mec-erían	

Imperativo

Singular	*Plural*
(not used); no (not used)	mez-amos; no mez-amos
mec-e; no mez-as	mec-ed; no mez-áis
mez-a; no mez-a	mez-an; no mez-an

Make compound tenses by adding the past participle mecido to pattern 83.
Translation possibilities are at pattern 88. Conjugation tips are at pattern 90.

Pattern 47: o ➠ ue when stressed.
Mover (mov-er) (to move, stir, sway, use, abort) is the pattern verb.
Present participle: mov-iendo   Past participle: mov-ido

47 mover

Singular		*Plural*	
Indicativo	*Subjuntivo*	*Indicativo*	*Subjuntivo*
Presente	*Presente*	*Presente*	*Presente*
muev-o	muev-a	mov-emos	mov-amos
muev-es	muev-as	mov-éis	mov-áis
muev-e	muev-a	muev-en	muev-an
Imperfecto	*Imperfecto*	*Imperfecto*	*Imperfecto*
mov-ía	mov-iera OR mov-iese	mov-íamos	mov-iéramos OR mov-iésemos
mov-ías	mov-ieras OR mov-ieses	mov-íais	mov-ierais OR mov-ieseis
mov-ía	mov-iera OR mov-iese	mov-ían	mov-ieran OR mov-iesen
Pretérito		*Pretérito*	
mov-í		mov-imos	
mov-iste		mov-isteis	
mov-ió		mov-ieron	
Futuro	*Futuro*	*Futuro*	*Futuro*
mov-eré	mov-iere	mov-eremos	mov-iéremos
mov-erás	mov-ieres	mov-eréis	mov-iereis
mov-erá	mov-iere	mov-erán	mov-ieren
Potencial		*Potencial*	
mov-ería		mov-eríamos	
mov-erías		mov-eríais	
mov-ería		mov-erían	

Imperativo

Singular	*Plural*
(not used); no (not used)	mov-amos; no mov-amos
muev-e; no muev-as	mov-ed; no mov-áis
muev-a; no muev-a	muev-an; no muev-an

Make compound tenses by adding the past participle movido to pattern 83.
Translation possibilities are at pattern 88. Conjugation tips are at pattern 90.

48 nacer

Pattern 48: c ➠ zc before a or o.
Nacer (nac-er) (to be born, to bud) is the pattern verb.
Present participle: nac-iendo Past participle: nac-ido

Singular		Plural	
Indicativo	*Subjuntivo*	*Indicativo*	*Subjuntivo*
Presente	*Presente*	*Presente*	*Presente*
nazc-o	nazc-a	nac-emos	nazc-amos
nac-es	nazc-as	nac-éis	nazc-áis
nac-e	nazc-a	nac-en	nazc-an
Imperfecto	*Imperfecto*	*Imperfecto*	*Imperfecto*
nac-ía	nac-iera OR nac-iese	nac-íamos	nac-iéramos OR nac-iésemos
nac-ías	nac-ieras OR nac-ieses	nac-íais	nac-ierais OR nac-ieseis
nac-ía	nac-iera OR nac-iese	nac-ían	nac-ieran OR nac-iesen
Pretérito		*Pretérito*	
nac-í		nac-imos	
nac-iste		nac-isteis	
nac-ió		nac-ieron	
Futuro	*Futuro*	*Futuro*	*Futuro*
nac-eré	nac-iere	nac-eremos	nac-iéremos
nac-erás	nac-ieres	nac-eréis	nac-iereis
nac-erá	nac-iere	nac-erán	nac-ieren
Potencial		*Potencial*	
nac-ería		nac-eríamos	
nac-erías		nac-eríais	
nac-ería		nac-erían	

Imperativo

Singular	Plural
(not used); no (not used)	nazc-amos; no nazc-amos
nac-e; no nazc-as	nac-ed; no nazc-áis
nazc-a; no nazc-a	nazc-an; no nazc-an

Make compound tenses by adding the past participle nacido to pattern 83.
Translation possibilities are at pattern 88. Conjugation tips are at pattern 90.

Pattern 49: add ig or y, i ➠ í or y. Similar to caer.
Oir (o-ir) (to hear, listen to) is the pattern verb.
Present participle: o-yendo   Past participle: o-ído

49 oír

Singular		Plural	
Indicativo	*Subjuntivo*	*Indicativo*	*Subjuntivo*
Presente	*Presente*	*Presente*	*Presente*
oig-o	oig-a	o-ímos	oig-amos
oy-es	oig-as	o-ís	oig-áis
oy-e	oig-a	oy-en	oig-an
Imperfecto	*Imperfecto*	*Imperfecto*	*Imperfecto*
o-ía	o-yera OR o-yese	o-íamos	o-yéramos OR o-yésemos
o-ías	o-yeras OR o-yeses	o-íais	o-yerais OR o-yeseis
o-ía	o-yera OR o-yese	o-ían	o-yeran OR o-yesen
Pretérito		*Pretérito*	
o-í		o-ímos	
o-íste		o-ísteis	
o-yó		o-yeron	
Futuro	*Futuro*	*Futuro*	*Futuro*
o-iré	o-yere	o-iremos	o-yéremos
o-irás	o-yeres	o-iréis	o-yereis
o-irá	o-yere	o-irán	o-yeren
Potencial		*Potencial*	
o-iría		o-iríamos	
o-irías		o-iríais	
o-iría		o-irían	

Imperativo

Singular	*Plural*
(not used); no (not used)	oig-amos; no oig-amos
oy-e; no oig-as	o-íd; no oig-áis
oig-a; no oig-a	oig-an; no oig-an

Make compound tenses by adding the past participle oído to pattern 83.
Translation possibilities are at pattern 88. Conjugation tips are at pattern 91.

50 oler

Pattern 50: o ➠ hue when stressed.
Oler (ol-er) (to smell, look into) is the pattern verb.
Present participle: ol-iendo   Past participle: ol-ido

Singular		*Plural*	
Indicativo	*Subjuntivo*	*Indicativo*	*Subjuntivo*
Presente	*Presente*	*Presente*	*Presente*
huel-o	huel-a	ol-emos	ol-amos
huel-es	huel-as	ol-éis	ol-áis
huel-e	huel-a	huel-en	huel-an
Imperfecto	*Imperfecto*	*Imperfecto*	*Imperfecto*
ol-ía	ol-iera OR ol-iese	ol-íamos	ol-iéramos OR ol-iésemos
ol-ías	ol-ieras OR ol-ieses	ol-íais	ol-ierais OR ol-ieseis
ol-ía	ol-iera OR ol-iese	ol-ían	ol-ieran OR ol-iesen
Pretérito		*Pretérito*	
ol-í		ol-imos	
ol-iste		ol-isteis	
ol-ió		ol-ieron	
Futuro	*Futuro*	*Futuro*	*Futuro*
ol-eré	ol-iere	ol-eremos	ol-iéremos
ol-erás	ol-ieres	ol-eréis	ol-iereis
ol-erá	ol-iere	ol-erán	ol-ieren
Potencial		*Potencial*	
ol-ería		ol-eríamos	
ol-erías		ol-eríais	
ol-ería		ol-erían	

Imperativo

Singular	*Plural*
(not used); no (not used)	ol-amos; no ol-amos
huel-e; no huel-as	ol-ed; no ol-áis
huel-a; no huel-a	huel-an; no huel-an

Make compound tenses by adding the past participle olido to pattern 83.
Translation possibilities are at pattern 88. Conjugation tips are at pattern 90.

Pattern 51: g ➡ gu before e to retain the hard g sound.
Pagar (pag-ar) (to pay, pay for) is the pattern verb.
Present participle: pag-ando   Past participle: pag-ado

51 pagar

Singular		Plural	
Indicativo	*Subjuntivo*	*Indicativo*	*Subjuntivo*
Presente	*Presente*	*Presente*	*Presente*
pag-o	pagu-e	pag-amos	pagu-emos
pag-as	pagu-es	pag-áis	pagu-éis
pag-a	pagu-e	pag-an	pagu-en
Imperfecto	*Imperfecto*	*Imperfecto*	*Imperfecto*
pag-aba	pag-ara OR pag-ase	pag-ábamos	pag-áramos OR pag-ásemos
pag-abas	pag-aras OR pag-ases	pag-abais	pag-arais OR pag-aseis
pag-aba	pag-ara OR pag-ase	pag-aban	pag-aran OR pag-asen
Pretérito		*Pretérito*	
pagu-é		pag-amos	
pag-aste		pag-asteis	
pag-ó		pag-aron	
Futuro	*Futuro*	*Futuro*	*Futuro*
pag-aré	pag-are	pag-aremos	pag-áremos
pag-arás	pag-ares	pag-aréis	pag-areis
pag-ará	pag-are	pag-arán	pag-aren
Potencial		*Potencial*	
pag-aría		pag-aríamos	
pag-arías		pag-aríais	
pag-aría		pag-arían	

Imperativo

Singular	Plural
(not used); no (not used)	pagu-emos; no pagu-emos
pag-a; no pagu-es	pag-ad; no pagu-éis
pagu-e; no pagu-e	pagu-en; no pagu-en

Make compound tenses by adding the past participle pagado to pattern 83.
Translation possibilities are at pattern 88. Conjugation tips are at pattern 89.

52 pedir

Pattern 52: e ➠ i.
Pedir (ped-ir) (to ask, ask for, request) is the pattern verb.
Present participle: pid-iendo Past participle: ped-ido

Singular		Plural	
Indicativo	*Subjuntivo*	*Indicativo*	*Subjuntivo*
Presente	*Presente*	*Presente*	*Presente*
pid-o	pid-a	ped-imos	pid-amos
pid-es	pid-as	ped-ís	pid-áis
pid-e	pid-a	pid-en	pid-an
Imperfecto	*Imperfecto*	*Imperfecto*	*Imperfecto*
ped-ía	pid-iera OR pid-iese	ped-íamos	pid-iéramos OR pid-iésemos
ped-ías	pid-ieras OR pid-ieses	ped-íais	pid-ierais OR pid-ieseis
ped-ía	pid-iera OR pid-iese	ped-ían	pid-ieran OR pid-iesen
Pretérito		*Pretérito*	
ped-í		ped-imos	
ped-iste		ped-isteis	
pid-ió		pid-ieron	
Futuro	*Futuro*	*Futuro*	*Futuro*
ped-iré	pid-iere	ped-iremos	pid-iéremos
ped-irás	pid-ieres	ped-iréis	pid-iereis
ped-irá	pid-iere	ped-irán	pid-ieren
Potencial		*Potencial*	
ped-iría		ped-iríamos	
ped-irías		ped-iríais	
ped-iría		ped-irían	

Imperativo

Singular	Plural
(not used); no (not used)	pid-amos; no pid-amos
pid-e; no pid-as	ped-id; no pid-áis
pid-a; no pid-a	pid-an; no pid-an

Make compound tenses by adding the past participle pedido to pattern 83.
Translation possibilities are at pattern 88. Conjugation tips are at pattern 91.

Pattern 53: e in stem ➠ ie when stressed.
Pensar (pens-ar) (to think, think over) is the pattern verb.
Present participle: pens-ando Past participle: pens-ado

53 pensar

Singular		Plural	
Indicativo	*Subjuntivo*	*Indicativo*	*Subjuntivo*
Presente	*Presente*	*Presente*	*Presente*
piens-o	piens-e	pens-amos	pens-emos
piens-as	piens-es	pens-áis	pens-éis
piens-a	piens-e	piens-an	piens-en
Imperfecto	*Imperfecto*	*Imperfecto*	*Imperfecto*
pens-aba	pens-ara OR pens-ase	pens-ábamos	pens-áramos OR pens-ásemos
pens-abas	pens-aras OR pens-ases	pens-abais	pens-arais OR pens-aseis
pens-aba	pens-ara OR pens-ase	pens-aban	pens-aran OR pens-asen
Pretérito		*Pretérito*	
pens-é		pens-amos	
pens-aste		pens-asteis	
pens-ó		pens-aron	
Futuro	*Futuro*	*Futuro*	*Futuro*
pens-aré	pens-are	pens-aremos	pens-áremos
pens-arás	pens-ares	pens-aréis	pens-areis
pens-ará	pens-are	pens-arán	pens-aren
Potencial		*Potencial*	
pens-aría		pens-aríamos	
pens-arías		pens-aríais	
pens-aría		pens-arían	

Imperativo

Singular	*Plural*
(not used); no (not used)	pens-emos; no pens-emos
piens-a; no piens-es	pens-ad; no pens-éis
piens-e; no piens-e	piens-en; no piens-en

Make compound tenses by adding the past participle pensado to pattern 83.
Translation possibilities are at pattern 88. Conjugation tips are at pattern 89.

54 placer

Pattern 54: c ➠ zc before a or o, pleg and plug are roots.
Placer (plac-er) (to please) is the pattern verb.
Present participle: plac-iendo Past participle: plac-ido

Singular		Plural	
Indicativo	*Subjuntivo*	*Indicativo*	*Subjuntivo*
Presente	*Presente*	*Presente*	*Presente*
plazc-o	plazc-a	plac-emos	plazc-amos
plac-es	plazc-as	plac-éis	plazc-áis
plac-e	plazc-a, plegu-e	plac-en	plazc-an
Imperfecto	*Imperfecto*	*Imperfecto*	*Imperfecto*
plac-ía	plac-iera OR plac-iese	plac-íamos	plac-iéramos OR plac-iésemos
plac-ías	plac-ieras OR plac-ieses	plac-íais	plac-ierais OR plac-ieseis
plac-ía	plac-iera, plugu-iera OR plac-iese, plugu-iese	plac-ían	plac-ieran OR plac-iesen
Pretérito		*Pretérito*	
plac-í		plac-imos	
plac-iste		plac-isteis	
plac-ió, plug-o		plac-ieron, plugu-ieron	
Futuro	*Futuro*	*Futuro*	*Futuro*
plac-eré	plac-iere	plac-eremos	plac-iéremos
plac-erás	plac-ieres	plac-eréis	plac-iereis
plac-erá	plac-iere, plug-iere	plac-erán	plac-ieren
Potencial		*Potencial*	
plac-ería		plac-eríamos	
plac-erías		plac-eríais	
plac-ería		plac-erían	

Imperativo

Singular	*Plural*
(not used); no (not used)	plazc-amos; no plazc-amos
plac-e; no plazc-as	plac-ed; no plazc-áis
plazc-a; no plazc-a	plazc-an; no plazc-an

Make compound tenses by adding the past participle placido to pattern 83.
Translation possibilities are at pattern 88. Conjugation tips are at pattern 90.

Pattern 55: e is deleted, é ➠ e, o ➠ u or ue, ó ➠ o.
Poder (pod-er) (to be able, to be possible) is the pattern verb.
Present participle: pud-iendo Past participle: pod-ido

55 poder

Singular		Plural	
Indicativo	*Subjuntivo*	*Indicativo*	*Subjuntivo*
Presente	*Presente*	*Presente*	*Presente*
pued-o	pued-a	pod-emos	pod-amos
pued-es	pued-as	pod-éis	pod-áis
pued-e	pued-a	pued-en	pued-an
Imperfecto	*Imperfecto*	*Imperfecto*	*Imperfecto*
pod-ía	pud-iera OR pud-iese	pod-íamos	pud-iéramos OR pud-iésemos
pod-ías	pud-ieras OR pud-ieses	pod-íais	pud-ierais OR pud-ieseis
pod-ía	pud-iera OR pud-iese	pod-ían	pud-ieran OR pud-iesen
Pretérito		*Pretérito*	
pud-e		pud-imos	
pud-iste		pud-isteis	
pud-o		pud-ieron	
Futuro	*Futuro*	*Futuro*	*Futuro*
pod-ré	pud-iere	pod-remos	pud-iéremos
pod-rás	pud-ieres	pod-réis	pud-iereis
pod-rá	pud-iere	pod-rán	pud-ieren
Potencial		*Potencial*	
pod-ría		pod-ríamos	
pod-rías		pod-ríais	
pod-ría		pod-rían	

Imperativo

Singular	*Plural*
(not used); no (not used)	pod-amos; no pod-amos
pued-e; no pued-as	pod-ed; no pod-áis
pued-a; no pued-a	pued-an; no pued-an

Make compound tenses by adding the past participle podido to pattern 83.
Translation possibilities are at pattern 88. Conjugation tips are at pattern 90.

56
podrir (and pudrir)

Pattern 56: podr and pudr are roots, plus o ➠ u.
Podrir (podr-ir) (to rot, putrefy) is the pattern verb.
Present participle: pudr-iendo   Past part.: podr-ido

Singular		*Plural*	
Indicativo	*Subjuntivo*	*Indicativo*	*Subjuntivo*
Presente	*Presente*	*Presente*	*Presente*
pudr-o	pudr-a	pudr-imos	pudr-amos
pudr-es	pudr-as	pudr-ís	pudr-áis
pudr-e	pudr-a	pudr-en	pudr-an
Imperfecto	*Imperfecto*	*Imperfecto*	*Imperfecto*
pudr-ía	pudr-iera OR pudr-iese	pudr-íamos	pudr-iéramos OR pudr-iésemos
pudr-ías	pudr-ieras OR pudr-ieses	pudr-íais	pudr-ierais OR pudr-ieseis
pudr-ía	pudr-iera OR pudr-iese	pudr-ían	pudr-ieran OR pudr-iesen
Pretérito		*Pretérito*	
pudr-í, podr-í		pudr-imos	
pudr-iste		pudr-isteis	
pudr-ió		pudr-ieron	
Futuro	*Futuro*	*Futuro*	*Futuro*
pudr-iré, podr-iré	pudr-iere	pudr-iremos	pudr-iéremos
pudr-irás	pudr-ieres	pudr-iréis	pudr-iereis
pudr-irá	pudr-iere	pudr-irán	pudr-ieren
Potencial		*Potencial*	
pudr-iría, podr-iría		pudr-iríamos	
pudr-irías		pudr-iríais	
pudr-iría		pudr-irían	

Imperativo

Singular	*Plural*
(not used); no (not used)	pudr-amos; no pudr-amos
pudr-e; no pudr-as	pudr-id; no pudr-áis
pudr-a; no pudr-a	pudr-an; no pudr-an

Make compound tenses by adding the past participle podrido to pattern 83. Translation possibilities are at pattern 88. Conjugation tips are at pattern 91.

Pattern 57: e is deleted, o ➟ u, add d or g, n ➟ s, plus other changes.
Poner (pon-er) (to put, set, lay, place) is the pattern verb.
Present participle: pon-iendo Past participle: pu-esto

57 poner

Singular		Plural	
Indicativo	*Subjuntivo*	*Indicativo*	*Subjuntivo*
Presente	*Presente*	*Presente*	*Presente*
pong-o	pong-a	pon-emos	pong-amos
pon-es	pong-as	pon-éis	pong-áis
pon-e	pong-a	pon-en	pong-an
Imperfecto	*Imperfecto*	*Imperfecto*	*Imperfecto*
pon-ía	pus-iera OR pus-iese	pon-íamos	pus-iéramos OR pus-iésemos
pon-ías	pus-ieras OR pus-ieses	pon-íais	pus-ierais OR pus-ieseis
pon-ía	pus-iera OR pus-iese	pon-ían	pus-ieran OR pus-iesen
Pretérito		*Pretérito*	
pus-e		pus-imos	
pus-iste		pus-isteis	
pus-o		pus-ieron	
Futuro	*Futuro*	*Futuro*	*Futuro*
pond-ré	pus-iere	pond-remos	pus-iéremos
pond-rás	pus-ieres	pond-réis	pus-iereis
pond-rá	pus-iere	pond-rán	pus-ieren
Potencial		*Potencial*	
pond-ría		pond-ríamos	
pond-rías		pond-ríais	
pond-ría		pond-rían	

Imperativo

Singular	Plural
(not used); no (not used)	pong-amos; no pong-amos
pon; no pong-as	pon-ed; no pong-áis
pong-a; no pong-a	pong-an; no pong-an

Make compound tenses by adding the past participle puesto to pattern 83.
Translation possibilities are at pattern 88. Conjugation tips are at pattern 90.

58 predecir

Pattern 58: e ➠ i, c ➠ g or j, plus other changes.
Predecir (predec-ir) (to predict) is the pattern verb.
Present participle: predic-iendo Past participle: predic-ho

Singular		*Plural*	
Indicativo	*Subjuntivo*	*Indicativo*	*Subjuntivo*
Presente	*Presente*	*Presente*	*Presente*
predig-o	predig-a	predec-imos	predig-amos
predic-es	predig-as	predec-ís	predig-áis
predic-e	predig-a	predic-en	predig-an
Imperfecto	*Imperfecto*	*Imperfecto*	*Imperfecto*
predec-ía	predij-era OR predij-ese	predec-íamos	predij-éramos OR predij-ésemos
predec-ías	predij-eras OR predij-eses	predec-íais	predij-erais OR predij-eseis
predec-ía	predij-era OR predij-ese	predec-ían	predij-eran OR predij-esen
Pretérito		*Pretérito*	
predij-e		predij-imos	
predij-iste		predij-isteis	
predij-o		predij-eron	
Futuro	*Futuro*	*Futuro*	*Futuro*
predec-iré	predij-ere	predec-iremos	predij-éremos
predec-irás	predij-eres	predec-iréis	predij-ereis
predec-irá	predij-ere	predec-irán	predij-eren
Potencial		*Potencial*	
predec-iría		predec-iríamos	
predec-irías		predec-iríais	
predec-iría		predec-irían	

Imperativo

Singular	*Plural*
(not used); no (not used)	predig-amos; no predig-amos
predic-e; no predig-as	predec-id; no predig-áis
predig-a; no predig-a	predig-an; no predig-an

Make compound tenses by adding the past participle predicho to pattern 83.
Translation possibilities are at pattern 88. Conjugation tips are at pattern 91.

Pattern 59: c ➠ zc or j, i is deleted.
Producir (produc-ir) (to produce, yield, beat) is the pattern verb.
Present participle: produc-iendo Past participle: produc-ido

59 producir

Singular		*Plural*	
Indicativo	*Subjuntivo*	*Indicativo*	*Subjuntivo*
Presente	*Presente*	*Presente*	*Presente*
produzc-o	produzc-a	produc-imos	produzc-amos
produc-es	produzc-as	produc-ís	produzc-áis
produc-e	produzc-a	produc-en	produzc-an
Imperfecto	*Imperfecto*	*Imperfecto*	*Imperfecto*
produc-ía	produj-era OR produj-ese	produc-íamos	peoduj-éramos OR produj-ésemos
produc-ías	produj-eras OR produj-eses	produc-íais	produj-erais OR produj-eseis
produc-ía	produj-era OR produj-ese	produc-ían	produj-eran OR produj-esen
Pretérito		*Pretérito*	
produj-e		produj-imos	
produj-iste		produj-isteis	
produj-o		produj-eron	
Futuro	*Futuro*	*Futuro*	*Futuro*
produc-iré	produj-ere	produc-iremos	produj-éremos
produc-irás	produj-eres	produc-iréis	produj-ereis
produc-irá	produj-ere	produc-irán	produj-eren
Potencial		*Potencial*	
produc-iría		produc-iríamos	
produc-irías		produc-iríais	
produc-iría		produc-irían	

Imperativo

Singular	*Plural*
(not used); no (not used)	produzc-amos; no produzc-amos
produc-e; no produzc-as	produc-id; no produzc-áis
produzc-a; no produzc-a	produzc-an; no produzc-an

Make compound tenses by adding the past participle producido to pattern 83.
Translation possibilities are at pattern 88. Conjugation tips are at pattern 91.

60 querer

Pattern 60: e ➠ ie or i, delete e, plus other changes.
Querer (quer-er) (to wish, want, desire) is the pattern verb.
Present participle: quer-iendo Past participle: quer-ido

Singular		Plural	
Indicativo	*Subjuntivo*	*Indicativo*	*Subjuntivo*
Presente	*Presente*	*Presente*	*Presente*
quier-o	quier-a	quer-emos	quer-amos
quier-es	quier-as	quer-éis	quer-áis
quier-e	quier-a	quier-en	quier-an
Imperfecto	*Imperfecto*	*Imperfecto*	*Imperfecto*
quer-ía	quis-iera OR quis-iese	quer-íamos	quis-iéramos OR quis-iésemos
quer-ías	quis-ieras OR quis-ieses	quer-íais	quis-ierais OR quis-ieseis
quer-ía	quis-iera OR quis-iese	quer-ían	quis-ieran OR quis-iesen
Pretérito		*Pretérito*	
quis-e		quis-imos	
quis-iste		quis-isteis	
quis-o		quis-ieron	
Futuro	*Futuro*	*Futuro*	*Futuro*
quer-ré	quis-iere	quer-remos	quis-iéremos
quer-rás	quis-ieres	quer-réis	quis-iereis
quer-rá	quis-iere	quer-rán	quis-ieren
Potencial		*Potencial*	
quer-ría		quer-ríamos	
quer-rías		quer-ríais	
quer-ría		quer-rían	

Imperativo

Singular	*Plural*
(not used); no (not used)	quer-amos; no quer-amos
quier-e; no quier-as	quer-ed; no quer-áis
quier-a; no quier-a	quier-an; no quier-an

Make compound tenses by adding the past participle querido to pattern 83.
Translation possibilities are at pattern 88. Conjugation tips are at pattern 90.

Pattern 61: raig and ray are roots, plus i ➠ í or y.
Raer (ra-er) (to scrape, scratch) is the pattern verb.
Present participle: ra-yendo Past participle: ra-ído

61 raer

Singular		Plural	
Indicativo	*Subjuntivo*	*Indicativo*	*Subjuntivo*
Presente	*Presente*	*Presente*	*Presente*
ra-o, raig-o, ray-o	raig-a, ray-a	ra-emos	raig-amos, ray-amos
ra-es	raig-as, ray-as	ra-éis	raig-áis, ray-áis
ra-e	raig-a, ray-a	ra-en	raig-an, ray-an
Imperfecto	*Imperfecto*	*Imperfecto*	*Imperfecto*
ra-ía	ra-yera OR ra-yese	ra-íamos	ra-yéramos OR ra-yésemos
ra-ías	ra-yeras OR ra-yeses	ra-íais	ra-yerais OR ra-yeseis
ra-ía	ra-yera OR ra-yese	ra-ían	ra-yeran OR ra-yesen
Pretérito		*Pretérito*	
ra-í		ra-ímos	
ra-íste		ra-ísteis	
ra-yó		ra-yeron	
Futuro	*Futuro*	*Futuro*	*Futuro*
ra-eré	ra-yere	ra-eremos	ra-yéremos
ra-erás	ra-yeres	ra-eréis	ra-yereis
ra-erá	ra-yere	ra-erán	ra-yeren
Potencial		*Potencial*	
ra-ería		ra-eríamos	
ra-erías		ra-eríais	
ra-ería		ra-erían	

Imperativo

Singular	*Plural*
(not used); no (not used)	raig-amos, ray-amos; no raig-amos, no ray-amos
ra-e; no raig-as, no ray-as	ra-ed; no raig-áis, no ray-áis
raig-a, ray-a; no raig-a, no ray-a	raig-an, ray-an; no raig-an, no ray-an

Make compound tenses by adding the past participle raído to pattern 83.
Translation possibilities are at pattern 88. Conjugation tips are at pattern 90.

62 regar

Pattern 62: e ➠ ie when stressed, g ➠ gu before e.
Regar (reg-ar) (to water, irrigate) is the pattern verb.
Present participle: reg-ando Past participle: reg-ado

Singular		*Plural*	
Indicativo	*Subjuntivo*	*Indicativo*	*Subjuntivo*
Presente	*Presente*	*Presente*	*Presente*
rieg-o	riegu-e	reg-amos	regu-emos
rieg-as	riegu-es	reg-áis	regu-éis
rieg-a	riegu-e	rieg-an	riegu-en
Imperfecto	*Imperfecto*	*Imperfecto*	*Imperfecto*
reg-aba	reg-ara OR reg-ase	reg-ábamos	reg-áramos OR reg-ásemos
reg-abas	reg-aras OR reg-ases	reg-abais	reg-arais OR reg-aseis
reg-aba	reg-ara OR reg-ase	reg-aban	reg-aran OR reg-asen
Pretérito		*Pretérito*	
regu-é		reg-amos	
reg-aste		reg-asteis	
reg-ó		reg-aron	
Futuro	*Futuro*	*Futuro*	*Futuro*
reg-aré	reg-are	reg-aremos	reg-áremos
reg-arás	reg-ares	reg-aréis	reg-areis
reg-ará	reg-are	reg-arán	reg-aren
Potencial		*Potencial*	
reg-aría		reg-aríamos	
reg-arías		reg-aríais	
reg-aría		reg-arían	

Imperativo

Singular	*Plural*
(not used); no (not used)	regu-emos; no regu-emos
rieg-a; no riegu-es	reg-ad; no regu-éis
riegu-e; no riegu-e	riegu-en; no riegu-en

Make compound tenses by adding the past participle regado to pattern 83.
Translation possibilities are at pattern 88. Conjugation tips are at pattern 89.

Pattern 63: e ➠ i or í, e is deleted, i ➠ í.
Reír (re-ír) (to laugh, laugh at) is the pattern verb.
Present participle: r-iendo Past participle: re-ído

63 reír

Singular		Plural	
Indicativo	*Subjuntivo*	*Indicativo*	*Subjuntivo*
Presente	*Presente*	*Presente*	*Presente*
rí-o	rí-a	re-ímos	ri-amos
rí-es	rí-as	re-ís	ri-áis
rí-e	rí-a	rí-en	rí-an
Imperfecto	*Imperfecto*	*Imperfecto*	*Imperfecto*
re-ía	r-iera OR r-iese	re-íamos	r-iéramos OR r-iésemos
re-ías	r-ieras OR r-ieses	re-íais	r-ierais OR r-ieseis
re-ía	r-iera OR r-iese	re-ían	r-ieran OR r-iesen
Pretérito		*Pretérito*	
re-í		re-ímos	
re-íste		re-ísteis	
r-ió		r-ieron	
Futuro	*Futuro*	*Futuro*	*Futuro*
re-iré	r-iere	re-iremos	r-iéremos
re-irás	r-ieres	re-iréis	r-iereis
re-irá	r-iere	re-irán	r-ieren
Potencial		*Potencial*	
re-iría		re-iríamos	
re-irías		re-iríais	
re-iría		re-irían	

Imperativo

Singular	*Plural*
(not used); no (not used)	ri-amos; no ri-amos
rí-e; no rí-as	re-íd; no ri-áis
rí-a; no rí-a	rí-an; no rí-an

Make compound tenses by adding the past participle reído to pattern 83.
Translation possibilities are at pattern 88. Conjugation tips are at pattern 91.

64 reñir

Pattern 64: e ➠ i, i is deleted.
Reñir (reñ-ir) (to fight, scold) is the pattern verb.
Present participle: riñ-endo Past participle: reñ-ido

Singular		Plural	
Indicativo	*Subjuntivo*	*Indicativo*	*Subjuntivo*
Presente	*Presente*	*Presente*	*Presente*
riñ-o	riñ-a	reñ-imos	riñ-amos
riñ-es	riñ-as	reñ-ís	riñ-áis
riñ-e	riñ-a	riñ-en	riñ-an
Imperfecto	*Imperfecto*	*Imperfecto*	*Imperfecto*
reñ-ía	riñ-era OR riñ-ese	reñ-íamos	riñ-éramos OR riñ-ésemos
reñ-ías	riñ-eras OR riñ-eses	reñ-íais	riñ-erais OR riñ-eseis
reñ-ía	riñ-era OR riñ-ese	reñ-ían	riñ-eran OR riñ-esen
Pretérito		*Pretérito*	
reñ-í		reñ-imos	
reñ-iste		reñ-isteis	
riñ-ó		riñ-eron	
Futuro	*Futuro*	*Futuro*	*Futuro*
reñ-iré	riñ-ere	reñ-iremos	riñ-éremos
reñ-irás	riñ-eres	reñ-iréis	riñ-ereis
reñ-irá	riñ-ere	reñ-irán	riñ-eren
Potencial		*Potencial*	
reñ-iría		reñ-iríamos	
reñ-irías		reñ-iríais	
reñ-iría		reñ-irían	

Imperativo

Singular	*Plural*
(not used); no (not used)	riñ-amos; no riñ-amos
riñ-e; no riñ-as	reñ-id; no riñ-áis
riñ-a; no riñ-a	riñ-an; no riñ-an

Make compound tenses by adding the past participle reñido to pattern 83.
Translation possibilities are at pattern 88. Conjugation tips are at pattern 91.

Pattern 65: roig and roy are roots, plus i ➠ í or y.
Roer (ro-er) (to nibble [at], gnaw) is the pattern verb.
Present participle: ro-yendo Past participle: ro-ído

65 roer

Singular		Plural	
Indicativo	*Subjuntivo*	*Indicativo*	*Subjuntivo*
Presente	*Presente*	*Presente*	*Presente*
ro-o, roig-o, roy-o	ro-a, roig-a, roy-o	ro-emos	ro-amos, roig-amos, roy-amos
ro-es	ro-as, roig-as, roy-as	ro-éis	ro-áis, roig-áis, roy-áis
ro-e	ro-a, roig-a, roy-a	ro-en	ro-an, roig-an, roy-an
Imperfecto	*Imperfecto*	*Imperfecto*	*Imperfecto*
ro-ía	ro-yera OR ro-yese	ro-íamos	ro-yéramos OR ro-yésemos
ro-ías	ro-yeras OR ro-yeses	ro-íais	ro-yerais OR ro-yeseis
ro-ía	ro-yera OR ro-yese	ro-ían	ro-yeran OR ro-yesen
Pretérito		*Pretérito*	
ro-í		ro-ímos	
ro-íste		ro-ísteis	
ro-yó		ro-yeron	
Futuro	*Futuro*	*Futuro*	*Futuro*
ro-eré	ro-yere	ro-eremos	ro-yéremos
ro-erás	ro-yeres	ro-eréis	ro-yereis
ro-erá	ro-yere	ro-erán	ro-yeren
Potencial		*Potencial*	
ro-ería		ro-eríamos	
ro-erías		ro-eríais	
ro-ería		ro-erían	

Imperativo

Singular	*Plural*
(not used); no (not used)	ro-amos, roig-amos, roy-amos; no ro-amos, no roig-amos, no roy-amos
ro-e; no ro-as, no roig-as, no roy-as	ro-ed; no ro-áis, no roig-áis, no roy-áis
ro-a, roig-a, roy-a; no ro-a, no roig-a, no roy-a	ro-an, roig-an, roy-an; no ro-an, no roig-an, no roy-an

Make compound tenses by adding the past participle roído to pattern 83.
Translation possibilities are at pattern 88. Conjugation tips are at pattern 90.

66 saber

Pattern 66: a ➠ e or u, e is deleted, b ➠ p.
Saber (sab-er) (to know, find out) is the pattern verb.
Present participle: sab-iendo Past participle: sab-ido

Singular		*Plural*	
Indicativo	*Subjuntivo*	*Indicativo*	*Subjuntivo*
Presente	*Presente*	*Presente*	*Presente*
s-é	sep-a	sab-emos	sep-amos
sab-es	sep-as	sab-éis	sep-áis
sab-e	sep-a	sab-en	sep-an
Imperfecto	*Imperfecto*	*Imperfecto*	*Imperfecto*
sab-ía	sup-iera OR sup-iese	sab-íamos	sup-iéramos OR sup-iésemos
sab-ías	sup-ieras OR sup-ieses	sab-íais	sup-ierais OR sup-ieseis
sab-ía	sup-iera OR sup-iese	sab-ían	sup-ieran OR sup-iesen
Pretérito		*Pretérito*	
sup-e		sup-imos	
sup-iste		sup-isteis	
sup-o		sup-ieron	
Futuro	*Futuro*	*Futuro*	*Futuro*
sab-ré	sup-iere	sab-remos	sup-iéremos
sab-rás	sup-ieres	sab-réis	sup-iereis
sab-rá	sup-iere	sab-rán	sup-ieren
Potencial		*Potencial*	
sab-ría		sab-ríamos	
sab-rías		sab-ríais	
sab-ría		sab-rían	

Imperativo

Singular	*Plural*
(not used); no (not used)	sep-amos; no sep-amos
sab-e; no sep-as	sab-ed; no sep-áis
sep-a; no sep-a	sep-an; no sep-an

Make compound tenses by adding the past participle sabido to pattern 83.
Translation possibilities are at pattern 88. Conjugation tips are at pattern 90.

Pattern 67: c ➠ qu before e to retain the k sound.
Sacar (sac-ar) (to take out, get out) is the pattern verb.
Present participle: sac-ando   Past participle: sac-ado

67 sacar

Singular		*Plural*	
Indicativo	*Subjuntivo*	*Indicativo*	*Subjuntivo*
Presente	*Presente*	*Presente*	*Presente*
sac-o	saqu-e	sac-amos	saqu-emos
sac-as	saqu-es	sac-áis	saqu-éis
sac-a	saqu-e	sac-an	saqu-en
Imperfecto	*Imperfecto*	*Imperfecto*	*Imperfecto*
sac-aba	sac-ara OR sac-ase	sac-ábamos	sac-áramos OR sac-ásemos
sac-abas	sac-aras OR sac-ases	sac-abais	sac-arais OR sac-aseis
sac-aba	sac-ara OR sac-ase	sac-aban	sac-aran OR sac-asen
Pretérito		*Pretérito*	
saqu-é		sac-amos	
sac-aste		sac-asteis	
sac-ó		sac-aron	
Futuro	*Futuro*	*Futuro*	*Futuro*
sac-aré	sac-are	sac-aremos	sac-áremos
sac-arás	sac-ares	sac-aréis	sac-areis
sac-ará	sac-are	sac-arán	sac-aren
Potencial		*Potencial*	
sac-aría		sac-aríamos	
sac-arías		sac-aríais	
sac-aría		sac-arían	

Imperativo

Singular	*Plural*
(not used); no (not used)	saqu-emos; no saqu-emos
sac-a; no saqu-es	sac-ad; no saqu-éis
saqu-e; no saqu-e	saqu-en; no saqu-en

Make compound tenses by adding the past participle sacado to pattern 83.
Translation possibilities are at pattern 88. Conjugation tips are at pattern 89.

68 salir

Pattern 68: i is deleted, add d or g.
Salir (sal-ir) (to leave, to go out) is the pattern verb.
Present participle: sal-iendo   Past participle: sal-ido

Singular		Plural	
Indicativo	*Subjuntivo*	*Indicativo*	*Subjuntivo*
Presente	*Presente*	*Presente*	*Presente*
salg-o	salg-a	sal-imos	salg-amos
sal-es	salg-as	sal-ís	salg-áis
sal-e	salg-a	sal-en	salg-an
Imperfecto	*Imperfecto*	*Imperfecto*	*Imperfecto*
sal-ía	sal-iera OR sal-iese	sal-íamos	sal-iéramos OR sal-iésemos
sal-ías	sal-ieras OR sal-ieses	sal-íais	sal-ierais OR sal-ieseis
sal-ía	sal-iera OR sal-iese	sal-ían	sal-ieran OR sal-iesen
Pretérito		*Pretérito*	
sal-í		sal-imos	
sal-iste		sal-isteis	
sal-ió		sal-ieron	
Futuro	*Futuro*	*Futuro*	*Futuro*
sald-ré	sal-iere	sald-remos	sal-iéremos
sald-rás	sal-ieres	sald-réis	sal-iereis
sald-rá	sal-iere	sald-rán	sal-ieren
Potencial		*Potencial*	
sald-ría		sald-ríamos	
sald-rías		sald-ríais	
sald-ria		sald-rían	

Imperativo

Singular	*Plural*
(not used); no (not used)	salg-amos; no salg-amos
sal; no salg-as	sal-id; no salg-áis
salg-a; no salg-a	salg-an; no salg-an

Make compound tenses by adding the past participle salido to pattern 83. Translation possibilities are at pattern 88. Conjugation tips are at pattern 91.

Pattern 69: a ➠ i, etc. as in hacer, plus a tú imperative.
Satisfacer (satisfac-er) (to satisfy) is the pattern verb.
Present participle: satisfac-iendo Past part.: satisfec-ho

69 satisfacer

Singular		Plural	
Indicativo	*Subjuntivo*	*Indicativo*	*Subjuntivo*
Presente	*Presente*	*Presente*	*Presente*
satisfag-o	satisfag-a	satisfac-emos	satisfag-amos
satisfac-es	satisfag-as	satisfac-éis	satisfag-áis
satisfac-e	satisfag-a	satisfac-en	satisfag-an
Imperfecto	*Imperfecto*	*Imperfecto*	*Imperfecto*
satisfac-ía	satisfic-iera OR satisfic-iese	satisfac-íamos	satisfic-iéramos OR satisfic-iésemos
satisfac-ías	satisfic-ieras OR satisfic-ieses	satisfac-íais	satisfic-ierais OR satisfic-ieseis
satisfac-ía	satisfic-iera OR satisfic-iese	satisfac-ían	satisfic-ieran OR satisfic-iesen
Pretérito		*Pretérito*	
satisfic-e		satisfic-imos	
satisfic-iste		satisfic-isteis	
satisfiz-o		satisfic-ieron	
Futuro	*Futuro*	*Futuro*	*Futuro*
satisfa-ré	satisfic-iere	satisfa-remos	satisfic-iéremos
satisfa-rás	satisfic-ieres	satisfa-réis	satisfic-iereis
satisfa-rá	satisfic-iere	satisfa-rán	satisfic-ieren
Potencial		*Potencial*	
satisfa-ría		satisfa-ríamos	
satisfa-rías		satisfa-ríais	
satisfa-ría		satisfa-rían	

Imperativo

Singular	Plural
(not used); no (not used)	satisfag-amos; no satisfag-amos
satisfaz, satisfac-e; no satisfag-as	satisfac-ed; no satisfag-áis
satisfag-a; no satisfag-a	satisfag-an; no satisfag-an

Make compound tenses by adding the past participle satisfecho to pattern 83.
Translation possibilities are at pattern 88. Conjugation tips are at pattern 90.

70 seguir

Pattern 70: e ➠ i, gu ➠ g before a or o.
Seguir (segu-ir) (to follow, pursue) is the pattern verb.
Present participle: sigu-iendo   Past participle: segu-ido

Singular		*Plural*	
Indicativo	*Subjuntivo*	*Indicativo*	*Subjuntivo*
Presente	*Presente*	*Presente*	*Presente*
sig-o	sig-a	segu-imos	sig-amos
sigu-es	sig-as	segu-ís	sig-áis
sigu-e	sig-a	sigu-en	sig-an
Imperfecto	*Imperfecto*	*Imperfecto*	*Imperfecto*
segu-ía	sigu-iera OR sigu-iese	segu-íamos	sigu-iéramos OR sigu-iésemos
segu-ías	sigu-ieras OR sigu-ieses	segu-íais	sigu-ierais OR sigu-ieseis
segu-ía	sigu-iera OR sigu-iese	segu-ían	sigu-ieran OR sigu-iesen
Pretérito		*Pretérito*	
segu-í		segu-imos	
segu-iste		segu-isteis	
sigu-ió		sigu-ieron	
Futuro	*Futuro*	*Futuro*	*Futuro*
segu-iré	sigu-iere	segu-iremos	sigu-iéremos
segu-irás	sigu-ieres	segu-iréis	sigu-iereis
segu-irá	sigu-iere	segu-irán	sigu-ieren
Potencial		*Potencial*	
segu-iría		segu-iríamos	
segu-irías		segu-iríais	
segu-iría		segu-irían	

Imperativo

Singular	*Plural*
(not used); no (not used)	sig-amos; no sig-amos
sigu-e; no sig-as	segu-id; no sig-áis
sig-a; no sig-a	sig-an; no sig-an

Make compound tenses by adding the past participle seguido to pattern 83.
Translation possibilities are at pattern 88. Conjugation tips are at pattern 91.

Pattern 71: e ➠ ie when stressed, e ➠ i.
Sentir (sent-ir) (to feel, sense, regret) is the pattern verb.
Present participle: sint-iendo Past participle: sent-ido

71 sentir

Singular		Plural	
Indicativo	*Subjuntivo*	*Indicativo*	*Subjuntivo*
Presente	*Presente*	*Presente*	*Presente*
sient-o	sient-a	sent-imos	sint-amos
sient-es	sient-as	sent-ís	sint-áis
sient-e	sient-a	sient-en	sient-an
Imperfecto	*Imperfecto*	*Imperfecto*	*Imperfecto*
sent-ía	sint-iera OR sint-iese	sent-íamos	sint-iéramos OR sint-iésemos
sent-ías	sint-ieras OR sint-ieses	sent-íais	sint-ierais OR sint-ieseis
sent-ía	sint-iera OR sint-iese	sent-ían	sint-ieran OR sint-iesen
Pretérito		*Pretérito*	
sent-í		sent-imos	
sent-iste		sent-isteis	
sint-ió		sint-ieron	
Futuro	*Futuro*	*Futuro*	*Futuro*
sent-iré	sint-iere	sent-iremos	sint-iéremos
sent-irás	sint-ieres	sent-iréis	sint-iereis
sent-irá	sint-iere	sent-irán	sint-ieren
Potencial		*Potencial*	
sent-iría		sent-iríamos	
sent-irías		sent-iríais	
sent-iría		sent-irían	

Imperativo

Singular	Plural
(not used); no (not used)	sint-amos; no sint-amos
sient-e; no sient-as	sent-id; no sint-áis
sient-a; no sient-a	sient-an; no sient-an

Make compound tenses by adding the past participle sentido to pattern 83.
Translation possibilities are at pattern 88. Conjugation tips are at pattern 91.

72 ser

Pattern 72: er, fu and se are roots, plus other changes.
Ser (s-er) (to be) (an auxiliary verb) is the pattern verb.
Present participle: s-iendo Past participle: s-ido

Singular		Plural	
Indicativo	*Subjuntivo*	*Indicativo*	*Subjuntivo*
Presente	*Presente*	*Presente*	*Presente*
s-oy	se-a	s-omos	se-amos
er-es	se-as	s-ois	se-áis
es	se-a	s-on	se-an
Imperfecto	*Imperfecto*	*Imperfecto*	*Imperfecto*
er-a	fu-era OR fu-ese	ér-amos	fu-éramos OR fu-ésemos
er-as	fu-eras OR fu-eses	er-ais	fu-erais OR fu-eseis
er-a	fu-era OR fu-ese	er-an	fu-eran OR fu-esen
Pretérito		*Pretérito*	
fu-i		fu-imos	
fu-iste		fu-isteis	
fu-e		fu-eron	
Futuro	*Futuro*	*Futuro*	*Futuro*
s-eré	fu-ere	s-eremos	fu-éremos
s-erás	fu-eres	s-eréis	fu-ereis
s-erá	fu-ere	s-erán	fu-eren
Potencial		*Potencial*	
s-ería		s-eríamos	
s-erías		s-eríais	
s-ería		s-erían	

Imperativo

Singular	*Plural*
(not used); no (not used)	se-amos; no se-amos
s-é; no se-as	s-ed; no se-áis
se-a; no se-a	se-an; no se-an

Make compound tenses by adding the past participle sido to pattern 83.
Translation possibilities are at pattern 88. Conjugation tips are at pattern 90.

Pattern 73: Some conjugations customarily are not used, plus o ➠ ue.
Soler (sol-er) (to be accustomed to [followed by a verb]).
Present participle: sol-iendo Past participle: sol-ido

73 soler

Singular		*Plural*	
Indicativo	*Subjuntivo*	*Indicativo*	*Subjuntivo*
Presente	*Presente*	*Presente*	*Presente*
suel-o	suel-a	sol-emos	sol-amos
suel-es	suel-as	sol-éis	sol-áis
suel-e	suel-a	suel-en	suel-an
Imperfecto	*Imperfecto*	*Imperfecto*	*Imperfecto*
sol-ía	sol-iera OR sol-iese	sol-íamos	sol-iéramos OR sol-iésemos
sol-ías	sol-ieras OR sol-ieses	sol-íais	sol-ierais OR sol-ieseis
sol-ía	sol-iera OR sol-iese	sol-ían	sol-ieran OR sol-iesen
Pretérito		*Pretérito*	
sol-í		sol-imos	
sol-iste		sol-isteis	
sol-ió		sol-ieron	
Futuro	*Futuro*	*Futuro*	*Futuro*
(not used)	(not used)	(not used)	(not used)
(not used)	(not used)	(not used)	(not used)
(not used)	(not used)	(not used)	(not used)
Potencial		*Potencial*	
(not used)		(not used)	
(not used)		(not used)	
(not used)		(not used)	

Imperativo	
Singular	*Plural*
(not used); no (not used)	(not used); no (not used)
(not used); no (not used)	(not used); no (not used)
(not used); no (not used)	(not used); no (not used)

Make compound tenses by adding the past participle solido to pattern 83.
Translation possibilities are at pattern 88. Conjugation tips are at pattern 90.

74 tener

Pattern 74: e ➠ ie or u, delete e, plus other changes.
Tener (ten-er) (to have) (an auxiliary verb) is the pattern verb.
Present participle: ten-iendo Past participle: ten-ido

Singular		Plural	
Indicativo	*Subjuntivo*	*Indicativo*	*Subjuntivo*
Presente	*Presente*	*Presente*	*Presente*
teng-o	teng-a	ten-emos	teng-amos
tien-es	teng-as	ten-éis	teng-áis
tien-e	teng-a	tien-en	teng-an
Imperfecto	*Imperfecto*	*Imperfecto*	*Imperfecto*
ten-ía	tuv-iera OR tuv-iese	ten-íamos	tuv-iéramos OR tuv-iésemos
ten-ías	tuv-ieras OR tuv-ieses	ten-íais	tuv-ierais OR tuv-ieseis
ten-ía	tuv-iera OR tuv-iese	ten-ían	tuv-ieran OR tuv-iesen
Pretérito		*Pretérito*	
tuv-e		tuv-imos	
tuv-iste		tuv-isteis	
tuv-o		tuv-ieron	
Futuro	*Futuro*	*Futuro*	*Futuro*
tend-ré	tuv-iere	tend-remos	tuv-iéremos
tend-rás	tuv-ieres	tend-réis	tuv-iereis
tend-rá	tuv-iere	tend-rán	tuv-ieren
Potencial		*Potencial*	
tend-ría		tend-ríamos	
tend-rías		tend-ríais	
tend-ría		tend-rían	

Imperativo

Singular	Plural
(not used); no (not used)	teng-amos; no teng-amos
ten; no teng-as	ten-ed; no teng-áis
teng-a; no teng-a	teng-an; no teng-an

Make compound tenses by adding the past participle tenido to pattern 83.
Translation possibilities are at pattern 88. Conjugation tips are at pattern 90.

Pattern 75: add ig or j, plus other changes.
Traer (tra-er) (to bring, carry) is the pattern verb.
Present participle: tra-yendo Past participle: tra-ído

75 traer

Singular		Plural	
Indicativo	*Subjuntivo*	*Indicativo*	*Subjuntivo*
Presente	*Presente*	*Presente*	*Presente*
traig-o	traig-a	tra-emos	traig-amos
tra-es	traig-as	tra-éis	traig-áis
tra-e	traig-a	tra-en	traig-an
Imperfecto	*Imperfecto*	*Imperfecto*	*Imperfecto*
tra-ía	traj-era OR traj-ese	tra-íamos	traj-éramos OR traj-ésemos
tra-ías	traj-eras OR traj-eses	tra-íais	traj-erais OR traj-eseis
tra-ía	traj-era OR traj-ese	tra-ían	traj-eran OR traj-esen
Pretérito		*Pretérito*	
traj-e		traj-imos	
traj-iste		traj-isteis	
traj-o		traj-eron	
Futuro	*Futuro*	*Futuro*	*Futuro*
tra-eré	traj-ere	tra-eremos	traj-éremos
tra-erás	traj-eres	tra-eréis	traj-ereis
tra-erá	traj-ere	tra-erán	traj-eren
Potencial		*Potencial*	
tra-ería		tra-eríamos	
tra-erías		tra-eríais	
tra-ería		tra-erían	

Imperativo

Singular	Plural
(not used); no (not used)	traig-amos; no traig-amos
tra-e; no traig-as	tra-ed; no traig-áis
traig-a; no traig-a	traig-an; no traig-an

Make compound tenses by adding the past participle traído to pattern 83.
Translation possibilities are at pattern 88. Conjugation tips are at pattern 90.

76 trocar

Pattern 76: o ➠ ue when stressed, c ➠ qu before e.
Trocar (troc-ar) (to exchange, barter) is the pattern verb.
Present participle: troc-ando   Past participle: troc-ado

Singular		Plural	
Indicativo	*Subjuntivo*	*Indicativo*	*Subjuntivo*
Presente	*Presente*	*Presente*	*Presente*
truec-o	truequ-e	troc-amos	troqu-emos
truec-as	truequ-es	troc-áis	troqu-éis
truec-a	truequ-e	truec-an	truequ-en
Imperfecto	*Imperfecto*	*Imperfecto*	*Imperfecto*
troc-aba	troc-ara OR troc-ase	troc-ábamos	troc-áramos OR troc-ásemos
troc-abas	troc-aras OR troc-ases	troc-abais	troc-arais OR troc-aseis
troc-aba	troc-ara OR troc-ase	troc-aban	troc-aran OR troc-asen
Pretérito		*Pretérito*	
troqu-é		troc-amos	
troc-aste		troc-asteis	
troc-ó		troc-aron	
Futuro	*Futuro*	*Futuro*	*Futuro*
troc-aré	troc-are	troc-aremos	troc-áremos
troc-arás	troc-ares	troc-aréis	troc-areis
troc-ará	troc-are	troc-arán	troc-aren
Potencial		*Potencial*	
troc-aría		troc-aríamos	
troc-arías		troc-aríais	
troc-aría		troc-arían	

Imperativo

Singular	Plural
(not used); no (not used)	troqu-emos; no troqu-emos
truec-a; no truequ-es	troc-ad; no troqu-éis
truequ-e; no truequ-e	truequ-en; no truequ-en

Make compound tenses by adding the past participle trocado to pattern 83.
Translation possibilities are at pattern 88. Conjugation tips are at pattern 89.

Pattern 77: e ➠ ie or i, delete i, add d or g, plus other changes.
Venir (ven-ir) (to come) is the pattern verb.
Present participle: vin-iendo Past participle: ven-ido

77 venir

Singular		Plural	
Indicativo	*Subjuntivo*	*Indicativo*	*Subjuntivo*
Presente	*Presente*	*Presente*	*Presente*
veng-o	veng-a	ven-imos	veng-amos
vien-es	veng-as	ven-ís	veng-áis
vien-e	veng-a	vien-en	veng-an
Imperfecto	*Imperfecto*	*Imperfecto*	*Imperfecto*
ven-ía	vin-iera OR vin-iese	ven-íamos	vin-iéramos OR vin-iésemos
ven-ías	vin-ieras OR vin-ieses	ven-íais	vin-ierais OR vin-ieseis
ven-ía	vin-iera OR vin-iese	ven-ían	vin-ieran OR vin-iesen
Pretérito		*Pretérito*	
vin-e		vin-imos	
vin-iste		vin-isteis	
vin-o		vin-ieron	
Futuro	*Futuro*	*Futuro*	*Futuro*
vend-ré	vin-iere	vend-remos	vin-iéremos
vend-rás	vin-ieres	vend-réis	vin-iereis
vend-rá	vin-iere	vend-rán	vin-ieren
Potencial		*Potencial*	
vend-ría		vend-ríamos	
vend-rías		vend-ríais	
vend-ría		vend-rían	

Imperativo

Singular	Plural
(not used); no (not used)	veng-amos; no veng-amos
ven; no veng-as	ven-id; no veng-áis
veng-a; no veng-a	veng-an; no veng-an

Make compound tenses by adding the past participle venido to pattern 83.
Translation possibilities are at pattern 88. Conjugation tips are at pattern 91.

78 ver

Pattern 78: e is added, é ➠ e, í ➠ i, ó ➠ o.
Ver (v-er) (to see, look at) is the pattern verb.
Present participle: v-iendo   Past participle: v-isto

Singular		*Plural*	
Indicativo	*Subjuntivo*	*Indicativo*	*Subjuntivo*
Presente	*Presente*	*Presente*	*Presente*
ve-o	ve-a	v-emos	ve-amos
v-es	ve-as	v-eis	ve-áis
v-e	ve-a	v-en	ve-an
Imperfecto	*Imperfecto*	*Imperfecto*	*Imperfecto*
ve-ía	v-iera OR v-iese	ve-íamos	v-iéramos OR v-iésemos
ve-ías	v-ieras OR v-ieses	ve-íais	v-ierais OR v-ieseis
ve-ía	v-iera OR v-iese	ve-ían	v-ieran OR v-iesen
Pretérito		*Pretérito*	
v-i		v-imos	
v-iste		v-isteis	
v-io		v-ieron	
Futuro	*Futuro*	*Futuro*	*Futuro*
v-eré	v-iere	v-eremos	v-iéremos
v-erás	v-ieres	v-eréis	v-iereis
v-erá	v-iere	v-erán	v-ieren
Potencial		*Potencial*	
v-ería		v-eríamos	
v-erías		v-eríais	
v-ería		v-erían	

Imperativo

Singular	*Plural*
(not used); no (not used)	ve-amos; no ve-amos
v-e; no ve-as	v-ed; no ve-áis
ve-a; no ve-a	ve-an; no ve-an

Make compound tenses by adding the past participle visto to pattern 83.
Translation possibilities are at pattern 88. Conjugation tips are at pattern 90.

Pattern 79: yag, yaz, yazc, and yazg are roots.
Yacer (yac-er) (to rest, lie somewhere, e.g., cattle) is the pattern verb.
Present participle: yac-iendo Past participle: yac-ido

79 yacer

Singular		Plural	
Indicativo	*Subjuntivo*	*Indicativo*	*Subjuntivo*
Presente	*Presente*	*Presente*	*Presente*
yazc-o, yazg-o, yag-o	yazc-a, yazg-a, yag-a	yac-emos	yazc-amos, yazg-amos, yag-amos
yac-es	yazc-as, yazg-as, yag-as	yac-éis	yazc-áis, yazg-áis, yag-áis
yac-e	yazc-a, yazg-a, yag-a	yac-en	yazc-an, yazg-an, yag-an
Imperfecto	*Imperfecto*	*Imperfecto*	*Imperfecto*
yac-ía	yac-iera OR yac-iese	yac-íamos	yac-iéramos OR yac-iésemos
yac-ías	yac-ieras OR yac-ieses	yac-íais	yac-ierais OR yac-ieseis
yac-ía	yac-iera OR yac-iese	yac-ían	yac-ieran OR yac-iesen
Pretérito		*Pretérito*	
yac-í		yac-imos	
yac-iste		yac-isteis	
yac-ió		yac-ieron	
Futuro	*Futuro*	*Futuro*	*Futuro*
yac-eré	yac-iere	yac-eremos	yac-iéremos
yac-erás	yac-ieres	yac-eréis	yac-iereis
yac-erá	yac-iere	yac-erán	yac-ieren
Potencial		*Potencial*	
yac-ería		yac-eríamos	
yac-erías		yac-eríais	
yac-ería		yac-erían	

Imperativo

Singular	*Plural*
(not used); no (not used)	yazc-amos, yazg-amos, yag-amos; no yazc-amos, yazg-amos, yag-amos
yaz, yac-e; no yazc-as	yac-ed; no yazc-áis
yazc-a, yazg-a, yag-a no yazc-a; no yazg-a; no yag-a	yazc-an, yazg-an, yag-an; no yazc-an, yazg-an, yag-an

Make compound tenses by adding the past participle yacido to pattern 83.
Translation possibilities are at pattern 88. Conjugation tips are at pattern 90.

80
reflexive "ar" verbs

Pattern 80: regular reflexive "ar" verbs.
Levantarse (levant-arse) (to get up) is the pattern.
Pres. part.: levant-ándose Past part.: levant-ado

Singular Indicativo	Singular Subjuntivo	Plural Indicativo	Plural Subjuntivo
Presente	*Presente*	*Presente*	*Presente*
me levant-o	me levant-e	nos levant-amos	nos levant-emos
te levant-as	te levant-es	os levant-áis	os levant-éis
se levant-a	se levant-e	se levant-an	se levant-en
Imperfecto	*Imperfecto*	*Imperfecto*	*Imperfecto*
me levant-aba	me levant-ara OR me levant-ase	nos levant-ábamos	nos levant-áramos OR nos levant-ásemos
te levant-abas	te levant-aras OR te levant-ases	os levant-abais	os levant-arais OR os levant-aseis
se levant-aba	se levant-ara OR se levant-ase	se levant-aban	se levant-aran OR se levant-asen
Pretérito		*Pretérito*	
me levant-é		nos levant-amos	
te levant-aste		os levant-asteis	
se levant-ó		se levant-aron	
Futuro	*Futuro*	*Futuro*	*Futuro*
me levant-aré	me levant-are	nos levant-aremos	nos levant-áremos
te levant-arás	te levant-ares	os levant-aréis	os levant-areis
se levant-ará	se levant-are	se levant-arán	se levant-aren
Potencial		*Potencial*	
me levant-aría		nos levant-aríamos	
te levant-arías		os levant-aríais	
se levant-aría		se levant-arían	

Imperativo

Singular	Plural
(not used); no (not used)	levant-émonos; no nos levant-emos
levánt-ate; no te levant-es	levant-aos; no os levant-éis
levánt-ese; no se levant-e	levánt-ense; no se levant-en

The letters in red on this page show how reflexive "ar" conjugations differ from non-reflexive "ar" conjugations in pattern 1 and elsewhere.
Make compound tenses by adding the past participle levantado to pattern 84.
Translation possibilities are at pattern 88. Conjugation tips are at pattern 89.

Pattern 81: regular reflexive "er" verbs.
Atreverse (atrev-erse) (to dare) is the pattern verb.
Pres. part.: atrev-iéndose Past part.: atrev-ido

81 reflexive "er" verbs

Singular		Plural	
Indicativo	*Subjuntivo*	*Indicativo*	*Subjuntivo*
Presente	*Presente*	*Presente*	*Presente*
me atrev-o	me atrev-a	nos atrev-emos	nos atrev-amos
te atrev-es	te atrev-as	os atrev-éis	os atrev-áis
se atrev-e	se atrev-a	se atrev-en	se atrev-an
Imperfecto	*Imperfecto*	*Imperfecto*	*Imperfecto*
me atrev-ía	me atrev-iera OR me atrev-iese	nos atrev-íamos	nos atrev-iéramos OR nos atrev-iésemos
te atrev-ías	te atrev-ieras OR te atrev-ieses	os atrev-íais	os atrev-ierais OR os atrev-ieseis
se atrev-ía	se atrev-iera OR se atrev-iese	se atrev-ían	se atrev-ieran OR se atrev-iesen
Pretérito		*Pretérito*	
me atrev-í		nos atrev-imos	
te atrev-iste		os atrev-isteis	
se atrev-ió		se atrev-ieron	
Futuro	*Futuro*	*Futuro*	*Futuro*
me atrev-eré	me atrev-iere	nos atrev-eremos	nos atrev-iéremos
te atrev-erás	te atrev-ieres	os atrev-eréis	os atrev-iereis
se atrev-erá	se atrev-iere	se atrev-erán	se atrev-ieren
Potencial		*Potencial*	
me atrev-ería		nos atrev-eríamos	
te atrev-erías		os atrev-eríais	
se atrev-ería		se atrev-erían	

Imperativo

Singular	Plural
(not used); no (not used)	atrev-ámonos; no nos atrev-amos
atrév-ete; no te atrev-as	atrev-eos; no os atrev-áis
atrév-ase; no se atrev-a	atrév-anse; no se atrev-an

The letters in red on this page show how reflexive "er" conjugations differ from non-reflexive "er" conjugations in pattern 2 and elsewhere.
Make compound tenses by adding the past participle atrevido to pattern 84.
Translation possibilities are at pattern 88. Conjugation tips are at pattern 90.

82

reflexive "ir" verbs

Pattern 82: regular reflexive "ir" verbs.
Aburrirse (aburr-irse) (to be bored) is the pattern.
Pres. part.: aburr-iéndose Past part.: aburr-ido

Singular		Plural	
Indicativo	*Subjuntivo*	*Indicativo*	*Subjuntivo*
Presente	*Presente*	*Presente*	*Presente*
me aburr-o	me aburr-a	nos aburr-imos	nos aburr-amos
te aburr-es	te aburr-as	os aburr-ís	os aburr-áis
se aburr-e	se aburr-a	se aburr-en	se aburr-an
Imperfecto	*Imperfecto*	*Imperfecto*	*Imperfecto*
me aburr-ía	me aburr-iera OR me aburr-iese	nos aburr-íamos	nos aburr-iéramos OR nos aburr-iésemos
te aburr-ías	te aburr-ieras OR te aburr-ieses	os aburr-íais	os aburr-ierais OR os aburr-ieseis
se aburr-ía	se aburr-iera OR se aburr-iese	se aburr-ían	se aburr-ieran OR se aburr-iesen
Pretérito		*Pretérito*	
me aburr-í		nos aburr-imos	
te aburr-iste		os aburr-isteis	
se aburr-ió		se aburr-ieron	
Futuro	*Futuro*	*Futuro*	*Futuro*
me aburr-iré	me aburr-iere	nos aburr-iremos	nos aburr-iéremos
te aburr-irás	te aburr-ieres	os aburr-iréis	os aburr-iereis
se aburr-irá	se aburr-iere	se aburr-irán	se aburr-ieren
Potencial		*Potencial*	
me aburr-iría		nos aburr-iríamos	
te aburr-irías		os aburr-iríais	
se aburr-iría		se aburr-irían	

Imperativo

Singular	*Plural*
(not used); no (not used)	aburr-ámonos; no nos aburr-amos
abúrr-ete; no te aburr-as	aburr-íos; no os aburr-áis
abúrr-ase; no se aburr-a	abúrr-anse; no se aburr-an

The letters in red on this page show how reflexive "ir" conjugations differ from non-reflexive "ir" conjugations in pattern 3 and elsewhere.
Make compound tenses by adding the past participle aburrido to pattern 84.
Translation possibilities are at pattern 88. Conjugation tips are at pattern 91.

Add the past participle (past p.) of the verb you want to conjugate (e.g., using hablar (1), add hablado after he to form he hablado).

83 compound non-reflexive verbs[1]

Singular		Plural	
Indicativo	*Subjuntivo*	*Indicativo*	*Subjuntivo*
Perfecto	*Perfecto*	*Perfecto*	*Perfecto*
he (past p.)	haya (past p.)	hemos (past p.)	hayamos (past p.)
has (past p.)	hayas (past p.)	habéis (past p.)	hayáis (past p.)
ha (past p.)	haya (past p.)	han (past p.)	hayan (past p.)
Pluscuamperfecto	*Pluscuamperfecto*	*Pluscuamperfecto*	*Pluscuamperfecto*
había (past p.)	hubiera (past p.) OR hubiese (past p.)	habíamos (past p.)	hubiéramos (past p.) OR hubiésemos (past p.)
habías (past p.)	hubieras (past p.) OR hubieses (past p.)	habíais (past p.)	hubierais (past p.) OR hubieseis (past p.)
había (past p.)	hubiera (past p.) OR hubiese (past p.)	habían (past p.)	hubieran (past p.) OR hubiesen (past p.)
Pretérito Anterior		*Pretérito Anterior*	
hube (past p.)		hubimos (past p.)	
hubiste (past p.)		hubisteis (past p.)	
hubo (past p.)		hubieron (past p.)	
Futuro Perfecto	*Futuro Perfecto*	*Futuro Perfecto*	*Futuro Perfecto*
habré (past p.)	hubiere (past p.)	habremos (past p.)	hubiéremos (past p.)
habrás (past p.)	hubieres (past p.)	habréis (past p.)	hubiereis (past p.)
habrá (past p.)	hubiere (past p.)	habrán (past p.)	hubieren (past p.)
Potencial Compuesto		*Potencial Compuesto*	
habría (past p.)		habríamos (past p.)	
habrías (past p.)		habríais (past p.)	
habría (past p.)		habrían (past p.)	

Imperativo	
Singular	*Plural*
(not used); no (not used)	(not used); no (not used)
(not used); no (not used)	(not used); no (not used)
(not used); no (not used)	(not used); no (not used)

[1]These conjugations are made using haber. Estar, ser, and tener can also be used to make compound verbs. All four verbs are, consequently, called auxiliary verbs. Translation possibilities are at pattern 88. Conjugation tips are at patterns 89-91. Compound present participle: habiendo (past p.)

 Add the past participle (past p.) of the verb you want to conjugate.

compound reflexive verbs[1]

Singular		Plural	
Indicativo	*Subjuntivo*	*Indicativo*	*Subjuntivo*
Perfecto me he (past p.) te has (past p.) se ha (past p.)	*Perfecto* me haya (past p.) te hayas (past p.) se haya (past p.)	*Perfecto* nos hemos (past p.) os habéis (past p.) se han (past p.)	*Perfecto* nos hayamos (past p.) os hayáis (past p.) se hayan (past p.)
Pluscuamperfecto me había (past p.)	*Pluscuamperfecto* me hubiera (past p.) OR me hubiese (past p.)	*Pluscuamperfecto* nos habíamos (past p.)	*Pluscuamperfecto* nos hubiéramos (past p.) OR nos hubiésemos (past p.)
te habías (past p.)	te hubieras (past p.) OR te hubieses (past p.)	os habíais (past p.)	os hubierais (past p.) OR os hubieseis (past p.)
se había (past p.)	se hubiera (past p.) OR se hubiese (past p.)	se habían (past p.)	se hubieran (past p.) OR se hubiesen (past p.)
Pretérito Anterior me hube (past p.) te hubiste (past p.) se hubo (past p.)		*Pretérito Anterior* nos hubimos (past p.) os hubisteis (past p.) se hubieron (past p.)	
Futuro Perfecto me habré (past p.) te habrás (past p.) se habrá (past p.)	*Futuro Perfecto* me hubiere (past p.) te hubieres (past p.) se hubiere (past p.)	*Futuro Perfecto* nos habremos (past p.) os habréis (past p.) se habrán (past p.)	*Futuro Perfecto* nos hubiéremos (past p.) os hubiereis (past p.) se hubieren (past p.)
Potencial Compuesto me habría (past p.) te habrías (past p.) se habría (past p.)		*Potencial Compuesto* nos habríamos (past p.) os habríais (past p.) se habrían (past p.)	

Imperativo	
Singular	*Plural*
(not used); no (not used)	(not used); no (not used)
(not used); no (not used)	(not used); no (not used)
(not used); no (not used)	(not used); no (not used)

[1]These compound verbs are made using haber. Estar, ser, and tener can also be used to make compound verbs. All four verbs, consquently, are called auxiliary verbs. Translation possibilities are at pattern 88. Conjugation tips are at patterns 89-91. Compound present participle: habiéndose (past p.)

progressive tenses of non-reflexive verbs

Singular		Plural	
Indicativo	*Subjuntivo*	*Indicativo*	*Subjuntivo*
Presente	*Presente*	*Presente*	*Presente*
estoy (pres. p.)	esté (pres. p.)	estamos (pres. p.)	estemos (pres. p.)
estás (pres. p.)	estés (pres. p.)	estáis (pres. p.)	estéis (pres. p.)
está (pres. p.)	esté (pres. p.)	están (pres. p.)	estén (pres. p.)
Imperfecto	*Imperfecto*	*Imperfecto*	*Imperfecto*
estaba (pres. p.)	estuviera (pres. p.) OR estuviese (pres. p.)	estábamos (pres. p.)	estuviéramos (pres. p.) OR estuviésemos (pres. p.)
estabas (pres. p.)	estuvieras (pres. p.) OR estuvieses (pres. p.)	estabais (pres. p.)	estuvierais (pres. p.) OR estuvieseis (pres. p.)
estaba (pres. p.)	estuviera (pres. p.) OR estuviese (pres. p.)	estaban (pres. p.)	estuvieran (pres. p.) OR estuviesen (pres. p.)
Pretérito		*Pretérito*	
estuve (pres. p.)		estuvimos (pres. p.)	
estuviste (pres. p.)		estuvisteis (pres. p.)	
estuvo (pres. p.)		estuvieron (pres. p.)	
Futuro	*Futuro*	*Futuro*	*Futuro*
estaré (pres. p.)	estuviere (pres. p.)	estaremos (pres. p.)	estuviéremos (pres. p.)
estarás (pres. p.)	estuvieres (pres. p.)	estaréis (pres. p.)	estuviereis (pres. p.)
estará (pres. p.)	estuviere (pres. p.)	estarán (pres. p.)	estuvieren (pres. p.)
Potencial		*Potencial*	
estaría (pres. p.)		estaríamos (pres. p.)	
estarías (pres. p.)		estaríais (pres. p.)	
estaría (pres. p.)		estarían (pres. p.)	

Imperativo

Singular	*Plural*
(not used); no (not used)	estemos (pres. p.); no estemos (pres. p.)
está (pres. p.); no estés (pres. p.)	estad (pres. p.); no estéis (pres. p.)
esté (pres. p.); no esté (pres. p.)	estén (pres. p.); no estén (pres. p.)

Translation possibilities are at pattern 88. Conjugation tips are at patterns 89-91.

86 Add the present participle (pres. p.) of the verb you want to conjugate.

progressive tenses of reflexive verbs

Singular		Plural	
Indicativo	*Subjuntivo*	*Indicativo*	*Subjuntivo*
Presente estoy (pres. p.)me estás (pres. p.-te está (pres. p.)se	*Presente* esté (pres. p.)me estés (pres. p.)te esté (pres. p.)se	*Presente* estamos (pres. p.)nos estáis (pres. p.)os están (pres. p.)se	*Presente* estemos (pres. p.)nos estéis (present p.)os estén (pres. p.)se
Imperfecto estaba (pres.p)me	*Imperfecto* estuviera (pres.p)me OR estuviese (pres. p.)me	*Imperfecto* estábamos (pres.p)nos	*Imperfecto* estuviéramos (pres.p)nos OR estuviésemos (pres. p.)nos
estabas (pres.p.)te	estuvieras (pres.p.)te OR estuvieses (pres. p.)te	estabais (pres.p.)os	estuvierais (pres.p.)os OR estuvieseis (pres. p.)os
estaba (pres. p.)se	estuviera (pres. p.)se OR estuviese (pres. p.)se	estaban (pres. p.)se	estuvieran (pres. p.)se OR estuviesen (pres. p.)se
Pretérito estuve (pres. p.)me estuviste (pres. p.)te estuvo (pres. p.)se		*Pretérito* estuvimos (pres. p.)nos estuvisteis (pres. p.)os estuvieron (pres. p.)se	
Futuro estaré (pres. p.)me estarás (pres.p.)te estará (pres. p.)se	*Futuro* estuviere (pres. p.)me estuvieres (pres.p.)te estuviere (pres. p.)se	*Futuro* estaremos (pres. p.)nos estaréis (pres.p.)os estarán (pres. p.)se	*Futuro* estuviéremos (pres.p.)nos estuviereis (pres.p.)os estuvieren (pres. p.)se
Potencial estaría (pres. p.)me estarías (pres. p.)te estaría (pres. p.)se		*Potencial* estaríamos (pres. p.)nos estaríais (pres. p.)os estarían (pres. p.)se	

Imperativo

Singular	Plural
(not used); no (not used)	estémonos (pres. p.); no nos estemos (pres. p.)
éstate (pres. p.); no te estés (pres. p.)	estaos (pres. p.); no os estéis (pres. p.)
éstese (pres. p.); no se esté (pres. p.)	éstense (pres. p.); no se estén (pres. p.)

Conjugation tips are at patterns 89-91.

Add the past participle (past p.) of the verb you want to conjugate.
Infinitive: ser (past p.)
Compound infinitive: haber sido (past p.)

87
passive voice

Singular		*Plural*	
Indicativo	*Subjuntivo*	*Indicativo*	*Subjuntivo*
Presente	*Presente*	*Presente*	*Presente*
soy (past p.)	sea (past p.)	somos (past p.)s	seamos (past p.)s
eres (past p.)	seas (past p.)	sois (past p.)s	seáis (past p.)s
es (past p.)	sea (past p.)	son (past p.)s	sean (past p.)s
Imperfecto	*Imperfecto*	*Imperfecto*	*Imperfecto*
era (past p.)	fuera (past p.) OR fuese (past p.)	éramos (past p.)s	fuéramos (past p.)s OR fuésemos (past p.)s
eras (past p.)	fueras (past p.) OR fueses (past p.)	erais (past p.)s	fuerais (past p.)s OR fueseis (past p.)s
era (past p.)	fuera (past p.) OR fuese (past p.)	eran (past p.)s	fueran (past p.)s OR fuesen (past p.)s
Pretérito		*Pretérito*	
fui (past p.)		fuimos (past p.)s	
fuiste (past p.)		fuisteis (past p.)s	
fue (past p.)		fueron (past p.)s	
Futuro	*Futuro*	*Futuro*	*Futuro*
seré (past p.)	fuere (past p.)	seremos (past p.)s	fuéremos (past p.)s
serás (past p.)	fueres (past p.)	seréis (past p.)s	fuereis (past p.)s
será (past p.)	fuere (past p.)	serán (past p.)s	fueren (past p.)s
Potencial		*Potencial*	
sería (past p.)		seríamos (past p.)s	
serías (past p.)		seríais (past p.)s	
sería (past p.)		serían (past p.)s	

Imperativo

Singular	*Plural*
(not used); no (not used)	seamos (past p.)s; no seamos (past p.)s
sé (past p.); no seas (past p.)	sed (past p.)s; no seáis (past p.)s
sea (past p.); no sea (past p.)	sean (past p.)s; no sean (past p.)s

Present participle: siendo (past p.)
Compound present participle: habiendo sido (past p.)
Past participle: sido (past p.)
Conjugation tips are at patterns 89-91.

88 translation possibilities

Translation possibilities using the verb hablar (to speak).

Singular		*Plural*	
Indicativo	*Subjuntivo*	*Indicativo*	*Subjuntivo*
Presente	*Presente*	*Presente*	*Presente*
I speak[1]	I speak[1]	we speak[2]	we speak[2]
you speak[3]	you speak[3]	you speak[4]	you speak[4]
he speaks[5]	he speaks[5]	they speak[6]	they speak[6]
Imperfecto	*Imperfecto*	*Imperfecto*	*Imperfecto*
I was speaking	I was speaking OR I was speaking	we were speaking	we were speaking OR we were speaking
you were speaking	you were speaking OR you were speaking	you were speaking	you were speaking OR you were speaking
he[7] was speaking	he[7] was speaking OR he[7] was speaking	they were speaking	they were speaking OR they were speaking
Pretérito		*Pretérito*	
I spoke		we spoke	
you spoke		you spoke	
he[8] spoke		they spoke	
Futuro	*Futuro*	*Futuro*	*Futuro*
I will speak	I will speak	we will speak	we will speak
you will speak	you will speak	you will speak	you will speak
he[8] will speak	he[8] will speak	they will speak	they will speak
Potencial		*Potencial*	
I would speak		we would speak	
you would speak		you would speak	
he[8] would speak		they would speak	

Imperativo

Singular	*Plural*
(not used); no (not used)	we must speak; we must not speak
you must speak; you must not speak	you must speak; you must not speak
he[8] must speak; he[8] must not speak	they must speak; they must not speak

[1]Also I do speak, I am speaking. [2]Also we do speak, we are speaking. [3]Also (familiar, singular) you do speak, are speaking. [4]Also (familiar, plural) you do speak, you are speaking. [5]Also (formal, singular) you speak, you do speak, you are speaking, he (she, it) speaks, he (she, it) does speak, he (she, it) is speaking. [6]Also(formal, plural) they do speak, they are speaking. [7]Also you were speaking, she was speaking, it was speaking. [8]Also you, she, it.

Tips on conjugating are shown by parentheses and footnotes.
Present participle: -ando
Past participle: -ado

89
tips on conjugating "ar" verbs

Singular		*Plural*	
Indicativo	*Subjuntivo*	*Indicativo*	*Subjuntivo*
Presente	*Presente*	*Presente*	*Presente*
-o	-e (yo)	-amos (presente)	-emos
-as	-es	-áis[1]	-éis[1]
-a[2] (Ud., él, ella, ello)	-e (Ud., él, ella, ello)	-an	-en
Imperfecto	*Imperfecto*	*Imperfecto*	*Imperfecto*
-aba (yo)	-ara[3] (yo) OR -ase[4] (yo)	-ábamos	-áramos[3] OR -ásemos[4]
-abas	-aras[3] OR -ases[4]	-abais[1]	-arais[1, 3] OR -aseis[1, 4]
-aba (Ud., él, ella, ello)	-ara[3] (Ud., él, ella, ello) OR -ase[4] (Ud., él, ella, ello)	-aban	-aran[3] OR -asen[4]
Pretérito		*Pretérito*	
-é		-amos (pretérito)	
-aste		-asteis[1]	
-ó		-aron	
Futuro	*Futuro*	*Futuro*	*Futuro*
-aré	-are[5] (yo)	-aremos	-áremos[5]
-arás	-ares[5]	-aréis[1]	-areis[1, 5]
-ará	-are[5] (Ud., él, ella, ello)	-arán	-aren[5]
Potencial		*Potencial*	
-aría (yo)		-aríamos	
-arías		-aríais[1]	
-aría (Ud., él, ella, ello)		-arían	

Imperativo

Singular	*Plural*
(not used); no (not used)	-emos; no -emos
-a[2] (tú); no -es	-ad;[1] no -éis[1]
-e(Ud., él, ella, ello); no -e (Ud., él, ella, ello)	-en; no -en

The parentheses indicate that a conjugation is not unique, so you need to tell your listener or reader which alternative you mean. By matching identical conjugations, you can tell which are paired together. Usually the choice is between yo and one of the following: Ud., él, ella, ello. Regarding footnote 2 only, the choice is between tú and Ud., él, ella, or ello. In one instance, the choice is between the presente and pretérito tense.

The footnotes are on page 182.

90 tips on conjugating "er" verbs

Tips on conjugating are shown by parentheses and footnotes.
Present participle: -iendo
Past participle: -ido

Singular		Plural	
Indicativo	*Subjuntivo*	*Indicativo*	*Subjuntivo*
Presente	*Presente*	*Presente*	*Presente*
-o	-a (yo)	-emos	-amos
-es	-as	-éis[1]	-áis[1]
-e[2] (Ud., él, ella, ello)	-a (Ud., él, ella, ello)	-en	-an
Imperfecto	*Imperfecto*	*Imperfecto*	*Imperfecto*
-ía (yo)	-iera[3] (yo) OR -iese[4] (yo)	-íamos	-iéramos[3] OR -iésemos[4]
-ías	-ieras[3] OR -ieses[4]	-íais[1]	-ierais[1, 3] OR -ieseis[1, 4]
-ía (Ud., él, ella, ello)	-iera[3] (Ud., él, ella, ello) OR -iese[4] (Ud., él, ella, ello)	-ían	-ieran[3] OR -iesen[4]
Pretérito		*Pretérito*	
-í		-imos	
-iste		-isteis[1]	
-ió		-ieron	
Futuro	*Futuro*	*Futuro*	*Futuro*
-eré	-iere[5] (yo)	-eremos	-iéremos[5]
-erás	-ieres[5]	-eréis[1]	-iereis[1, 5]
-erá	-iere[5] (Ud., él, ella, ello)	-erán	-ieren[5]
Potencial		*Potencial*	
-ería (yo)		-eríamos	
-erías		-eríais[1]	
-ería (Ud., él, ella, ello)		-erían	

Imperativo	
Singular	*Plural*
(not used); no (not used)	-amos; no -amos
-e[2] (tú); no -as	-ed;[1] no -áis[1]
-a (Ud., él, ella, ello); no -a (Ud., él, ella, ello)	-an; no -an

The parentheses indicate that a conjugation is not unique, so you need to tell your listener or reader which alternative you mean. By matching identical conjugations, you can tell which are paired together. Usually the choice is between yo and one of the following: Ud., él, ella, ello. Regarding footnote 2 only, the choice is between tú and Ud., él, ella, or ello.

The footnotes are on page 182.

Tips on conjugating are shown by parentheses and footnotes.
Present participle: -iendo
Past participle: -ido

tips on conjugating "ir" verbs

Singular		*Plural*	
Indicativo	*Subjuntivo*	*Indicativo*	*Subjuntivo*
Presente	*Presente*	*Presente*	*Presente*
-o	-a (yo)	-imos (presente)	-amos
-es	-as	-ís[1]	-áis[1]
-e[2] (Ud., él, ella, ello)	-a (Ud., él, ella, ello)	-en	-an
Imperfecto	*Imperfecto*	*Imperfecto*	*Imperfecto*
-ía (yo)	-iera[3] (yo) OR -iese[4] (yo)	-íamos	-iéramos[3] OR -iésemos[4]
-ías	-ieras[3] OR -ieses[4]	-íais[1]	-ierais[1, 3] OR -ieseis[1, 4]
-ía (Ud., él, ella, ello)	-iera[3] (Ud., él, ella, ello) OR -iese[4] (Ud., él, ella, ello)	-ían	-ieran[3] OR -iesen[4]
Pretérito		*Pretérito*	
-í		-imos (pretérito)	
-iste		-msteis[1]	
-ió		-ieron	
Futuro	*Futuro*	*Futuro*	*Futuro*
-iré	-iere[5] (yo)	-iremos	-iéremos[5]
-irás	-ieres[5]	-iréis[1]	-iereis[1, 5]
-irá	-iere[5] (Ud., él, ella, ello)	-irán	-ieren[5]
Potencial		*Potencial*	
-iría (yo)		-iríamos	
-irías		-iríais[1]	
-iría (Ud., él, ella, ello)		-irían	

Imperativo

Singular	*Plural*
(not used); no (not used)	-amos; no -amos
-e[2] (tú); no -as	-id;[1] no -áis[1]
-a (Ud., él, ella, ello); no -a (Ud., él, ella, ello)	-an; no -an

The parentheses indicate that a conjugation is not unique, so you need to tell your listener or reader which alternative you mean. By matching identical conjugations, you can tell which are paired together. Usually the choice is between yo and one of the following: Ud., él, ella, ello. Regarding footnote 2 only, the choice is between tú and Ud., él, ella, or ello. In one instance, the choice is between the presente and pretérito tense.

The footnotes are on page 182.

footnotes to patterns 89-91

[1]Use the ustedes (Uds.) conjugations rather than the vosotros (and vosotras) conjugations when communicating with people in the Americas.

[2]These two conjugations are identical for most non-reflexive verbs, but not for reflexive verbs. Some frequently used non-reflexive verbs, including haber, are exceptions.

The other imperative conjugations of non-reflexive verbs, and reflexive imperative conjugations preceded by "no", are identical to the related present subjunctive tense, except the affirmative vosotros (and vostoras).

The affirmative vosotros (and vosotras) of non-reflexive verbs replace the final "r" of the infinitive form of the verb with "d". The affirmative vosotros (and vosotras) of reflexive verbs replace the final "r" of the infinitive form of the verb with "os".

[3]This form usually is preferred in unpublished writing.

[4]This form usually is preferred in published writing.

[5]The present indicative and subjunctive conjugations are preferred nowadays over the future subjunctive. Similarly, the compound present indicative and subjunctive conjugations are preferred nowadays over the compound future subjunctive.

The tips on conjugating Spanish verbs in patterns 89, 90 and 91 are identical, except that in pattern 90 (i.e., for "er" verbs), you do not have to tell your listener or reader whether you mean the presente or pretérito tense.

Pronunciation Guide

Columns: 1 = Spanish letter; 2 = Spanish examples; 3 = English word with similar sound; 4 = description

1	2	3	4
Vowels			
a	**casa**	*father*	
e	**dedo** **estado**	*pay* *net*	When stressed. When unstressed.
i	**fin**	*marine*	
o	**sol**	*obey*	
u	**luna** **quince** **guerra** **guiar** **agüero** **güiro**	*rule*	The u is silent when preceded by q or in gue or gui, unless marked with a dieresis (ü). When u has a dieresis (ü), it is pronounced like the wee in the English word week.
y	**y**	*see*	As a word, like ee in the English word see.
y	**yeso, suyo**	*young*	At the beginning of a word, or between vowels, y is pronounced like y in the English word young. In Argentina and Uruguay, y sounds similar to s in the English word vision.
	inyectar	*judge*	In some of Spanish America, when y follows an n, y sounds like j in the English word judge. See also y below in diphthongs and triphthongs.

Diphthongs (two vowel sounds in one syllable)

ai, ay	**caigo, hay**		Like the wi in wide.
au	**causa**		Like the ou in round.
ei, ey	**reina, rey**		Like the ey in they.
eu	**deuda**		Like the combined vowel sounds of hey, you!
ia, ya	**estudiar, haya**		Like the ya in yarn.

Columns: 1 = Spanish letter; 2 = Spanish examples; 3 = English word with similar sound; 4 = description

1	2	3	4
Diphthongs (two vowel sounds in one syllable) (continued)			
ie, ye	**sierra, yermo**		Like the ye in yes.
io, yo	**región, yodo**		Like the yo in yoke.
iu, yu	**ciudad, yugo**		Like the yu in Yule.
oi, oy	**oigo, voy, soy**		Like the oy in toy.
ua	**cuanto**		Like the wa in wand.
ue	**buena**		Like the we in went.
ui	**ruido**		Like the wee in week.
uo	**cuota**		Like the uo in quote.
Triphthongs (three vowel sounds in one syllable)			
iai	**estudiáis**		Like the yi in yipes.
iau	**miau**		Like the eow in meow.
iei	**estudiéis**		Like yea.
uai, uay	**continuáis, Uruguay**		Like the wi in wide.
uau	**guau**		Like wow.
uei, uey	**continuéis, buey**		Like the wei in weigh.
Consonants			
b	**bomba**	*bib*	At the beginning of a word or after m, similar to English b.
	labio, tabla	*lever*	Between vowels or before l or r, more like the v in lever.
c	**casa**	*cat*	Before a,o,u, or a consonant. The hard c in Spanish is not aspirated as it is in English.
	cerdo	*thick* *six*	Before e or i, in most of Spain, similar to the th in English thick; in southern Spain and Spanish America, similar to the s in six.

Columns: 1 = Spanish letter; 2 = Spanish examples; 3 = English word with similar sound; 4 = description

1	2	3	4
	acción		When a word contains a double c, the first is pronounced like the c in cat. In most of Spain, the second c is pronounced like the th in English thick; in southern Spain and Spanish America, similar to the s in six.
ch	**mucho**	*cheese*	
d	**dar**	*dog*	At the beginning of a word or after n or l, similar to the English d, but not aspirated.
	lodo	*rather*	At all other positions, similar to the th in the English word rather.
f	**sofa**	*fat*	
g	**gato**	*gain*	Before a, o, or u; the group ue or ui; or a consonate, g sounds like the g in English gain. The hard g is not aspirated as it is in English.
	general	*ha!*	Before e or i, similar to the strongly aspirated ha! in English.
h	**ahora**		It is always silent.
j	**joven**	*ha!*	Similar to the strongly aspirated ha! in English.
k	**kilo**	*kick*	Not aspirated as in English. Found only in words of foreign origin.
l	**libro**	*lid*	
ll	**silla**	*million*	In most of Spain, similar to the lli in million.
		yet *jar*	In southern Spain and most of Spanish America, similar to y in the English word yet or j in the English word jar.
		vision	In Argentina and Uruguay, similar to s in the English word vision.
m	**tomo**	*map*	
n	**tono**	*no*	

Columns: 1 = Spanish letter; 2 = Spanish examples; 3 = English word with similar sound; 4 = description

1	2	3	4
ñ	**paño**	*onion*	Similar to ni in the English word onion.
p	**parte**	*pot*	Not aspirated as p is in English.
q	**queso**	*coal*	Similar to c in the English word coal without the aspiration. Q is always followed by ue or ui and the u is always silent.
r	**roca**		At the beginning of a word or following l, n, or s, the letter r is strongly trilled by flapping the tip of the tongue against the roof of the mouth several times.
	caro		In all other positions, r is pronounced with a single flap of the tongue.
rr	**carro**		Double r is strongly trilled.
s	**cosa**	*so*	
t	**toma**	*tip*	Similar to t in the English word tip but generally softer. Not aspirated as in English.
v	**vino**	*bib*	At the beginning of a word, similar to b in the English word bib.
	salvo	*lever*	In all other positions, the v is softer, more like v in the English word lever.
w	**warrant**		Although not part of the Spanish alphabet, w is used in spelling foreign words. Pronounced like either the English v or w, or sometimes like the gu in Guam.
x	**examen**	*expand*	Generally like x in the English word expand.
	mixta	*so*	Before a consonant, x is sometimes pronounced like the s in the English word so.
	México	*ha!*	Sounds like the aspirated h in ha!
z	**zona**	*thick*	In most of Spain.
		so	In southern Spain and Spanish America.

Stress and the accent mark

Stress the next to last syllable in words which end in n , s, or a vowel: **to**man, **chi**cos, **na**da, inge**nie**ro.

Stress the last syllable in words which end in a consonant other than n or s: ho**tel**, Ma**drid**, me**jor**, fe**liz**.

Words which do not follow the above rules carry a written accent over the stressed syllable: a**llí**, in**glés**, auto**bús**, invita**ción**, te**lé**fono, ki**ló**metro.

Differences in meaning between certain words are shown by using an accent: sí (yes) and si (if); él (he) and el (the, masculine); sé (I know) and se (reflexive pronoun).

Question words carry an accent and are preceded by an inverted question mark: ¿dónde? (where?); ¿cuándo? (when?); and ¿qué? (what?).

Pronouncing words as though they were one word

If a word ends in a vowel and is followed by a word beginning with a vowel, the two words are pronounced as one word. When the two vowels are the same, they are pronounced as one vowel: ¿Cómo_está_usted? ¿Habla_español? No_está_aqui.

What the Pattern Verbs Illustrate

Outline

Description

A. Regular verbs

Category	Pattern verb	Pattern Verb #
Verbs ending in ar	hablar	1
Verbs ending in er	comer	2
Verbs ending in ir	vivir	3

B. Verbs containing spelling changes that retain pronunciation (These are sometimes called orthographic-changing verbs.)

The change	When	Retained Sound	Pattern Verb	Translation	Pattern Verb #
c ➠ qu	before e	k	sacar	to take out	67
c ➠ z	before a, o	s or th	mecer	to rock, to swing	46
g ➠ gu	before e	hard g	pagar	to pay	51
g ➠ j	before a, o	ha	coger	to catch, to pick	23
gu ➠ g	before a, o	hard g	distinguir	to distinguish	30
gu ➠ gü	before e	gw	aguar	to dilute, to water	7
qu ➠ c	before a, o	k	delinquir	to be delinquent	29
z ➠ c	before e	s or th	cazar	to hunt	21

C. Irregular verbs

C.1. Vowels change

a ➠ i or ie, á ➠ a, e ➠ é, é ➠ e or í, ó ➠ io, y (a vowel sound) is added.
Dar (27) (to give) is the pattern verb.

e ➠ i.
Pedir (52) (to ask) is the pattern verb.

e ➠ i, i is deleted.
Reñir (64) (to fight) is the pattern verb.

e ➠ i or í, e is deleted, i ➠ í.
Reír (63) (to laugh) is the pattern verb.

e in stem ➠ ie when stressed.
Pensar (53) (to think) is the pattern verb.

e ➠ ie when stressed, e ➠ i.
Sentir (71) (to feel) is the pattern verb.

e is added, é ➠ e, í ➠ i, ó ➠ o, irregular past participle.
Ver (78) (to see) is the pattern verb.

e is deleted, é ➠ e, o ➠ u or ue, ó ➠ o.
Poder (55) (to be able) is the pattern verb.

i in stem ➠ ie when stressed.
Adquirir (5) (to acquire) is the pattern verb.

i ➠ y between two vowels, and i ➠ í when the weak vowel i is in the same syllable as a strong vowel and the weak vowel receives the stress.
Creer (26) (to believe) is the pattern verb.

i ➠ y between vowels in some instances, y is added between vowels in other instances.
Huir (42) (to flee) is the pattern verb.

i ➠ y between two vowels in some instances, y is added between vowels in other instances, as in huir (42) (to flee), and ü ➠ u before y.
Argüir (12) (to imply, to argue) is the pattern verb.

i is deleted before e or o.
Bruñir (17) (to polish) is the pattern verb.

o ➠ hue when stressed.
Oler (50) (to smell) is the pattern verb.

o ➠ ue when stressed.
Contar (25) (to count) is the pattern verb ending in ar.
Mover (47) (to move) is the pattern verb ending in er.

o ➠ ue when stressed, o ➠ u when unstressed and the following syllable contains stressed a, ie, or ió.
Dormir (31) (to sleep) is the pattern verb.

o ➠ üe when stressed. The result is a change in pronunciation from a hard g to gw.
Agorar (6) (to predict) is the pattern verb.

y (a vowel sound) is added before e in stem when e is stressed.
Errar (37) (to be mistaken) is the pattern verb.

C.2. Vowels change, plus spelling changes that retain pronunciation

e ➠ i, gu ➠ g before a or o. Seguir, the pattern verb, is conjugated like pedir (52) (to ask), plus distinguir (30) (to distinguish).
Seguir (70) (to follow) is the pattern verb.

e ➠ ie when stressed, g ➠ gu before e. Regar, the pattern verb, conjugates like pensar (53) (to think), plus pagar (51) (to pay).
Regar (62) (to water, to irrigate) is the pattern verb.

e in stem ➠ ie when stressed, z ➠ c before e. Empezar, the pattern verb, conjugates like pensar (53) (to think), plus cazar (21) (to hunt).
Empezar (34) (to begin) is the pattern verb.

o ➠ ue when stressed, c ➠ qu before e. Trocar, the pattern verb, is conjugated like mover (47) (to move), plus sacar (67) (to take out).
Trocar (76) (to exchange) is the pattern verb.

o ➡ ue when stressed, c ➡ z before a or o. Cocer, the pattern verb, is conjugated like mover (47) (to move), plus mecer (46) (to rock, to swing).
Cocer (22) (to cook, to boil) is the pattern verb.

o ➡ ue when stressed, g ➡ gu before e. Colgar, the pattern verb, is conjugated like contar (25) (to count), plus pagar (51) (to pay).
Colgar (24) (to hang, as a curtain) is the pattern verb.

o ➡ ue when stressed, z ➡ c before e. Forzar, the pattern verb, is conjugated like contar (25) (to count), plus cazar (21) (to hunt).
Forzar (39) (to force) is the pattern verb.

o ➡ üe when stressed, z ➡ c before e. Avergonzar, the pattern verb, conjugates like agorar (6) (to foretell), plus cazar (21) (to hunt).
Avergonzar (15) (to shame) is the pattern verb.

u ➡ ue when stressed, g ➡ gu before e.
Jugar (44) (to play, gamble, risk) is the pattern verb.

C.3. Consonants change

c ➡ zc before a or o.
Nacer (48) (to be born, to bud) is the pattern verb.

c ➡ zc or j, i is deleted.
Producir (59) (to produce, to yield, to beat) is the pattern verb.

g is added.
Asir (13) (to grasp) is the pattern verb.

C.4. Vowels and consonants change

a ➡ e or u, e is deleted, b ➡ p. The following conjugations are irregular yo in the present tense, and yo and usted in the past (pretérito) tense.
Saber (66) (to know, to find out) is the pattern verb.

a ➡ e or u, e ➡ a, o ➡ e, b ➡ y, delete a, e and b. Hay is the impersonal usted form. Haber, the pattern verb, like estar, ser, and tener (all called auxiliary verbs), is used with other verbs (e.g., hablar) to make compound verbs.
Haber (40) (to have) is the pattern verb.

a ➡ i, c ➡ g or z, delete c or e, irregular past participle.
Hacer (41) (to make, to do) is the pattern verb.

a ➡ i, c ➡ g or z, delete c or e, irregular past participle, as in hacer (41) (to make, to do), plus a regular form of the tú imperative as an alternative.
Satisfacer (69) (to satisfy) is the pattern verb.

a ➡ i or ie, é ➡ e, ó ➡ o, uv is added. Andar, the pattern verb, has some similarities to estar (38) (to be, to stand, to look).
Andar (10) (to walk, to move, to go) is the pattern verb.

a ➡ i or ie, é ➡ e, ó ➡ o, add uv or y, accents are added in the imperative mood. Estar, the pattern verb, has some similarities to andar (10) (to walk, to move, to go). Estar, the pattern verb, like haber, ser, and tener (all called auxiliary verbs) is used with other verbs (e.g., hablar with haber) to make compound verbs.
Estar (38) (to be) is the pattern verb.

e ➡ i, delete ec, delete i, c ➡ g or j, irregular final letter in the past (pretérito) tense of yo and usted. Decir, the pattern verb, has some similarities to predecir (58) (to predict). Decir and predecir have unusual past participles.
Decir (28) (to say, to tell, to talk) is the pattern verb.

e ➡ i, delete i, c ➡ g or j, irregular final letter in the past (pretérito) tense of yo and usted. Predecir, the pattern verb, has some similarities to decir (28) (to say, to tell). Decir and predecir have unusual past participles.
Predecir (58) (to predict) is the pattern verb.

e ➡ i, g ➡ j, plus an additional past participle electo.
Elegir (32) (to elect, to choose, to select) is the pattern verb.

e ➡ ie or i, delete, i, add d or g, delete the final vowel in the tú form of the verb in the imperative mood.
Venir (77) (to come) is the pattern verb.

e ➡ ie or i, delete e, r ➡ s, irregular ending in the yo and usted conjugations of the past (pretérito) tense.
Querer (60) (to want, to need, to love) is the pattern verb.

e ➡ ie or u, delete e, add d or g, n ➡ v, irregular ending in the yo and usted conjugations of the past (pretérito) tense. Tener, like haber, estar, and ser (all called auxiliary verbs) is used with other verbs (e.g., hablar with haber) to make compound tenses.
Tener (74) (to have, to own, to hold) is the pattern verb.

e is deleted, o ➡ u, add d or g, n ➡ s, irregular ending in yo and usted past (pretérito) conjugation, irregular past participle.
Poner (57) (to put, to set, to lay, to place) is the pattern verb.

i is deleted, add d or g. Salir, the pattern verb, has some similarities to asir (13) (to grasp).
Salir (68) (to leave, to go out) is the pattern verb.

ig or j is added, i in the ending is deleted, irregular ending in the yo and usted past (pretérito) conjugation. The present and past participles are irregular.
Traer (75) (to bring, to carry, to wear) is the pattern verb.

ig is added, i ➠ í or y. Caer, the pattern verb, has some similarities to oír (49) (to hear).

Caer (20) (to fall, to decline) is the pattern verb.

ig or y is added, i ➠ í or y. Oír, the pattern verb, has some similarities to caer (20) (to fall).

Oír (49) (to hear) is the pattern verb.

C.5. Vowels and consonants change, plus spelling changes that retain pronunciation

a ➠ u or e, b ➠ p, c ➠ qu before e (because of a change in the stem from "a" to "e"), e is deleted.

Caber (18) (to fit, to fit into) is the pattern verb.

D. Accent mark

Accent mark An accent mark is used when a weak vowel (i or u) appears in the same syllable with a strong vowel (a, e or o) and the weak vowel is stressed, or when h (a silent letter) separates a stressed weak vowel from a strong vowel.

D.1. Accent mark is on a stressed weak vowel

i ➠ í (or u ➠ ú in verbs that follow the pattern of the verb actuar [to act]) when the weak vowel i (or the weak vowel u) and a strong vowel appear in the same syllable and the weak vowel is stressed.

Airar (9) (to anger, to irritate) is the pattern verb for i ➠ í.

Actuar is not shown as a separate pattern verb. The u ➠ ú occurs in the verb actuar in the same conjugations as the i ➠ í occurs in the verb airar.

D.2. Accent mark is on a stressed weak vowel, plus changes that retain pronunciation

i ➠ í when stressed, c ➠ qu before e to retain the k sound. Ahincar, the pattern verb, conjugates like airar (9) (to anger, to irritate), plus sacar (67) (to take out).

Ahincar (8) (to urge) is the pattern verb.

i ➠ í when stressed, g ➠ gu before e. Cabrahigar, the pattern verb, conjugates like airar (9) (to anger, to irritate), plus pagar (51) (to pay).

Cabrahigar (19) (to pollinate, such as fruit trees by bees) is the pattern verb.

i ➠ í when stressed, z ➠ c before e. Enraizar, the pattern verb, conjugates like airar (9) (to anger, to irritate), plus cazar (21) (to hunt).

Enraizar (35) (to grow roots, to take root) is the pattern verb.

E. Verbs having more than one root

Pattern Verb	Roots	Explanation
erguir	ergu irg yerg	+ gu ➠ g before a or o. Erguir (36) (to become erect, to straighten up) is th pattern verb.
ir	v va vay ib fu	+ e or i ➠ a, i ➠ y, í ➠ i, ie ➠ e, delete i or í. The verb ir has no stem; the infinitive form of the verb is a verb ending only. Roots are added in some conjugations, but not in all conjugations, but not in all conjugations, in order to have a stem plus an ending. Ir has only one root in each conjugation. Ir (43) (to go) is the pattern verb.
placer	plac plazc plegu plug plugu	+ c ➠ zc before a or o, g ➠ gu before e or i to retain the hard g sound. Placer (54) (to please) is the pattern verb.
podrir	podr pudr	+ o ➠ u. Podrir (56) (to rot) is the pattern verb.
raer	ra raig ray	+ i ➠ í or y. Except for the additional roots, raer is like caer (20) (to fall, to decline) and the verb roer (65) (to gnaw). Raer (61) (to scrape, to scratch, to become worn or frayed) is the pattern verb.
roer	ro roig roy	+ i ➠ í or y. Roer is conjugated like raer (61) (to scrape) except for keeping moreregular roots as alternatives. Roer (65) (to gnaw) is the pattern verb.
ser	s er fu se	+ e ➠ é or o, plus other changes. Ser, like estar, haber, and tener, is used with other verbs to make compound verbs. For example, hablar is used with haber to make compound verbs. Ser (72) (to be) is the pattern verb.
yacer	yac yag yaz yazc yazg	Yacer (79) (to lie somewhere, to rest, e.g., cattle at night) is the pattern verb.

F. **Verbs customarily not used in some conjugations** (seven categories)

abolir (4) (to abolish, to annul) is the pattern verb for the first category.

aplacer (11) (to please, to satisfy) is the pattern verb for the second category.

atañer (14) (to concern) is the pattern verb for the third category.

balbucir (16) (to stammer) is the pattern verb for the fourth category.

embaír (33) (to deceive) is the pattern verb for the fifth category. Embaír is usually used in the same positions as abolir (4) (to abolish), plus i ➠ y between two vowels, and i ➠ í, as in creer (26) (to believe).

llover (45) (to rain) is the pattern verb for the sixth category. o ➠ ue. Llover, and other "impersonal verbs," some of which refer to atmospheric phenomenia, typically are used only in the third person singular as shown by llover.

soler (73) (to be accustomed to [followed by a verb in the infinitive form]) is the pattern verb for the seventh category. o ➠ ue when stressed, as in mover (47) (to move).

G. Other categories of verb conjugations

Reflexive verbs (80, 81, 82) (sometimes called pronomial verbs). They always require a reflexive pronoun. The subject of the verb receives the action of the verb. In the list of 15,000 Spanish verbs, these verbs, (because they are listed in their infinitive form) end in "arse", "erse", or "irse".

Compound verbs (non-reflexive verbs follow pattern 83, reflexive verbs follow pattern 84). Compound verbs are formed by using two verbs, one of which is haber, estar, ser, or tener.

Progressive tense (non-reflexive verbs follow pattern 85, reflexive verbs follow pattern 86).

Passive voice (87). The passive voice does not have an explicit subject of the verb. The passive voice is formed by adding ser or estar to the participle of the main verb.

Pattern Verbs Contained Here That Are Not in Other Verb Books

501 Spanish Verbs

abolir 4
agorar 6
aplacer 11
argüir 12
atañer 14
avergonzar .. 15
balbucir 16
cabrahigar .. 19
cocer 22
embaír 33
enraizar 35
podrir 56
roer 65
trocar 76

Bescherelle. ***El Arte de Conjugar en Español***

aplacer 11
argüir 12
atañer 14
balbucir 16
llover 45

Das Spanische Verb

agorar 6
aguar 7
ahincar 8
aplacer 11
argüir 12
atañer 14
avergonzar .. 15
balbucir 16
cabrahigar ... 19
cocer 22
colgar 24
elegir 32
embaír 33
empezar 34
enraizar 35
forzar 39
llover 45
predecir 58
raer 61
regar 62
reír 63
roer 65
sacar 67
satisfacer .. 69
seguir ... 70
soler 73
trocar ... 76

Langenscheidts Verb-Tabellen Spanisch

ahincar 8
aplacer 11
argüir 12
asir 13
atañer 14
avergonzar ... 15
balbucir 16
cabrahigar ... 19
cocer 22
colgar 24
elegir 32
embaír 33
empezar 34
enraizar 35
forzar 39
llover 45
mecer 46
podrir 56
predecir 58
raer 61
regar 62
reñir 64
roer 65
satisfacer .. 69
seguir 70
trocar ... 76

Larousse da la Conjugación and ***Larousse Verbformen Spanisch***

aplacer 11
argüir 12
atañer 14
balbucir 16
creer 26
huir 42
llover 45
soler 73

Los Quince Mil Verbos Españoles

adquirir 5
agorar 6
aguar 7
ahincar 8
airar 9
argüir 12
avergonzar .. 15
cabrahigar ... 19
cazar 21
cocer 22
coger 23
colgar 24
delinquir 29
distinguir 30
elegir 32
empezar 34
enraizar 35
mecer 46
pagar 51
querer 60
regar 62
sacar 67
seguir 70
trocar 76

VerbiCard: Todos los Verbos Catellanos Conjugados

agorar 6
aguar 7
ahincar 8
aplacer 11
cabrahigar .. 19
embaír 33
enraizar 35
mecer 46
trocar 76